Thames & Hudson world of art

This famous series provides the widest available
range of illustrated books on art in all its aspects.

If you would like to receive a complete list
of titles in print please write to:

THAMES & HUDSON
181A High Holborn
London WC1V 7QX

In the United States please write to:

THAMES & HUDSON INC.
500 Fifth Avenue
New York, New York 10110

Printed in China

National Gallery of Art

with 315 illustrations, 312 in color

Thames & Hudson world of art

Frontispiece
JEAN-HONORÉ
FRAGONARD,
A Young Girl Reading
(see p. 173)

The texts in this volume were contributed by

Nancy Anderson

E.P. Bowron

Florence E. Coman

Philip Conisbee

Nancy E. Edwards

Gail Feigenbaum

Frances Feldman

Margaret Morgan Grasselli

Sarah Greenough

John Hand

Gretchen Hirschauer

Kimberly Jones

Franklin Kelly

Alice Kreindler

Alison Luchs

Donna Mann

Donald Myers

Margaret O'Neil

Nicholas Penny

Marla Prather

Lynn Russell

Julie Springer

Jill Steinberg

Jeremy Strick

Susan B. Taylor

Diane Waggoner

Jeffrey Weiss

Arthur Wheelock

William J. Williams

Christopher B. With

Martha Wolff

First published in the United States of America in 1992 by
Thames & Hudson Inc., 500 Fifth Avenue,
New York, New York 10110

thamesandhudsonusa.com

Second edition 2006

Library of Congress Catalog Card Number 2005904459
ISBN-13: 978-0-500-20390-3
ISBN-10: 0-500-20390-3

Printed and bound in China

Contents

Foreword

Museum visitors are travelers through time and space. Staying within the realm of the National Gallery of Art's permanent collection, it is possible, moving from gallery to gallery, to journey from the Byzantine empire of the thirteenth century to contemporary America, with innumerable options and diversions along the way.

A good guide is like an accurate map. It can convey the distinguishing features of a landscape, suggest its terrain, and give the user, whether a first-time or repeat traveler, a sense of what to expect along the way. This publication plays much the part of a map, giving a valuable overview of a crucial part of the National Gallery of Art domain: its permanent collection of paintings, sculpture, graphic arts, photography, and decorative arts. The book follows the Gallery's policy of grouping the collection according to school while arranging it along general chronological lines within those divisions. Here, in a convenient format, it is possible to get a sense of the remarkable works of art that have been secured for the nation.

The story of the collection and the institution that houses and cares for it is a happy and inspiring one. In 1937 Andrew W. Mellon, a man whose life embraced both public service and private wealth, founded the National Gallery of Art with a three-part gift. It included his own collection, a splendid physical plant to shelter it as well as the many additional donations that have come because of it, and an endowment for certain key activities. The Gallery opened to the public in March 1941 and has been blessed with steady growth and progress ever since. This successful undertaking has been continuously reinforced by the public-private partnership conceived for the Gallery from its creation. Each work of art in the permanent collection is a private donation, acquired either directly or with contributed funds. Although the Gallery has never relied on federally appropriated funds for obtaining art, it has depended on the Federal Government for essential support. Enabling legislation, passed by the 75th Congress, assured the maintenance of a secure home for the nation's art collection and a staff to care for it. The fruits of this public-private partnership were made dramatically evident once again in 1978, when the East Building of the National Gallery opened. This new building was a gift from Andrew Mellon's children, Ailsa Mellon Bruce and Paul Mellon, and the foundation they created and named for their father. Perhaps the most often and best perceived result of the cooperation between the public and private sectors is the Gallery's continuing ability to open its doors without charging an admission fee.

The enrichment and presentation of the permanent collection is a multi-faceted endeavor that depends on curatorial, conservation, publication, and education programs of the highest standards. The Gallery is also committed to a dynamic and ambitious program of temporary exhibitions. Working internationally to borrow art from public and private collections, this institution has been able to exhibit a remarkable range of the world's best art to an audience that has come to average more than six million visitors annually. Many of these temporary exhibitions amplify the Gallery's impressive holdings in the visual arts. It is that permanent core that this volume addresses and the reader is urged to visit.

Earl A. Powell III
Director, National Gallery of Art

Italian Painting
OF THE XIII–EARLY XVI CENTURIES

The Renaissance celebration of human moral freedom or self-determination had a profound effect on the visual arts. Immersed in Greek and Latin learning, humanist thinkers were emboldened in their understanding that the human being had been placed at the center of the universe. Whereas medieval art focused on otherworldly truths, Renaissance art was nurtured on the principles of humanism which also paid tribute to visible reality. Interest in the classical past did not preclude Christian devotion; although secular forms emerged, religious art remained dominant.

Tuscany was the cradle for the new humanist concerns. While Duccio's *Maestà* altarpiece for Siena Cathedral owes much to his Byzantine predecessors, certain elements derive from the painter's direct observation of nature. The Florentine painter Giotto, a narrator and draftsman of genius, succeeded in expressing complex human emotions in his frescoes in the Arena Chapel at Padua.

During the fifteenth century, artists were challenged to depict the visual world in a naturalistic manner, and endeavored to deepen their understanding of light and shadow, of space and anatomy. The idealized statuary of classical antiquity served as models, while in architecture the classical orders were applied to Renaissance buildings.

The prosperous mercantile economy of Florence helped to nurture the arts, with commissions coming from the church, the state, and the wealthier families. Heroes and heroines, both classical and biblical, were portrayed as examples of virtue and moral fortitude. However, to view the art of the Renaissance as an exclusively Tuscan preserve or as a mere conquest of naturalistic representation would overlook the complexity of the period. Carlo Crivelli painted sumptuous altarpieces in a boldly ornamental manner, and Cosimo Tura frequently departed from logical, naturalistic norms in favor of an energetic idiom with an eccentric elegance. Portraiture flourished during the Renaissance, and the Venetians – foremost among them Giorgione and Bellini – excelled in their depictions of pastoral landscape.

In the early sixteenth century, the center of patronage in the arts shifted to Rome. Pope Julius II recruited the finest artists of the day for his ambitious building program; Raphael and Michelangelo were heirs to Leonardo's High Renaissance style, characterized by classical balance, controlled movement, and an elevated conception. Raphael learned from Leonardo that a fully resolved composition was reached only after unrelenting study of the human figure. His frescoes for the Pope's private apartments display a noble grandeur, vitality and rhetorical power, while in the Sistine Chapel ceiling frescoes, Michelangelo created ideal figures of awesome physical power.

Detail:
SANDRO BOTTICELLI,
The Adoration of the Magi

BYZANTINE
ARTIST/SCHOOL
13th century

*Enthroned Madonna and
Child, c.1280*

Wood. 131.1 × 76.8 cm.
(51⅝ × 30¼ in.)

Gift of Mrs. Otto H. Kahn
1949.7.1

During the thirteenth century, the art of the Catholic West and Orthodox East intermingled, resulting in a Byzantine style in Italy. This icon or "holy image," probably painted by a Greek artist working in Italy, is a perfect example of this fusion. Known also as the "Kahn Madonna" from the name of the previous owner, the large panel represents a full-length figure of Mary enthroned as Queen of Heaven. She holds the infant Christ who, true to medieval convention, is a miniature adult. In the flanking medallions, archangels hold orbs and scepters, emphasizing Mary's imperial role. In this, the "Hodegetria" type of Madonna, she directs the viewer's attention to Christ, thus pointing the way to salvation.

There are distinct similarities in style and subject matter between this painting and the Byzantine icons painted in the East for the Greek Orthodox Church. The graceful movement of the figures, the gold striations on the drapery which simulate shimmering light, and the flowing, rhythmic lines identify the artist as a Greek painter. But an Italian influence is notable in the tooled decoration of the halos, the perspective of the wooden throne with its high back, the delicate gradations of light and shade, and the distinctly Tuscan scheme of the rectangular panel with a full-length depiction of the enthroned Virgin.

This three-part panel comes from the front predella, the separate horizontal band of narrative scenes at the base of the great *Maestà* altarpiece that depicts Mary, the patron saint of Siena, in majesty with angels and saints. A contract of 1308 states that the huge altarpiece for the cathedral of Siena was to be painted entirely by Duccio di Buoninsegna; it is probable, however, that the artist took on assistants to help carry out the project.

In the *Nativity*, Duccio employed conventional Byzantine elements, such as the cave setting, the glowing colors, and the multi-scene composition. Mary is shown in the usual Byzantine manner – larger than the figures around her – yet, her large size also underscores the importance the Virgin held for the Sienese. The bracketing side panels portray Old Testament prophets holding scrolls that foretell the birth of Christ.

Duccio's unique contribution to the Byzantine style is his use of elegantly flowing lines, most evident here in the drapery folds and mountain ridges. The soft, undulating brushstrokes downplay the austerity of the earlier style, as do the sensitive rendering of the Virgin's face and the individual characterizations of Isaiah and Ezekiel, expressing a true sense of human feeling.

DUCCIO DI
BUONINSEGNA
(Sienese, *c.*1255–1318)

Nativity with Prophets Isaiah and Ezekiel,
1308/11

Wood. Middle panel:
43.8 × 44.4 cm. (17¼ × 17½ in.);
side panels, each:
43.8 × 16.5 cm. (17¼ × 6½ in.)

Andrew W. Mellon Collection
1937.1.8a–c

GIOTTO
(Florentine, probably
1266–1337)

Madonna and Child,
probably *c.*1320/30

Wood. 85.5 × 62 cm.
(33⅝ × 24⅜ in.)

Samuel H. Kress Collection
1939.1.256

Giotto's explorations and innovations in art during the early fourteenth century developed, a full century later, into the Italian Renaissance. Besides making panel paintings, he executed many fresco cycles, the most famous at the Arena Chapel, Padua, and he also worked as an architect and sculptor.

Transformed by Giotto, the stylized figures in paintings such as the *Enthroned Madonna and Child* (p.10) took on human, believable qualities. Whereas his Sienese contemporary Duccio concentrated on line, pattern, and shape arranged on a flat plane, the Florentine Giotto emphasized mass and volume, a classical approach to form. By giving his figures a blocky, corporeal character, the artist introduced great three-dimensional plasticity to painting.

Painted during the latter part of Giotto's career, the *Madonna and Child* was the central part of a five-section polyptych, or altarpiece in many panels. Giotto utilized a conservative Byzantine-style background in gold leaf, symbolizing the realm of heaven, and the white rose is a traditional symbol of Mary's purity as well as a reference to the innocence lost through Original Sin. Yet, the *Madonna and Child* introduces a new naturalistic trend in painting. Instead of making the blessing gesture of a philosopher, the infant Christ grasps his mother's left index finger in a typically babylike way as he playfully reaches for the flower that she holds.

entile da Fabriano's patrons were princes, the church, and various city governments as well as the customary merchant clients. His art has a cosmopolitan flavor, in which brilliant color, textural richness, and ornamental pattern are combined.

In the *Madonna and Child*, painted in Florence, Mary sits on a bench covered by floral material that falls onto an elaborately tiled floor. The elegantly attired figures are surrounded by four angels, barely visible, which have been incised into the gold-leaf background. In contrast to earlier devotional images in which the Madonna and Child appear as a celestial vision, the holy figures here appear very corporeal. As if to emphasize Mary's role as Divine Mother, the Christ Child gestures with his right hand toward the Latin word *Mater* inscribed on the collar of her mantle. The string in his other hand tethers a butterfly, a traditional symbol of Christ's resurrection from the tomb.

Gentile's art is typical of the International Style, a manner of painting which became popular at courts throughout Europe in the late fourteenth and early fifteenth centuries. Characterized by a refined decorative elegance, a concern for continuous rhythms, and the lavish use of gold and bright colors, this aristocratic manner fused the stylized art of the Middle Ages with the emerging naturalistic interests of the Renaissance.

GENTILE DA FABRIANO
(Umbrian, *c.*1370–1427)

Madonna and Child,
*c.*1422

Wood. 95.9 × 56.5 cm.
(37¾ × 22¼ in.)

Samuel H. Kress Collection
1939.1.255

13

Giovanni di Paolo's *Annunciation* is believed to be one of five predella panels that belonged to the lower portion of a large, as yet unidentified, Sienese altarpiece. The central area of the panel shows the most important part of the painted narrative – the Archangel Gabriel announcing the impending birth of the Christ Child to the Virgin Mary. Outside her elegant Italian Gothic house, a lush garden reflects the spring season of the Annunciation. The fertile landscape also provides an appropriate setting for the secondary representation at the left – Adam and Eve's dramatic expulsion from the Garden of Eden. Giovanni used the figure of God the Father, who occupies the celestial realm in the upper left corner, to link the Expulsion to the Annunciation. God both points out the exiled couple's disgrace and looks ahead toward the Annunciation in anticipation of divine redemption. Finally, at the right, Joseph warms his hands at a fireplace, symbolic of Jesus' future birth in the winter.

Disregarding naturalistic detail in favor of flat, decorative pattern, Giovanni was nevertheless aware of current Renaissance experiments in linear perspective, as exemplified by the receding floor tiles in both the central loggia and Joseph's cubicle. The artist's decision, however, not to follow realistic spatial and scale relationships completely, and his use of willowy, elegantly dressed figures, place him firmly within the medieval pictorial tradition, now reappearing as the International Style.

ITALIAN PAINTING XIII–XVI.

This brilliantly colored, richly decorated circular panel presents a splendid vision of the arrival of the Magi, accompanied by a courtly entourage. A 1492 inventory of Lorenzo de' Medici's estate possibly identifies this picture as the most valuable in the collection of the powerful Florentine family, and attributes it to Fra Angelico. The *Adoration of the Magi* actually appears to be the product of two artists; Fra Angelico may only have started the altarpiece, the greatest part of the work having been taken up by Fra Filippo Lippi.

Fra Angelico was a Dominican known for his great monastic devotion; his saintly deportment is mirrored in the quiet piety of his paintings. The representation of the Virgin Mary here characterizes his style in the pure, simple form of her head and the gentle refinement of her features. Fra Filippo's earthy style appeals to the viewer in the portrayal of massive forms and well-articulated figures. In the *Adoration*, the richly attired wise men and their attendants, as well as the broad-faced Joseph beside the Virgin, are usually attributed to him.

While several elements of the painting can be seen as symbolic – for example, the peacock was considered a symbol of immortality – the *Adoration* can also simply be appreciated for its sparkling color, delightful details, and festive gaiety.

FRA ANGELICO AND
FRA FILIPPO LIPPI
(Florentine, *c.*1400–55;
*c.*1406–69)

*The Adoration of the Magi, c.*1445

Wood. Diameter 137.2 cm. (54 in.)

Samuel H. Kress Collection
1952.2.2

DOMENICO VENEZIANO
(Florentine, c.1410–61)

Saint John in the Desert,
c.1445

Wood. 28.4 × 32.4 cm.
(11⅛ × 12¾ in.)

Samuel H. Kress Collection
1943.4.48

One of Domenico Veneziano's major works is an altarpiece that he painted about 1445 for the Church of Santa Lucia dei Magnoli, Florence. The incident illustrated in this panel of the altarpiece is John's act of exchanging his rich, worldly clothes for a rough, camel-hair coat. In the few known representations of John in the wilderness that preceded Domenico's version, the emphasis was placed either on the divine origin of the saint's animal skin or on his preaching. Domenico, however, shifted attention from mere narration to the spiritual significance of John's decision to forsake luxury in favor of a life of piety.

Rather than showing the saint in the usual manner, as a mature, bearded hermit, Domenico painted a youthful figure. Clearly classical in appearance, his saint is one of the earliest embodiments of the Renaissance preoccupation with antique models. However, a fusion of pagan and Christian ideas is suggested; the Grecian type is transformed into a religious being by the golden halo above his head. Another innovative combination of elements exists in the arrangement of this antique nude in a landscape that retains artistic features from the High Gothic era of the late Middle Ages. Symbolic rather than realistic, the rugged mountains enliven the drama of John's decision by emphasizing the desolate nature of his chosen environment.

The Youthful David is unique in Renaissance art. It is the only example of a painted shield that can be attributed to a great master, and it is decorated with a narrative scene instead of the typical coat of arms. Rather than for protection in battle, it was intended for display in ceremonial parades.

The subject was especially appropriate for a Florentine audience of the fifteenth century. As the smallest major power on the political stage of Italy, the city saw itself as a young David contending with such powerful Goliaths as the Pope, the Duke of Milan, the King of Naples, and the Doge of Venice. In Castagno's shield, David is depicted preparing to attack Goliath, having already chosen a smooth stone from the riverbank for his sling. The conclusion appears at the bottom of the shield; the terrible giant's severed head, with the stone embedded in its forehead, lies at David's feet as a warning to any potential enemies of Florence.

For this interpretation of the Old Testament hero, Castagno chose a young athlete, whose pose shows the painter's awareness of classical prototypes. Castagno demonstrated his knowledge of the new science of anatomy by modeling the figure in light and shadow, articulating the muscles and veins of the arms and legs, and giving powerful activity to David's running pose and windblown garments.

ANDREA DEL CASTAGNO
(Florentine, 1417/19–1457)

The Youthful David,
c.1450

Leather on wood. 115.6 × 76.9
to 41 cm. (45½ × 30¼ to 16⅛ in.)

Widener Collection
1942.9.8

17

COSIMO TURA
(Ferrarese,
before 1430–1495)

*Madonna and Child in a
Garden, c.*1455

Wood. 52.7 × 37.2 cm.
(20¾ × 14⅝ in.)

Samuel H. Kress Collection
1952.5.29

This work shows the Madonna and Child seated in a garden that represents Eden. The orange trees bloom with pure white flowers that symbolize Mary's virginity. An Annunciation scene appears in the raised and gilded foliate scrolls at the top of the painting.

Since antiquity, sleep was regarded as "the brother of death," and during the Renaissance, representations of the sleeping Christ Child were considered prefigurations of the death that he would suffer for mankind. In Cosimo Tura's painting, death is also foreshadowed by the stone sarcophagus on which Mary is seated.

Cosimo Tura is considered the first great painter in Renaissance Ferrara, a city in northern Italy. He spent most of his professional life in the service of the noble d'Este family, the dukes of Ferrara. Because Ferrara lacked strong artistic traditions, Cosimo was free to develop a very personal style. He may have been inspired by the works of Tuscan and Paduan artists, as well as by the Flemish, some of whose paintings figured in Ferrarese collections in the fifteenth century. In this early work, Cosimo showed an eccentric tendency to exaggerate human anatomy for expressive ends, as seen in the treatment of the Virgin's elongated hands. Purposeful distortions increase in his later works, which reverberate with spiritual and emotional fervor.

CARLO CRIVELLI
(Venetian, *c*.1430–*c*.1495)

*Madonna and Child
Enthroned with Donor,*
c.1470

Wood. 129.5 × 54.5 cm.
(51 × 21⅜ in.)

Samuel H. Kress Collection
1952.5.6

"Remember me, O Mother of God. O Queen of Heaven, rejoice." These words, taken from an Easter psalm sung in the Virgin's honor, appear on the golden arch at the top of Carlo Crivelli's *Madonna and Child Enthroned with Donor.* The donor, the Albanian ecclesiastic Prenta di Giorgio, kneels in prayer near the Virgin's crown.

Crivelli's painting originally constituted the central section of a polyptych in the parish church at Porto San Giorgio, near Fermi. The crisp, sculptural forms reflect Crivelli's probable training in the humanist center of Padua. Yet the manner in which Crivelli's figures are modeled in light and shade also expresses a broader Renaissance concern with direct observation of nature.

Crivelli's very personal, almost metallic style must in large part be explained by the events of his life. He was born in Venice where the Gothic tradition lingered well into the fifteenth century. After spending some time in Padua, he settled in the Marches on the Adriatic, and there remained relatively unaffected by new trends.

LEONARDO DA VINCI
(Florentine, 1452–1519)

Ginevra de' Benci, c.1474

Wood. Obverse:
38.8 × 36.7 cm. (15¼ × 14½ in.);
reverse: 38.2 × 36.7 cm.
(15 × 14½ in.)

Ailsa Mellon Bruce Fund
1967.6.1a–b

Although a portrait of Ginevra de' Benci by Leonardo is mentioned by three sixteenth-century writers, the attribution of the Washington painting to that artist has been the cause of much debate. It is now accepted by virtually all Leonardo scholars. The date of the portrait, generally given as c.1474, and its commission, however, are still discussed. The sitter, born into a wealthy Florentine family, was married to Luigi Niccolini in 1474 at the age of sixteen. It was a customary practice to have a likeness painted on just such an occasion. Recently, however, the humanist Bernardo Bembo has been identified as a possible patron. He was the Venetian Ambassador to Florence from 1474–76 and again in 1478–80, dates that have been suggested for the portrait. Bembo and Ginevra, both married to others, were known to have had a platonic affair, an accepted convention at the time. The heraldic motif on the painted porphyry reverse side of the portrait, with the motto "Beauty adorns Virtue," praises her, and juniper plants symbolize chastity, considered an appropriate choice for a marriage portrait. The juniper bush, *ginepro* in Italian, is also a pun on her name.

Leonardo has painted a sensitive and finely modeled image of Ginevra. The undulating curls of her hair are set against her pale flesh, the surface of the paint smoothed by the artist's own hands. Leonardo's portrait was cut down at the bottom sometime in the past by as much as one-third. Presumably the lower section would have shown her hands, possibly folded or crossed, resting in her lap.

B oth this panel of Ginevra Bentivoglio and the companion portrait of her husband, *Giovanni II Bentivoglio*, also in the National Gallery of Art, were created when the family was at the height of its power. Giovanni, a major political figure in northern Italy, ruled the city of Bologna from 1463 until his expulsion for tyranny in 1506. For the most part, *Ginevra Bentivoglio* is unemotional, and the lifeless gaze, masklike features, and impenetrable stare reveal little of the sitter's personality.

Renaissance profile portraits recalled the images of emperors and deities on the ancient Roman coins and medals that were so highly prized at the time. Moreover, the profile format, which isolates the sitter from the observer, was particularly appropriate to Giovanni's position as a strong-willed lord.

Ercole de' Roberti absorbed Francesco del Cossa's and Cosimo Tura's eccentric style; yet he was also aware of the meticulous realism of contemporary Flemish art, as is indicated by the lustrous pearls and gems so prominently displayed on Ginevra's sleeve. But the single most salient element in Ercole's style is his superior draftsmanship. An energetic yet nervous line describes the flowing contours of Ginevra's head, the swirling concentric rhythms of her hair, and the stiff, parallel folds of her kerchief.

ERCOLE DE' ROBERTI
(Ferrarese, 1451/56–1496)

Ginevra Bentivoglio,
*c.*1480

Wood. 53.7 × 38.7 cm.
(21⅛ × 15¼ in.)

Samuel H. Kress Collection
1939.1.220

SANDRO BOTTICELLI
(Florentine, 1444 or
1445–1510)

Adoration of the Magi,
early 1480s

Wood. 70.2 × 104.2 cm.
(27⅝ × 41 in.)

Andrew W. Mellon Collection
1937.1.22

Sandro Botticelli, a Florentine, painted several versions of the theme of the Adoration of the Magi. The Magi, or wise men, were particularly venerated in Florence, as one of the city's leading religious confraternities was dedicated to them. The members of the confraternity took part in pageants organized every five years, when the journey to Bethlehem of the Magi and their retinue, often numbering in the hundreds, was re-enacted through the streets of Florence.

The Washington *Adoration* was probably painted in 1481 or 1482 in Rome, where Pope Sixtus IV had called the artist to fresco the walls of the Sistine Chapel, along with other leading Florentine masters of the day. Botticelli's linear and decorative *Adoration* is set in the ruin of a classical temple instead of a humble stable. This setting emphasizes the belief that Christianity arose from the ruins of paganism, and suggests a continuity between ancient and Christian philosophy.

Earlier Renaissance paintings of this theme, such as the Gallery's tondo by Fra Angelico and Fra Lippi (p. 15), emphasize the pomp and pageantry of the scene. As painted by Botticelli in this late version, the religious aspect is stressed. Each figure is an expression of piety, the postures of their hands and bodies revealing devotion, reverence and contemplation on the divine mystery before them.

Pietro Vannucci, called Perugino after the city in which he often lived, collaborated with other celebrated painters in one of the most prestigious commissions of the late fifteenth century – the decoration of the walls of the Sistine Chapel in 1481–82. He headed active workshops in Perugia and Florence, where he would eventually be overshadowed by his greatest pupil, Raphael.

Perugino's *Crucifixion with Saints*, painted for a chapel in the Dominican church in San Gimignano near Siena, shows Christ hanging on the cross with Mary and Saint John the Evangelist at his feet. In the two side panels, Saint Jerome with his lion, and Mary Magdalene gaze up at the figure of Christ. However, the work does not attempt to depict the actual event or place, but is a visual meditation on the theme of the Crucifixion. The serene mood is reflected in the landscape, which also reveals the influence of Flemish painting which had recently been introduced into Florence.

From the late seventeenth to the early twentieth century Perugino's *Crucifixion* was thought to be the work of his pupil Raphael. When it was discovered that the donor of the triptych died in 1497, when Raphael would have been only fourteen, Perugino's authorship once again became clear.

PERUGINO
(Umbrian, probably 1445–1523)

Crucifixion with the Virgin, Saint John, Saint Jerome and Saint Mary Magdalene, c.1485

Transferred from wood to canvas. Middle panel: 101.3 × 56.5 cm. (39⅞ × 22¼ in.); side panels: 95.2 × 30.5 cm. (37½ × 12 in.)

Andrew W. Mellon Collection 1937.1.27 a–c

FILIPPINO LIPPI
(Florentine, *c*.1457–1504)

Portrait of a Youth,
c.1485

Wood. 51 × 35.5 cm.
(20 × 13⅞ in.)

Andrew W. Mellon Collection
1937.1.20

Filippino Lippi was the son of the painter Fra Filippo Lippi, who was undoubtedly the boy's first master. After his father died in 1469, he became a pupil of Botticelli, who had a profound influence on his style. In fact, the Washington portrait comes so close to Botticelli's style that there has been considerable disagreement among scholars as to exactly which artist was responsible for it. Although it has been attributed more often to Botticelli than to Filippino, most recent authors are now agreed that it is by the younger painter. In 1483 or 1484, Filippino was assigned the task of finishing Masaccio's great frescoes in the Brancacci Chapel in Florence. This portrait bears a great resemblance to a young man portrayed there by Filippino.

During the Gothic era and early Renaissance, donors of a painting would often be portrayed as tiny figures praying at the lower edge of a painting, as in Crivelli's *Madonna Enthroned with Donor*. During the Renaissance a new interest in the individual, in human character and feeling, gave rise to the genre of portraiture as an artistic expression. Filippino's likeness of an unknown sitter shows a young man dressed in the typically plain costume of a well-to-do Florentine of the time.

The central scene of the eccentric Florentine artist Piero di Cosimo's *Visitation* depicts the meeting of the Virgin Mary and the elderly Saint Elizabeth, the mother of John the Baptist. Saint Nicholas on the left, identified by his attribute of three gold balls alluding to his charity towards the daughters of an impoverished nobleman, and Saint Anthony Abbot on the right, identified by his cane, bell and ever-present pig, sit in the foreground as studious witnesses to the event. Additional scenes relating to the birth of Christ are depicted in the background: the Annunciation painted on a distant church wall, the Nativity and Adoration of the Shepherds on the left, and the Massacre of the Innocents in the middle ground.

Piero's *Visitation* has an unbroken history, having been first described in 1550 by the artist-biographer Giorgio Vasari in his *Lives of the Artists* as an altarpiece painted for the Capponi family chapel in the church of Santo Spirito in Florence. The heightened realism of the painting probably has its source in Flemish art, in vogue in Florence at the time. Piero's composition, with a main central group and a saint on either side, recalls the traditional triptych format. However, its pyramidal quality, with the saints forming a base and the heads of Mary and Elizabeth as the apex, reflects the influence of recent work by Leonardo da Vinci.

PIERO DI COSIMO
(Florentine, 1462–1521)

Visitation with Saint Nicholas and Saint Anthony Abbot, c.1490

Wood. 184.2 × 188.6 cm.
(72½ × 74¼ in.)

Samuel H. Kress Collection
1939.1.361

ANDREA MANTEGNA
(Paduan, 1431–1506)

Judith and Holofernes,
*c.*1495

Wood. 30.2 × 18.1 cm.
($11\frac{7}{8} \times 7\frac{1}{8}$ in.)

Widener Collection
1942.9.42

The story of Judith and Holofernes comes from the Old Testament Apocrypha, sacred texts that were excluded from the Bible. Besieged by the Assyrians, the beautiful Israelite widow Judith went into the enemy camp of Holofernes to win his confidence. During a great banquet Holofernes became drunk, and later in his tent Judith seized his sword and cut off his head. Their leader gone, the enemy was soon defeated by the Israelites. This ancient heroine was understood in the Renaissance as a symbol of civic virtue, of intolerance of tyranny, and of a just cause triumphing over evil. The moralizing subject was a favorite of the artist.

Judith is portrayed as if she were a classical statue. The drapery folds of her costume, a clinging white gown, fall in sculptural forms, and her stance, the twisting *contrapposto* prevalent in Renaissance figures, derives from ancient models. The heroine is serene and calm, detached from the gruesome scene as her victim's head is dropped into a sack held by the servant.

Mantegna was trained in the Paduan workshop of Squarcione, but he was strongly influenced by the Florentine sculptor Donatello. He married the daughter of the Venetian artist Jacopo Bellini, and was influenced by his work, as well as that of his brother-in-law Giovanni Bellini.

L otto's panel can be dated to early in his career because of stylistic similarities to another *Allegory* signed by him and dated 1505, also in the National Gallery. That Lotto *Allegory* was made as a cover to a portrait of *Bernardo de' Rossi*. The *Maiden's Dream* probably served a similar function.

The subject of the panel has been the cause for much discussion. A variety of interpretations have been suggested, including the classical, *Plutus and the Nymph Rhodos*, and the literary, Petrarch's poetic vision of Laura. The painting is now referred to with the vague title of *A Maiden's Dream*, for the young woman, dressed in white, reclines in a hilly landscape resting her head in her hand. A cupid showers her with flower petals, while a female satyr gazes around a tree at a male satyr, who is more interested in his jug of wine. The composition is divided horizontally in two parts, the maiden and cupid seen on one level, the satyrs on a lower, baser level. It can be read as a choice between virtue and pleasure, *virtus* and *voluptas*, the chaste maiden in repose, or the satyr couple, symbolic in the Renaissance of lust and even evil. It was considered quite appropriate to associate such moralizing themes with portraits.

LORENZO LOTTO
(Venetian, c.1480–1556)

A Maiden's Dream,
*c.*1505

Wood. 42.9 × 33.7 cm.
(16⅞ × 13¼ in.)

Samuel H. Kress Collection
1939.1.147

GIORGIONE
(Venetian, 1477 or
1478–1510)

*Adoration of the
Shepherds*, c.1505/10

Wood. 90.8 × 110.5 cm.
(35¾ × 43½ in.)

Samuel H. Kress Collection
1939.1.289

Giorgione has always been considered one of the greatest artists of the Renaissance and one whose influence on following generations of painters was considerable. For all his fame, very little of fact is known about his life, and few paintings can be attributed to him without dispute. He initially studied with Giovanni Bellini, seems to have been influenced by Leonardo, and could claim Titian and Sebastiano del Piombo as his pupils. He died of the plague at the young age of thirty-two or thirty-three.

The *Adoration of the Shepherds* or the *Allendale Nativity*, as it is commonly known after one of the previous owners, is now generally accepted as by Giorgione. However, the debate on its attribution continues, with Bellini and the young Titian considered as possible authors. This important work had an immediate impact on Venetian painting. The composition is divided into two parts, the dark cave on the right and a luminous Venetian landscape on the left. The shimmering draperies of Joseph and Mary are set off by the darkness behind them, and are also contrasted with the tattered dress of the shepherds. The scene is one of intense meditation; the rustic shepherds are the first to recognize Christ's divinity and they kneel accordingly. Mary and Joseph also participate in the adoration, creating an atmosphere of intimacy.

Raphael was born in Urbino, a central Italian duchy noted for its elegant gentility and Renaissance scholarship. After training under Perugino, he moved to Florence toward the end of 1504.

Saint George and the Dragon, one of two versions of the theme by the artist, belonged to a series of miniature panels which Raphael painted in Florence for the celebrated court of Urbino. A Roman soldier of Christian faith, Saint George saved the daughter of a pagan king by subduing a dragon with his lance; the princess then led the dragon to the city, where the saint killed it with his sword, prompting the king and his subjects to convert to Christianity.

One unusual feature of the painting is the saint's blue garter on his armor-covered leg. Its inscription, HONI, begins the phrase "*Honi soit qui mal y pense*" or "Disgraced be he who thinks ill of it," the motto of the chivalric Order of the Garter, of which George is the patron saint. Duke Guidobaldo da Montefeltro of Urbino was made a knight of the prestigious order in 1504 by King Henry VII of England. Recent scholarship has shown that the panel was made for the king's emissary, Gilbert Talbot, and not as a gift directly for the king as was previously thought.

RAPHAEL
(Umbrian, 1483–1520)

Saint George and the Dragon, c.1506

Wood. 28.5 × 21.5 cm.
(11¼ × 8¾ in.)

Andrew W. Mellon Collection
1937.1.26

RAPHAEL
(Umbrian, 1483–1520)

Alba Madonna, c. 1510

Transferred from wood to
canvas. Diameter: 94.5 cm.
(37¼ in.)

Andrew W. Mellon Collection
1937.1.24

After only four years in Florence, Raphael moved to Rome in 1508, probably to seek more monumental commissions under the papal reign of Julius II. The major work in America from Raphael's Roman period is the *Alba Madonna*. In this "Madonna of Humility" – where, instead of on a heavenly throne or a sumptuous cushion, the Virgin is seated directly on the ground – the artist grouped the figures in a broad low pyramid, aligning them within a circle in such a way that they not only conform to their space, but dominate it as well. The tondo, or round painting or sculpture, is a predominantly Florentine format, and the influence of the Florentine masters Michelangelo and Leonardo is also apparent in the work.

Although retrospective in composition, the *Alba Madonna* is Roman in style and feeling. It has a delicacy of color and mood, with figures draped in rose pink, pale blue, and green, set in an idealized, classical landscape. The Madonna is dressed in an antique costume of turban, sandals, and flowing robes.

The serene, bucolic atmosphere of Raphael's tondo belies its emotional meaning. The Christ Child's gesture of accepting the cross from the Baptist is the focus of attention of all three figures, as if they know of Christ's future sacrifice for mankind.

Giovanni Bellini's *Feast of the Gods* is one of the greatest Renaissance paintings in America by the father of Venetian art. In this illustration of a scene from Ovid's *Fasti*, the gods, Jupiter, Neptune, and Apollo among them, revel in a wooded pastoral setting, eating and drinking, attended by nymphs and satyrs. According to the tale, Priapus, the god of fertility, approached the sleeping nymph Lotis. But Silenus' ass brayed, alerting the deities who laughed at Priapus' misadventure.

The *Feast* was the first in a series of mythologies or bacchanals commissioned by Duke Alfonso d'Este to decorate the *camerino d'alabastro*, or alabaster study, of his castle in Ferrara. The Duke also ordered works by Raphael and Fra Bartolomeo, who both died before their contributions could be finished. The patron then transferred these commissions to Titian, who painted three canvases for the room. In addition, he reworked part of Bellini's canvas; a dramatic, mountain landscape at the left partly covers Bellini's band of trees, and an intermediate landscape – probably by Dosso Dossi – has also been painted out, perhaps to create a canvas more in harmony with Titian's three later scenes for the *camerino*. The original tonalities and intensity of the colors have recently been restored, and the painting has regained its sense of depth and spaciousness.

GIOVANNI BELLINI
(Venetian, *c.*1430–1516)
and TITIAN
(Venetian, *c.*1490–1576)

The Feast of the Gods,
1514/29

Canvas. 170.2 × 188 cm.
(67 × 74 in.)

Widener Collection
1942.9.1

31

SEBASTIANO DEL PIOMBO
(Venetian, 1485–1547)

Cardinal Bandinello
Sauli, His Secretary and
Two Geographers, 1516

Transferred from wood to
canvas. 121.8 × 150.4 cm.
(48 × 59¼ in.)

Samuel H. Kress Collection
1961.9.37

One of the earliest Italian group portraits, this painting depicts Cardinal Bandinello Sauli and three companions gathered around a table covered with a Turkish carpet. Set within a narrow space closed off by a rich green wall hanging, the figures appear to have been discussing the geography manuscript lying open before them.

Bandinello Sauli of Genoa was elevated to the rank of cardinal by Pope Julius II in 1511. In 1516, when this painting was completed, Sauli was at the height of his prestige and influence in Rome. His fortunes quickly changed, for he was imprisoned in 1517 for plotting against Pope Leo X.

The artist, Sebastiano Luciani, is better known as Sebastiano del Piombo from his appointment in 1531 to the office of Keeper of the Papal Seal, or *piombo*. Probably born in Venice, his earliest artistic influences were undoubtedly Giovanni Bellini and Giorgione. The portrait of Sauli and his companions, with its varying shades of red, green, white, and black, reflects the Venetian love of resonant color. In 1511 Sebastiano moved to Rome to study the works of the High Renaissance artists there. The solidity and clarity of his life-sized figures reveal in particular the impact of Michelangelo, who befriended the young Venetian shortly after his arrival. Remaining in Rome until 1527, Sebastiano became one of the most sought after portraitists in the city.

The obscure iconography of Dosso's canvas has caused much speculation. In the past it has been titled simply *Scene from a Legend* and, more often, *Departure of the Argonauts*. The present title refers instead to an event in Virgil's *Aeneid*. Designed to celebrate the origin and growth of the Roman Empire, the *Aeneid* tells the story of Aeneas, who after the fall of Troy and seven years wandering, founded a settlement on the Italian peninsula, establishing the Roman state. The story of *Aeneas and Achates* is taken from Book I of the *Aeneid*, where Aeneas and his faithful companion Achates, their journey just begun, take refuge on the Libyan coast after their ships are wrecked in a storm.

Two other surviving scenes from the *Aeneid* by Dosso have been located, one in England, the other in Canada, and along with the Washington canvas have been identified as part of a frieze of ten pictures painted by the artist for the *camerino*, or study of Alfonso d'Este in his castle at Ferrara. Dosso Dossi was greatly influenced by Venetian art, especially the use of color and treatment of landscape as seen in works by Titian and Giorgione. He was perhaps best known in his time for soft, feathery landscapes and scenes of everyday life that are nevertheless infused with a touch of fantasy.

DOSSO DOSSI
(Ferrarese, active 1512–42)

Aeneas and Achates on the Libyan Coast, c.1520

Canvas. 58.7 × 87.6 cm.
(23⅛ × 34½ in.)

Samuel H. Kress Collection
1939.1.250

Netherlandish and Flemish Painting

At the end of the Middle Ages some of the most active centers of painting were in the Netherlands, an area corresponding to present-day Holland, Belgium, Luxembourg, and parts of France. Here artists rivaled even well-known Italian masters. Rich patrons – foremost among them the ruling house of Burgundy, but also religious orders and private citizens of the prosperous towns of Ghent, Bruges, Brussels and Tournai – commissioned paintings, sculpture, tapestries, vessels of precious metal, jewelry and illuminated books.

One of the most renowned Netherlandish artists, Jan van Eyck, revolutionized painting by substituting oil for tempera. He was court painter to Philip the Good, Duke of Burgundy, but his religious subjects and portraits were also in great demand among the merchants and bankers of Bruges. Painters such as Robert Campin and Rogier van der Weyden continued to produce works rich in detail and symbolism, as foreign artists flocked to the region, eager to learn the new techniques. Antwerp gradually took over from Bruges to become the leading art center and the wealthiest city of all Europe in the sixteenth century, attracting talented painters such as Gerard David and Jan Gossaert.

While most artists of the Low Countries showed great respect for tradition, Hieronymus Bosch stands out for his extraordinary independence and flights of imagination. Pieter Bruegel the Elder later incorporated many of Bosch's fantasies into his work, some of which reflected the political unrest and religious troubles of his own day.

Detail:
JAN VAN EYCK,
The Annunciation

In 1568 the northern provinces of the Low Countries broke away from Spanish control, eventually to become the Dutch Republic. In the southern Netherlands, which were ruled by the Spanish Regents, the Catholic church and the court continued to be the most important patrons of the arts. Perhaps most characteristic of late sixteenth-century court art is the dignified, formal portraiture of Antonis Mor. Mor's reputation was eclipsed in the seventeenth century by that of Anthony van Dyck, who eventually became court painter to Charles I.

The most sought-after Flemish painter of the seventeenth century was van Dyck's teacher, Peter Paul Rubens. After working in Italy for eight years, he returned to Antwerp, where he was besieged with commissions from the nobility and religious orders of Europe for portraits, altarpieces, mythological scenes and allegories. A scholar, linguist and diplomat, his stirring works were admired for qualities ranging from theatricality to emotional tenderness.

ROGIER VAN DER
WEYDEN
(c.1399/1400– 1464)

*Saint George and the
Dragon, c.*1432/35

Wood. 15.2 × 11.8 cm.
(6 × 4⅝ in.)

Ailsa Mellon Bruce Fund
1966.1.1

The special mixture of reality, fantasy, and virtuosity that is particular to early Netherlandish painting is nowhere more apparent than in this exquisite panel. In an episode from the popular legend, Saint George in black Gothic armor pins the dragon to the ground with his lance; at the left kneels the fashionably attired Princess Cleodolinda who was to have been sacrificed to the dragon. George was a Roman soldier living in third-century Cappadocia, but the setting has here been transformed from ancient Asia Minor to the contemporary Belgian countryside.

Passing through a series of overlapping hills, we come upon a walled city surrounded by water and dominated by a castle perched atop a fantastic mountain. This scene is almost certainly imaginary and yet is rendered with the greatest clarity and realism. The attention to specific detail has led to the suggestion that the artist made use of a magnifying glass.

The artist's interest in the depiction of light – reflecting on George's armor and the dragon's scales – and atmospheric effects shows the influence of Jan van Eyck. The painting is also stylistically related to manuscript illumination that would suggest this is an early work. The panel may originally have been part of a larger ensemble, perhaps a diptych, and was most likely used for private devotion.

This large panel painting by a follower of Robert Campin combines the new interest in nature of the fifteenth-century Netherlandish artists with a long tradition of symbolic religious painting. There is a thoroughly believable quality about the heavy folds of drapery, the delicate leaves of the flowers, and the shallow space within the garden walls. Yet this world is invested with mystical overtones through the figures' quiet poses and the minutely observed details which are painted in glowing oil colors and displayed in a steady light.

John the Baptist holds a lamb, recalling his recognition of Christ as the "Lamb of God." Seated on the left is Catherine of Alexandria with her sword and wheel, the instruments of her martyrdom. Saint Barbara offers Jesus an apple or a quince, an age-old symbol of love. Her special attribute is the impregnable tower, a symbol of her chastity. Half-hidden by Saint Anthony's robe, a pig beside him symbolizes gluttony, recalling his triumph over temptation.

The walled garden refers to a passage from the Song of Solomon where a bridegroom speaks of his beloved as "a garden enclosed . . . a fountain sealed." To early Christian and medieval theologians, Mary became associated with this bride, and the enclosed garden symbolized her virginity and also the lost Eden which is regained through Christ's birth. Even the doorway recalls Christ's saying, "I am the door. No man cometh unto the Father but by me."

Follower of
ROBERT CAMPIN
(active mid-15th century)

Madonna and Child with Saints in the Enclosed Garden, *c.*1440/60

Wood. 122.2 × 151.2 cm.
(48¼ × 59⅝ in.)

Samuel H. Kress Collection
1959.9.3

37

PETRUS CHRISTUS
(active 1444–72/73)

*The Nativity, c.*1450

Wood. 130.2 × 97.2 cm.
(51¼ × 38¼ in.)

Andrew W. Mellon Collection
1937.1.40

The *Nativity*, one of Petrus Christus' most important devotional paintings, emphasizes the sacrificial nature of Christ's coming and shows the scene as part of a chain of events in the story of the Fall and Redemption of humankind. In the foreground, a sculpted archway displays scenes of the Fall as described in Genesis. Below Adam and Eve, Atlas-like figures symbolize humanity burdened by Original Sin. The artist's depiction of the scene is like an act from a mystery or Passion play, the figures clothed in simple Flemish costume and provided with a landscape backdrop of what, at first, appears to be a Netherlandish town. However, with its two domed buildings, it would be understood as Jerusalem, the scene of the events of Christ's Passion.

Christus depicted not only the historical moment of Jesus' birth but also the enactment of the first Mass, an image deriving in part from the revelation of Saint Bridget, which had become the conventional visualization of the Nativity by the early fifteenth century. The angels wear eucharistic vestments of the subministers of the Mass, though none wears the chasuble worn by the principal celebrant, suggesting that Christ himself is here both priest and sacrifice.

This painting is an outstanding example of the abstract elegance characteristic of Rogier's late portraits. Although the identity of the sitter is unknown, her air of self-conscious dignity suggests that she is a member of the nobility. Her costume and severely plucked eyebrows and hairline are typical of those favored by highly placed ladies of the Burgundian court.

The stylish costume does not distract attention from the sitter. The dress, with its dark bands of fur, almost merges with the background. The spreading headdress frames and focuses attention upon her face. Light falls with exquisite beauty along the creases of the sheer veiling over her head, and gentle shadows mark her fine bone structure. In contrast to the spareness of execution in most of the painting, the gold filigree of her belt buckle is rendered with meticulous precision. The scarlet belt serves as a foil to set off her delicately clasped hands.

Rogier excelled as a portrait painter because he so vividly presented the character of the persons he portrayed. The downcast eyes, the firmly set lips, and the tense fingers reflect this woman's mental concentration. Rogier juxtaposed the strong sensation of the sitter's acute mental activity to his rigid control of the composition and the formality of her costume and pose, presenting the viewer with an image of passionate austerity.

ROGIER VAN DER WEYDEN
(c.1399/1400–1464)

*Portrait of a Lady, c.*1460

Wood. 36.8 × 27.3 cm.
(14½ × 10¾ in.)

Andrew W. Mellon Collection
1937.1.44

JAN VAN EYCK
(c.1390–1441)

The Annunciation,
c.1434/36

Transferred from wood to
canvas. 92.7 × 36.7 cm.
(36½ × 14½ in.)

Andrew W. Mellon Collection
1937.1.39

The Annunciation described by Saint Luke is interpreted in terms of actuality in this painting, which was probably once the left wing of a triptych. The forms – even that of the archangel – seem to have weight and volume. Light and shadow play over them in a natural way, and with amazing skill, Jan van Eyck has distinguished between the textures of materials ranging from hard, polished stone to the soft, fragile petals of flowers.

Yet religious symbolism speaks from every detail, expounding the significance of the Annunciation, and the relationship of the Old Testament to the New. The structure of the church can be interpreted symbolically; the dark upper story, with its single, stained-glass window of Jehovah, may refer to the former era of the Old Testament, while the lower part of the building, already illuminated by the "Light of the World" and dominated by transparent, triple windows symbolizing the Trinity, may refer to the Era of Grace of the New Testament. The idea of passing from old to new is further manifested in the transition from the Romanesque round-arched windows of the upper story to the early Gothic pointed arches of the lower zone, and also in the depictions on the floor tiles: David beheading Goliath and Samson destroying the Philistine temple are both Old Testament events in the salvation of the Jewish people which prefigure the salvation of humankind through the coming of Christ.

HIERONYMUS BOSCH
(c.1450–1516)

Death and the Miser,
c.1485/90

Wood. 93 × 30.8 cm.
(36⅝ × 12⅛ in.)

Samuel H. Kress Collection
1952.5.33

In this panel Bosch shows us the last moments in the life of a miser, just before his eternal fate is decided. A little monster peeping out from under the bed-curtains tempts the miser with a bag of gold, while an angel kneeling at the right encourages him to acknowledge the crucifix in the window. Death, holding an arrow, enters at the left.

Oppositions of good and evil occur throughout the painting. A lantern containing the fire of Hell, carried by the demon atop the bed canopy, balances the cross which emits a single ray of divine light. The figure in the middle ground, perhaps representing the miser earlier in his life, is shown as hypocritical; with one hand he puts coins into the strongbox where they are collected by a rat-faced demon, and with the other he fingers a rosary, attempting to serve God and Mammon at the same time. A demon emerging from underneath the chest holds up a paper sealed with red wax – perhaps a letter of indulgence or a document that refers to the miser's mercenary activities.

This type of deathbed scene derives from an early printed book, the *Ars Moriendi* or "Art of Dying," which enjoyed great popularity in the second half of the fifteenth century. The panel may have been the left wing of an altarpiece; the other panels – now missing – would have clarified the meaning of some aspects of the scene, such as the discarded and broken armor and weapons in the foreground.

HANS MEMLING
(active 1465–94)

Madonna and Child with Angels, after 1479

Wood. 58.8 × 48 cm.
(23⅛ × 18⅞ in.)

Andrew W. Mellon Collection
1937.1.41

In the tradition of his Flemish predecessors, Memling's painting contains a wealth of religious meaning; it is filled with symbols which explain the importance of Christ's mission on earth. Jesus reaches out for an apple, emblem of Original Sin; his attitude of acceptance foreshadows his future sacrifice on the cross. The angel who offers the fruit of redemption is in fact dressed in a dalmatic, the liturgical vestment worn by a deacon during the solemn High Mass. Around the arch is a carved vine of grapes referring to the wine of the eucharistic rite. On the crystal and porphyry columns stand David, as an ancestor of Christ, and Isaiah, one of the prophets who foretold the Virgin Birth.

Memling adhered closely to the northern tradition in art; the format and details of the enthroned Madonna theme recall Jan van Eyck. It is believed that Memling worked in the studio of Rogier van der Weyden at Brussels before settling in Bruges; here, he adopted Rogier's angular figural types clothed in heavy, crisp drapery, but transformed the older artist's dramatic intensity into a calm and graceful elegance. The framing archway was a device used by a number of Flemish painters including Rogier. While combining various influences, Hans Memling's own tender and pious sentiment made him the most popular artist of his day in Bruges.

This unusually large panel painting depicts three facets of Marian iconography: the Virgin's corporeal assumption, the Immaculate Conception – the crescent moon and the radiance behind her identify Mary as the Woman of the Apocalypse, mentioned in Revelation 12:1 – and the Coronation of the Virgin. The painting is of great interest to musicologists in that it depicts Renaissance instruments with great accuracy and also reflects contemporary performance practices in the arrangement of the music-making angels. At the top, a full orchestra plays before the three figures of the Trinity. The ensemble around the Virgin is a mixed consort composed of "loud" instruments (trumpets and shawms) and "soft" instruments (vielle, lute, and harp). Two of the singing angels hold books bearing legible lyrics and notations. This music, which is the source of the painting's title, has been identified as derived from a setting of the Marian antiphon, *Ave Regina Caelorum*, by Walter Frye (d. 1474/75), an English composer whose works were popular on the Continent, particularly at the Burgundian court.

Historians refer to the artist as the Master of the Saint Lucy Legend because his principal work, an altarpiece dated 1480, depicts episodes from the life of that saint. His style is characterized in both paintings by oval faces that are restrained in expression, the use of extraordinarily intense color, and a tendency to over-emphasize elaborate textures.

MASTER OF THE SAINT LUCY LEGEND
(active *c*.1480–*c*.1510)

Mary, Queen of Heaven,
c.1485/1500

Wood. 201.5 × 163.8 cm.
(79⅜ × 64½ in.)

Samuel H. Kress Collection
1952.2.13

GERARD DAVID
(*c*.1460–1523)

*The Rest on the Flight
into Egypt, c.*1510

Wood. 44.3 × 44.9 cm.
(17½ × 17¾ in.)

Andrew W. Mellon Collection
1937.1.43

The short biblical account of the Flight into Egypt (Matt.2:13–14) was elaborated upon by Early Christian and medieval theologians. In one of these apocryphal legends, the weary family paused during their journey after three days of travel. The Virgin longed for food, but the date-palm branches were too high for Joseph to pick any fruit. Thereupon Jesus commanded the tree to lower its branches. David deemphasized this miracle by giving Joseph a sturdy stick and by replacing the date palm with a Flemish chestnut tree, but a sixteenth-century audience would have remembered the apocryphal story. There are also indications of the special significance of the family: the Madonna wears robes in her symbolic colors of red and blue; fine rays of golden light emanate from the mother's head and that of the child; and the bunch of grapes held by the Madonna is a well-known symbol of the Eucharist.

David created a mood of calm equilibrium. The Madonna and Child are centrally placed, while receding diagonals and alternating bands of light and dark skillfully lead back into the landscape and harmoniously relate the figures to their surroundings. The predominance of the restful color blue throughout the composition unifies the work. All in all, *The Rest on the Flight into Egypt* is one of Gerard David's loveliest and most peaceful creations.

The pairing of unequal couples has a literary history dating back to antiquity when Plautus, a third-century BC Roman comic poet, cautioned elderly men against courting younger ladies. By the late fifteenth and early sixteenth centuries, the coupling of old men with young women or old women with young men had become popular themes in northern European art and literature.

This painting provides a clear illustration of the ideas that old age, especially lecherous old age, leads to foolishness – with the fool participating in the deception by helping to rob the old man's purse – and that women's sexual powers cause men to behave absurdly and to lose their wits and their money. The deck of cards may allude to competition between the sexes, morally loose or amorous behavior, and the loss and gain of money through gambling, themes to be found in such works as Sebastian Brandt's *Ship of Fools* and Erasmus' *Praise of Folly*.

The painting is an example of Massys' ability to assimilate elements from both northern and Italian art. Apparently familiar with Leonardo da Vinci's grotesque drawings of physiognomy and distortion, Massys adapted the facial type for the old lecher from one of Leonardo's caricatures, and the complicated pose of the suitor from Leonardo's lost drawing of an ill-matched pair, known today through a later copy.

QUENTIN MASSYS
(c.1465/66–1530)

Ill-Matched Lovers,
c.1520/25

Wood. 43.2 × 63 cm.
(17 × 24⅞ in.)

Ailsa Mellon Bruce Fund
1971.55.1

45

JAN GOSSAERT
(c.1478–1532)

Portrait of a Merchant,
*c.*1530

Wood. 63.6 × 47.5 cm.
(25 × 18¾ in.)

Ailsa Mellon Bruce Fund
1967.4.1

Gossaert's portrait shows a merchant seated in a cramped yet cozy space, surrounded by the tools of his trade. Scattered over the table are such useful items as a talc shaker used to dry ink, an ink pot, a pair of scales for testing the weight (and hence the quality) of coins, and a metal receptacle for sealing wax, quill pens, and paper. Attached to the wall are balls of twine and batches of papers labeled "miscellaneous letters" and "miscellaneous drafts." The monogram on the sitter's hat pin and index finger ring have led to his tentative identification as Jerome Sandelin, who was a tax collector in Zeeland. This region, on the southern coast of present-day Holland, was also the home of Jan Gossaert for approximately the last ten years of his life.

The artist's Netherlandish love of detail and texture combine with his admiration for the massiveness of Italian High Renaissance art to achieve here what might be termed a monumentality of the particular. At the same time, the sitter's furtive glance and prim mouth are enough to inform us of the insecurity and apprehension that haunted bankers in the 1530s, when the prevailing moral attitude was summed up by the Dutch humanist Erasmus, who asked, "When did avarice reign more largely and less punished?"

46

Legends of Anthony Abbot relate how the pious early Christian, forsaking society, journeyed into the wilderness to seek God. Anthony appears twice in this painting; in his foreground retreat, he resists the Devil's manifold temptations. After failing to yield to the evil lures, he is shown again being physically tortured while carried aloft by demons. Yet, the saint was saved by the purity of his soul.

The religious subject is presented in a revolutionary fashion; generations of earlier artists had tended to treat landscape as an unobtrusive backdrop of secondary importance, whereas now the landscape dominates the subject to such an extent that the temptation of Saint Anthony seems only incidental. This change of emphasis marks an important advance toward the development of pure landscape painting, in which Pieter Bruegel the Elder was an instrumental figure. Already, that delight in the natural world is apparent here in the shadowy depths of leafy forests, contrasting with open vistas of waterways, villages, and towns bathed in pearly light.

Perhaps the juxtaposition of a peaceful landscape with the temptations and attacks of demons was a subtle statement by this Bruegel follower on the political and moral brutalities of his time. Possibly Saint Anthony is meant allegorically to represent Everyman caught up in a world gone mad.

Follower of PIETER BRUEGEL THE ELDER

*The Temptation of Saint Anthony, c.*1550/75

Wood. 58.5 × 85.7 cm. (23 × 33¾ in.)

Samuel H. Kress Collection 1952.2.19

ANTONIS MOR
(c.1516/20–c.1575/76)

Portrait of a Gentleman,
1569

Wood. 119.7 × 88.3 cm.
(47⅛ × 34¾ in.)

Andrew W. Mellon Collection
1937.1.52

Although the identity of the sitter is unknown, his elegant dress and bearing suggest that he was an individual of wealth and distinction. The inclusion of a hunting dog was quite common in portraits of aristocrats, and the gold chains are a usual sign of honor. The suggestion of a military identification is enhanced by the gesture of his hand fisted at his waist, and the standing, three-quarter-length pose was generally used by Mor in his paintings of aristocrats as opposed to the more informal poses he used in his likenesses of middle-class subjects.

The most likely precedent for this painting is the *Portrait of Charles V* (Prado, Madrid), done in 1532 or 1533 by the Venetian artist Titian. From Titian, Mor adapted the compositional arrangement for his depiction of a standing man with a dog. Similarly, the way that light is employed, brilliantly illuminating selective portions of the figure while arbitrarily obscuring other parts in dark shadow, is thoroughly Titianesque. Mor's style also reveals his training in his native Flanders, in his close attention to detail and delight in depicting textures.

The deft handling of paint and the astute psychological presentation clearly demonstrate why Mor was such a sought-after portraitist during the sixteenth century, anticipating the achievements of the great portraitist of the aristocracy in the following century, Anthony van Dyck.

The Old Testament Book of Daniel recounts how the biblical hero was condemned to spend the night in the lions' den for worshipping God rather than the Persian king Darius. Depicted here is the moment on the following morning when, after the stone sealing the entrance was rolled away, Daniel was revealed giving thanks to his God for having been brought through the night safely. For theologians, the image of Daniel being freed from the cave symbolized the resurrection of Christ from the sepulcher.

Rubens masterfully combined realism and theatricality in such a way as to produce a strong emotional impact. Several of the lions, for instance, stare directly at the viewer; because of this suggestion that the spectator shares the same space as the lions, he is drawn into the painting and, like Daniel, is menaced by the savage predators. This immediacy is heightened by the fact that the beasts are portrayed full-size on the huge canvas and depicted with convincing realism. The lifelike movement of the lions and their superbly rendered fur results from Rubens' direct observation and sketches made in the royal menagerie in Brussels. Complementing this veracity is the dramatic lighting and the exaggerated emotionalism of Daniel's prayerful pose.

SIR PETER PAUL RUBENS
(1577–1640)

Daniel in the Lions' Den,
*c.*1615

Canvas. 224.3 × 330.4 cm.
(88¼ × 130⅛ in.)

Ailsa Mellon Bruce Fund
1965.13.1

SIR ANTHONY
VAN DYCK
(1599–1641)

Marchesa Elena Grimaldi,
Wife of Marchese Nicola
Cattaneo, probably 1623

Canvas. 246.4 × 172.7 cm.
(97 × 68 in.)

Widener Collection
1942.9.92

Anthony van Dyck's portraits of the Genoese nobility are generally recognized as one of the supreme achievements of Western portraiture and as the high point of the artist's career. Of these, his portrayal of Elena Grimaldi is the most brilliant. A marchesa both by birth and by marriage, the elegant Italian noblewoman is depicted in a stately setting expressive of her social status; she steps out of a Corinthian-columned portico onto a balustraded terrace. Behind her extends a luxuriant estate beneath a dramatically cloud-filled sky.

The painting hangs in an arrangement at the National Gallery similar to its original placement in the Cattaneo palace: flanked by van Dyck's sensitive portraits of the marchesa's two children, Filippo and Clelia. The entire composition of the mother's portrait – the low viewpoint, the two diagonals created by the advancing servant and the parasol handle, and the stairway balustrade – is planned to draw attention to her face.

In an oil sketch for this portrait (Smithsonian Institution), the marchesa wears a red flower at her right cheek. A careful study of the large, completed painting in the National Gallery reveals that the artist revised the final composition, replacing the flower with a parasol. This brilliant scarlet ellipse sets off her fair complexion, and the parasol's radiating spokes converge on her head.

SIR PETER
PAUL RUBENS
(1577–1640)

*Deborah Kip, Wife of Sir
Balthasar Gerbier, and
Her Children,* 1629/30

Canvas. 165.8 × 177.8 cm.
(65¼ × 70 in.)

Andrew W. Mellon Fund
1971.18.1

Aman of great integrity, probity, and discretion, Rubens was often
entrusted with delicate diplomatic missions which could be
accomplished under cover of his activities as an artist. So it was that in
an effort to secure peace between Spain and England he spent, in 1629,
several months in London as the guest of Balthasar Gerbier, himself a
diplomatic agent, artist, and advisor to the Duke of Buckingham.
Gerbier's wife, Deborah Kip, was the daughter of a well-to-do
member of the Dutch community in London.

Deborah Kip and four of her children are shown on a terrace
elaborately appointed with entwined caryatids who support a bower, a
setting that indicates the status of the family group. Further richness is
evident in Deborah Kip's elegantly embroidered skirt and lustrous
blouse and cap. Perched on the back of her chair is a blue-gray parrot, a
symbol of aristocratic wealth and an allusion, in Christian art, to the
perfect mother, the Virgin Mary. At the rear George holds back a
curtain; Elizabeth, dressed entirely in black, is serene and composed;
and Susan rests her arms on her mother's knee and tilts her head,
returning our gaze. Despite the elegant setting and the bravura
brushwork, Rubens controlled the composition so that we are not
allowed to lose sight of the tender relationship between a mother and
her children.

In 1632 Anthony van Dyck was invited to England to work at the court of Charles I. There he painted many impressive portraits, including this depiction of Queen Henrietta Maria at the age of twenty-four. The French-born queen exerted a strong influence on court fashion and protocol, introducing to England the fashions of the Continent; she is shown here wearing a delicate lace collar instead of the stiff Elizabethan ruff.

The queen's love of amusement is symbolized by the presence of the dwarf and monkey, both royal favorites. Jeffrey Hudson, the fourteen-year-old dwarf, had been given to her as a gift and remained a faithful companion until her death.

The portrait is a superb demonstration piece of van Dyck's working methods and the reasons for his phenomenal success. Henrietta probably posed only briefly for a sketch, so the painting itself had to be executed from a model or mannequin attired in the queen's costume. The artist shows a tall woman with an oval face, pointed chin, and long nose. According to sketches done from life, however, she actually was a tiny person with a petite figure, round head, and small features. She thus has been greatly idealized. The fluted column emphasizes her already exaggerated height, and the crown and cloth of gold signify her royalty.

SIR ANTHONY
VAN DYCK (1599–1641)

*Queen Henrietta Maria
with Her Dwarf,*
probably 1633

Canvas. 219.1 × 134.8 cm.
(86¼ × 53⅛ in.)

Samuel H. Kress Collection
1952.5.39

German Painting

Given Germany's large size and – throughout history – its territorial and political divisions, it is no wonder that the country's art is marked by a strong regionalism. During the second half of the fourteenth century a major school of art developed in Bohemia, centered in the university city of Prague and patronized by Charles IV (1316–78). This style – as seen in the diptych *The Death of Saint Clare* – shares many traits with the International Gothic style imported by French and Italian artists.

The sixteenth century was a heroic age of German art; the best known and arguably the greatest German artist, Albrecht Dürer, was born in Nuremberg in 1471. His trips to Italy, where he became acquainted with Gentile and Giovanni Bellini and with theories of perspective and proportions, were of inestimable importance for the history of northern European art.

The intensity of religious sentiment that preceded the Protestant Reformation, as well as the upheaval of the Reformation itself, had a decisive impact upon German life. The *Small Crucifixion* is a tangible expression of the faith of Matthias Grünewald, whose mysticism and genius as a colorist were rediscovered in the early twentieth century and particularly admired by the German expressionists. Lucas Cranach the Elder was a close friend of Martin Luther and *The Crucifixion with the Converted Centurion*, alluding to salvation by faith alone, may be considered a Protestant subject. Hans Holbein the Younger was one painter who did not thrive in post-Reformation Germany; he left for England in 1526 and eventually became portraitist to Henry VIII.

German art did not maintain its brilliance into the seventeenth century, in part because of the disruption of the Thirty Years' War (1618–48) and in part because of the allure of other artistic centers. Two of the finest artists of the period – Adam Elsheimer and Johann Liss – worked mainly in Italy.

Although the development of German art in the eighteenth and nineteenth centuries roughly paralleled that of other countries, there is a unique character to German romanticism, involving an almost mystical love of and identification with the hidden forces of nature. The German romantic painter Arnold Böcklin died in 1901 yet several aspects of his style, his symbolist vocabulary and emphasis on intuition and empathy are essential to an understanding of the art of the twentieth century.

Detail:
LUCAS CRANACH, the Elder,
The Crucifixion with the Converted Centurion

MASTER OF
HEILIGENKREUZ
(active early 15th century)

The Death of Saint Clare,
*c.*1410

Wood. 66.4 × 54.5 cm.
(26⅛ × 21¾ in.)

Samuel H. Kress Collection
1952.5.83

S aint Clare, a wealthy woman from the central Italian town of Assisi, gave up all her possessions to pursue the goals of poverty and service preached by Saint Francis. She founded an order of nuns known as the Poor Clares, which was recognized by the Pope in 1253. This painting depicts the vision of the death of Saint Clare as experienced by one of her followers, Sister Benvenuta of Diambra.

In the vision of Saint Benvenuta, the Virgin Mary and a procession of virgin martyrs appeared to Saint Clare on her deathbed. Here Mary, dressed in a rich brocade robe, supports Saint Clare's head, while the other elegantly robed and crowned saints follow behind, identified by the tiny attributes they hold.

The work of the Master of Heiligenkreuz, who was probably active in Lower Austria, illustrates the cosmopolitan aspect of the International Style, which flourished around 1400. While his exaggerated figures with their bulbous foreheads and clinging drapery are characteristically Austrian, the anonymous painter must also have been aware of the most advanced art produced at the courts of Paris and Prague. Thus the surface of the panel is worked in a variety of different techniques to fashion a particularly splendid object.

·I·II·T·I·

The anonymous master who painted this work was the leading painter in Cologne shortly after 1400. His name derives from his finest work, *Saint Veronica with the Sudarium*, preserved in the Alte Pinakothek, Munich. In this *Crucifixion* the attenuated boneless figures, the sinuous contours of the drapery folds, and the delicate colors set off against the gold ground are all hallmarks of the International Gothic style. The subject is Christ's suffering and death on the cross and the grief of the weeping Virgin Mary and Saint John the Evangelist; yet, the sorrow of the event is softened by the figures' gentle expressions. Even the tiny angels who catch the blood flowing from Christ's wounds add a decorative and fanciful touch.

The painting was probably used as a focus for prayers and meditation by a Carthusian monk, since a member of that monastic order is shown kneeling at the right of the cross. The painting's small size would make it suitable for such use, probably in the monk's cell.

Cologne was the largest and most densely populated city in Germany at the end of the Middle Ages. It supported a wealthy middle class and many religious institutions, including the Charterhouse of Saint Barbara, for which this *Crucifixion* may have been painted.

MASTER OF
SAINT VERONICA
(active *c*.1395–1420)

The Crucifixion,
c.1400/10

Wood. 46 × 31.4 cm.
(18⅛ × 12⅜ in.)

Samuel H. Kress Collection
1961.9.29

JOHANN KOERBECKE
(c.1420–91)

The Ascension, 1456/57

Wood. 92.6 × 64.8 cm.
(36½ × 25½ in.)

Samuel H. Kress Collection
1959.9.5

Looking up in amazement as Christ ascends into heaven are the twelve apostles. Kneeling with them is the Virgin, the only one to have a halo. Although few of the men can be identified, John the Evangelist is recognizable. He is the blond, beardless youth dressed in green who solicitously puts his arm around Mary. Surrounding the risen Christ are a group of Old Testament personages who either predicted or foreshadowed events of his life on earth.

The gold background, bright colors, and compact space reveal the lingering influence of the International Gothic. However, a new spirit of visual observation also can be detected. The sharp, angular folds of the drapery evoke the perception of real human forms beneath the material. Further, the faces of the apostles reveal a broad variety of human emotions.

This panel was once part of the high altar in the Cistercian abbey church of Marienfeld at Münster. At its center was a richly gilded sculpture of the Virgin and Child. Folding wings extended from this core with pictures on the fronts and backs. When the shutters were open, eight scenes – including the National Gallery's painting – revealed the story of Mary's life. In the closed positions, eight other subjects recounted Christ's Passion.

Saints played a very important role in the popular piety of the late Middle Ages. They were considered to be not only patrons and protectors against all manner of ills, but also mediators between the individual worshiper and God.

In this unusual scene, fourteen saints participate as witnesses at the Baptism of Christ. All the saints are vividly characterized by costume and attributes. They include the giant Christopher carrying the Christ Child on his shoulders, Catherine of Alexandria with sword and wheel of her martyrdom, Augustine holding his heart pierced by the arrow of divine love, Mary Magdalene with her ointment jar, and the chivalrous George kneeling on his dragon. The gold background, the luminescent cloud on which the saints float, and the unrealistic island setting for the Baptism itself all impart a visionary quality to the scene.

The Master of the Saint Bartholomew Altar, named after his monumental altarpiece now in Munich, was active in Cologne. Early in his career he seems to have worked as a manuscript illuminator, and this tradition is evident in his fluid paint handling and sparkling treatment of decorative details.

MASTER OF THE SAINT
BARTHOLOMEW ALTAR
(active c.1475–1510)

The Baptism of Christ,
c.1485/1510

Wood. 106.1 × 170.5 cm.
(41¾ × 67⅛ in.)

Samuel H. Kress Collection
1961.9.78

ALBRECHT DÜRER
(1471–1528)

Madonna and Child,
*c.*1496/99

Wood. 50.2 × 39.7 cm.
(19¾ × 15⅝ in.)

Samuel H. Kress Collection
1952.2.16a

Dürer was born in Nuremberg and received a typical medieval training from his goldsmith father and from the Nuremberg painter Michael Wolgemut. Yet he was one of the major transmitters of the ideas of the Italian Renaissance to artists in the North. This was the result of direct experience acquired on two trips to Italy, as well as of his own diligent study of ideal figural proportions and perspective.

Dürer traveled to Venice in 1494/95 and 1505/07. While there, he became well acquainted with Giovanni Bellini, whose influence is evident in the *Madonna and Child.* The athletic Christ Child, the stable pyramid of the Virgin's form, the strong and almost sculptural modeling of the figures, and the contrast of clear blue and red setting off Mary's shape all recall Bellini's treatment of the same subject.

On the other hand, Mary's placement in the corner of a room with a window open on a distant view indicates Dürer's familiarity with Netherlandish devotional images. The minute treatment of the Alpine landscape and the careful delineation of all textures and surfaces equally remind one of Dürer's persistent fascination with the North's tradition of visual exactitude.

The *Madonna and Child* probably was intended for private devotion. The diminutive coat-of-arms in the lower left corner identifies the patron as a member of the wealthy Nuremberg mercantile family of Haller von Hallerstein.

This scene is painted on the reverse side of Dürer's *Madonna and Child*. The story of Lot and his daughters comes from the nineteenth chapter of the Book of Genesis. In the foreground, Lot and his two children are portrayed fleeing from the destruction of Sodom and Gomorrah, which erupt in blinding explosions of fire in the background. Lot's wife is visible on the path at the upper left in the middle distance. She has been turned into a pillar of salt for disobeying the divine command by looking back on the scene of retribution.

This scene was important for the moral lesson it taught. Like the story of Noah and the flood, that of Lot and the desolation of Sodom and Gomorrah was an allegory demonstrating the power of God to save the righteous.

Since the combination of the story of Lot with the depiction of the Virgin and Child is extremely unusual, the exact relation of the two images remains unclear. However, they could be understood as two examples of the value of a just life and of the pervasive grace of God, especially if the *Madonna and Child* on the obverse was intended as a private devotional image.

ALBRECHT DÜRER
(1471–1528)

Lot and His Daughters,
c.1496/99

Wood. 50.2 × 39.7 cm.
(19¾ × 15⅝ in.)

Samuel H. Kress Collection
1952.2.16b

BERNHARD STRIGEL
(*c.*1460/61–1528)

*Saint Mary Salome and
Her Family, c.*1520/28

Wood. 12.4 × 62.9 cm.
(49 × 25¾ in.)

Samuel H. Kress Collection
1961.9.89

*S*aint Mary Salome and Her Family together with its companion piece *Saint Mary Cleophas and Her Family*, also in the National Gallery, were wings from an altarpiece combining painting and sculpture that was dedicated to the Holy Kinship or extended family of Christ. There was a fascination with the details of the life of the Holy Family as well as a growing desire to experience the Gospels on a human level in the late Middle Ages. According to the *Golden Legend*, written about 1270 as a compilation of earlier tales, Saint Anne married three times, her third husband being the father of Mary Salome, who was thus the half-sister of the Virgin Mary.

Strigel, who worked in Memmingen, a small city in the southern German province of Bavaria, makes Mary Salome the center of a comfortable domestic scene. Her father Salomas, wearing characteristic Jewish headgear, hovers behind her, while her husband Zebedee sits beside her. Their two small sons James and John are identifiable by the names inscribed on their halos. They will grow up to be disciples of Christ, and indeed Saint John is already busy writing a book in Hebrewlike characters, foretelling his future activity as one of the four authors of the Gospels.

Among the outstanding German artists of the period around 1500 was Hans Baldung Grien, a printmaker and painter. He produced book illustrations, devotional woodcuts, stained-glass window designs, portraits, and morality paintings as well as religious panels such as this one.

John the Baptist is here depicted to the left of Jesus. He simultaneously gestures to the lamb at his feet and to the infant, visually alluding to his own description of Christ as "the Lamb of God." The Virgin's mother, Saint Anne, although dressed in a sixteenth-century wimple, wears her traditional robe of red, a symbol of divine love. Garbed in green, symbolic of rebirth and eternal life, Mary offers Jesus an apple. This fruit, associated with the fall of Adam and Eve, here signifies Mary as the new Eve and Christ as the second Adam.

Baldung Grien's figures are symbolically, rather than realistically, depicted. Mary, for instance, is represented as a very young girl. And, although John and Jesus historically were about the same age, the Baptist is portrayed as an adult to emphasize his prophetic message. The painting was discovered in a small village church in Alsace, an area where the artist spent most of his life.

HANS BALDUNG GRIEN
(c.1484/85–1545)

Saint Anne with the Christ Child, the Virgin, and Saint John the Baptist, c.1511

Wood. 87 × 75.9 cm.
(34¼ × 29⅞ in.)

Samuel H. Kress Collection
1961.9.62

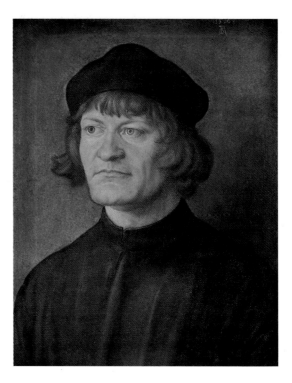

ALBRECHT DÜRER
(1471–1528)

*Portrait of a Clergyman
(Johann Dorsch ?)*, 1516

Parchment on canvas.
42.9 × 33.2 cm. (16⅞ × 13 in.)

Samuel H. Kress Collection
1952.2.17

Although the sitter's identity is not verified, he is possibly Johann Dorsch, a cleric in Nuremberg. The clergyman's ardor, spiritual zeal, and intense determination are communicated through the turn of the head, the fixed, staring eyes, and the tight, compressed lips.

With great respect for reality, Dürer has recorded every detail of the man's appearance regardless of how small or unimportant it may be: the wrinkles and lines of the face, the individual strands of fine hair, the coarse skin texture, and even the reflection of window panes in the irises of the eyes. This incisive clarity and accuracy derive in large part from Dürer's experience in the graphic arts.

The portrait is of further interest for having been painted on parchment rather than on wood, which was still the most common support. Experimenting with techniques and materials, Dürer also used silk and linen at times. The animal skin gives the paint surface a fine, smooth quality and lends amazing richness to the oil colors.

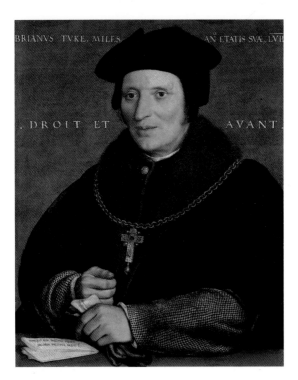

The political strength of Henry VIII's regime lay in his ability to choose advisors who were both wise and learned. One of these men was Sir Brian Tuke. As Master of the Posts, he organized and established England's postal service. In 1528 Sir Brian was appointed treasurer and secretary of the royal household, a position he held until his death in 1545. He was also admired as an eloquent speaker and literary figure who authored a preface to an edition of Chaucer.

The portrait, which shows Tuke at the age of fifty-seven, exemplifies the qualities most praised in Holbein's work: precise observation of detail and impartial, accurate portrayal of the face. Yet the image is also tinged with gentle sorrow. On the table beneath Tuke's left hand is a folded paper bearing a quotation from the Book of Job (10:20) which begins, "Are not my days few?" The gravity of the sentiment is echoed in Tuke's countenance; his faint smile is pained and his eyes, fixed but not focused, seem melancholy.

HANS HOLBEIN,
the Younger
(1497/98–1543)

Sir Brian Tuke, c.1527

Wood. 49.2 × 38.7 cm.
(19⅜ × 15¼ in.)

Andrew W. Mellon Collection
1937.1.65

Matthias Grünewald's *Small Crucifixion* is a masterful example of that artist's ability to translate his deep spiritual faith into pictorial form. Each individual, according to Grünewald, must re-experience within himself not only the boundless joy of Christ's triumphs but also the searing pains of his Crucifixion.

In order to communicate this mystical belief, Grünewald resorted to a mixture of ghastly realism and coloristic expressiveness. Silhouetted against a greenish-blue sky and illuminated by an undefined light source, Christ's haggard and emaciated frame sags limply on the cross. The details – the twisted and gnarled feet and hands, the crown of thorns, the agonized look upon Jesus' face, and the ragged loincloth – bear strident witness to physical suffering and emotional torment. This abject mood is intensified by the anguished expressions and demonstrative gestures of John the Evangelist, the Virgin Mary, and the kneeling Mary Magdalene.

Grünewald's dissonant, eerie colors were also rooted in biblical fact. The murky sky, for instance, corresponds to Saint Luke's description of "a darkness over all the earth." Grünewald, who himself witnessed a full eclipse in 1502, has recreated here the dark and rich tonalities associated with such natural phenomena.

Today, only twenty paintings by Grünewald are extant, and *The Small Crucifixion* is the only one of them in America.

MATTHIAS GRÜNEWALD
(*c*.1475/80–1528)

The Small Crucifixion,
c.1511/20

Wood. 61.6 × 46 cm.
(24¼ × 18⅛ in.)

Samuel H. Kress Collection
1961.9.19

LUCAS CRANACH,
the Elder (1472–1553)

The Crucifixion with the Converted Centurion,
1536

Wood. 50.8 × 34.9 cm.
(20 × 13¾ in.)

Samuel H. Kress Collection
1961.9.69

In *The Crucifixion with the Converted Centurion,* Lucas Cranach the Elder chose to portray a scene of religious redemption. The crucified Christ, silhouetted against a darkened and troubled sky, is at the point of death; his last words from the cross are inscribed above him in German: VATER IN DEIN HET BEFIL ICH MEIN GAIST (Father, into thy hand I commend my spirit [Luke 23:46]). At that moment, a Roman centurion, astride a white charger, recognizes Christ's divinity and pronounces: WARLICH DISER MENSCH IST GOTES SVN GEWEST (Truly, this man was the Son of God [Mark 15:39]).

The theme of *The Crucifixion with the Converted Centurion* especially appealed to Protestants because it clearly illustrated the doctrine of salvation by faith alone, the central precept of their creed. The centurion, clothed in contemporary armor, symbolized the "Knight of Christ" who steadfastly defends his new-won belief despite all adversity.

From 1505 until his death, Cranach was the court painter to three successive electors of Saxony. He became close friends with Luther – who lived in the Saxon town of Wittenberg – and is considered the foremost artist of the Reformation.

Hans Mielich was the leading painter in Bavaria in the mid-sixteenth century. His art was greatly influenced by Albrecht Altdorfer with whom he worked in Regensburg from about 1536 to 1538. After a trip to Rome in 1542, Mielich settled in his native Munich, becoming court painter to Albrecht V, the Duke of Bavaria.

This sitter's identification with the Fröschl family derives from the presence of their coat-of-arms painted on the reverse of the panel. The man might be Jakob Fröschl of Wasserburg. A grain merchant and city councilor in Wasserburg, he married in 1539, and thus this may be his wedding portrait.

The sitter's large scale, dignified bearing, and richly decorated padded black jacket all suggest someone of great power and importance. In the background, visible through the wood-trimmed window, is a landscape with trees, a house, and a man and a horse plowing. Clearly, the man was a substantial landowner as well.

Beyond its representational fascination, the portrait is a wonderful study in the abstract interplay of pattern, form, and outline. The massive, simple expanse of the black jacket contrasts with the intricately marbleized decor of the wall which, in turn, mimics the irregular configurations of the trees.

HANS MIELICH
(1516–73)

A Member of the Fröschl Family, c.1539/40

Wood. 61.6 × 47 cm.
(24¼ × 18½ in.)

Gift of David Edward Finley and Margaret Eustis Finley, 1984.66.1

PARVVLE PATRISSA, PATRIÆ VIRTVTIS ET HÆRES
ESTO, NIHIL MAIVS MAXIMVS ORBIS HABET.
GNATVM VIX POSSVNT COELVM ET NATVRA DEDISSE,
HVIVS QVEM PATRIS, VICTVS HONORET HONOS.
ÆQVATO TANTVM, TANTI TV FACTA PARENTIS,
VOTA HOMINVM, VIX QVO PROGREDIANTVR, HABENT
VINCITO, VICISTI, QVOT REGES PRISCVS ADORAT
ORBIS, NEC TE QVI VINCERE, POSSIT, ERIT.

HANS HOLBEIN,
the Younger
(1497–1543)

Edward VI as a Child,
probably *c.*1538

Wood. 56.8 × 44.1 cm.
(22⅜ × 17⅜ in.)

Andrew W. Mellon Collection
1937.1.64

After the Reformation had brought social and political upheaval to Germany, creating an unfavorable climate for artists, Holbein moved to England in 1526. He first painted for Sir Thomas More's circle of high servants of the crown and then became painter to the King himself, Henry VIII. As court painter Holbein produced portraits, festival sets and other decorations intended to exalt the King and the Tudor dynasty, and also designs for jewelry and metalwork.

In his portraits Holbein endowed his sitters with a powerful physical presence which was increasingly held in check by the psychological reserve and elegance of surface appropriate to a court setting. This portrait of Henry VIII's only legitimate son and much desired male heir exemplifies these qualities. Edward was born on 12 October 1537 to Henry's third wife, Jane Seymour, and this portrait appears to be the one given to the King on the New Year of 1539. The form of the portrait and the long Latin verse provided by the poet Richard Morison flatter the royal father and emphasize the succession.

Holbein depicted the baby prince as erect and self-possessed, one hand holding a scepter and the other open in a gesture of blessing. His frontal pose before a parapet is a type reserved for royalty or for images of holy figures.

FONTIS NYMPHA SACRI SOM-
NVM NE RVMPE QVIESCO ·

A note of ambiguity or unease often gives a piquant quality to German adaptations of the Renaissance ideal. Cranach's painting of a classical nymph represents an Italian theme but gives it a moralizing twist common to late Gothic courtly and amorous subjects.

The nymph reclines beside a spring, perhaps a reference to a legendary ancient Roman fountain with which a Latin verse was associated. The text was translated by Alexander Pope in 1725:

> *Nymph of the grot, these springs I keep,*
> *And to the murmurs of these waters sleep;*
> *Ah, spare my slumbers, gently tread the cave!*
> *And drink in silence, or in silence lave!*

The inscription on this painting – *I am the nymph of the sacred spring, do not disturb my sleep. I am resting* – may be an allusion to the poem. Though exposed by modern scholarship as a fifteenth-century counterfeit, the poem influenced Italian garden decoration, which not infrequently included fountains with attendant reclining nymphs. However, the proportions of Cranach's nude are more Gothic than classical, and the robe on which she rests her head is that of a German court lady. Far from sleeping, she admires herself beguilingly through lowered eyelids. The painting is intended both as an enticement and a warning to Cranach's sophisticated patrons.

LUCAS CRANACH,
the Elder (1472–1553)

*The Nymph of the
Spring*, after 1537

Wood. 48.5 × 72.9 cm.
(19 × 28⅝ in.)

Gift of Clarence Y. Palitz
1957.12.1

JOHANN LISS
(c.1597–1631)

*The Satyr
and the Peasant,*
probably c.1623/26

Canvas. 133.5 × 166.5 cm.
(52½ × 65½ in.)

Widener Collection
1942.9.39

The unusual subject of this painting comes from one of Aesop's fables. In his *Man and the Satyr*, he related how a demigod helped a peasant who was lost on a wintry day. When the mortal put his chilled fingers to his mouth to breathe warmth onto them, the immortal satyr was astonished. Later, in thanks for the satyr's guidance, the peasant invited him to eat. The soup being hot, the man blew on his spoon to cool it. Johann Liss portrayed the tale's climax when the satyr jumps up in disgust, proclaiming, "From this moment I renounce your friendship, for I will have nothing to do with one who blows hot and cold with the same breath" – the moral being that all humans are hypocrites because they inconsistently blow hot and cold.

Johann Liss was among the initiators of the dynamic baroque style of the 1600s. The sonorous color scheme shows his knowledge of past Venetian masters such as Titian and Veronese, while the dramatic conflict of light and shadow reveals an acquaintance with the spotlighting which Caravaggio concurrently employed in Rome. But the main influences here are the energized movement and robust figure types derived from the contemporary Antwerp geniuses, Jacob Jordaens and Peter Paul Rubens.

In Arnold Böcklin's *Sanctuary of Hercules*, three soldiers kneel reverently on the outer step of a shrine, while a fourth looks defiantly off into the distance. The sky, a rich panoply of gray, blue, and white, signals an approaching storm, and a strong wind whips through the trees, scattering the leaves and ruffling the plumes on the soldiers' helmets. At the painting's focal point is the sanctuary itself, constructed of stones which are trimmed with polished marble and rest upon an equally smooth circular base. Within the enclosure is a sacred grove of massive trees and at the back, seen in darkened profile, a statue of Hercules, mythical hero and protector from danger.

At first glance, the subject appears very realistic and the shrine archaeologically accurate. Yet the scene also conveys a definite mood of mystery. The stones' pure and richly harmonious colors glow with an unnatural radiance. The gloom inside the grove is equaled by the dark ominous clouds, lit by flashes of lightning on the horizon. Indebted to the romantics of the first half of the nineteenth century, Böcklin rejected the idea of painting solely *from* nature, and strove to express his own feelings *through* nature, with the use of vibrant coloration and dramatic lighting.

ARNOLD BÖCKLIN
(1827–1901)

The Sanctuary of Hercules, 1884

Wood. 113.8 × 180.5 cm.
(44⅞ × 71⅛ in.)

Andrew W. Mellon Fund
1976.36.1

Spanish Painting

The earliest Spanish paintings in the National Gallery date from the age of Ferdinand and Isabella, who reigned from 1474 until 1504. Known as *Los Reyes Católicos* ("the Catholic Kings") because of their religious zeal, they sought to impose religious unity over the varied provinces of the Iberian peninsula as a means of achieving political hegemony. *The Marriage at Cana*, one of several works in the collection that reflect Isabella's preference for devotional subjects painted in the Flemish style, is of historic as well as aesthetic interest; it not only represents a biblical wedding but may also document two contemporary weddings that brought Spain into the mainstream of European history, by establishing lasting ties between the Spanish royal house and the Habsburgs of Austria.

Spain's preoccupation with spiritual matters remained largely undiluted by the new humanistic ideas of the Renaissance. In the wake of the great schism caused by the Protestant Reformation, the Catholic church set strict guidelines for artists requiring that they express the dogma vividly and convincingly in order to stir the emotions and encourage piety and devotion. Domenikos Theotokopoulos, called El Greco, was well able to meet that challenge; his expressive spatial and figural distortions and flickering lights and darks carried the world of the spirit as far as it could go. The next century's interest in the material world fostered a new realism in painting and saw the introduction of secular subjects such as still life and genre scenes. Dominated by such masters as Juan van der Hamen y León, Francisco de Zurbarán, Bartolomé Esteban Murillo, Juan de Valdés Leal, and, above all Diego Velázquez, the seventeenth century has since been thought of as a Golden Age, not only in painting but in literature as well.

There were no immediate successors to the great Spanish painters of the seventeenth century; in the eighteenth century, the Bourbons who succeeded the Habsburgs on the Spanish throne commissioned foreign artists, among them Anton Raphael Mengs and Giovanni Battista Tiepolo, to decorate their palaces. The first native painter of genius since Velázquez was Francisco de Goya, whose innovations anticipated much that painting and the graphic arts would explore in the nineteenth century, a time of great artistic ferment, when romanticists, realists, symbolists, impressionists and expressionists – each for different reasons – would claim him as their antecedent.

Detail:
EL GRECO,
Laocoön

MASTER OF THE
CATHOLIC KINGS
(Hispano-Flemish, active
late 15th century)

The Marriage at Cana,
*c.*1495/97

Wood. 153.1 × 92.6 cm.
(60¾ × 36¾ in.)

Samuel H. Kress Collection
1952.5.42

hrist is shown here at the scene of his first miracle – the transformation of water into wine. He stands at the banquet table, his right hand raised in a gesture of benediction, while a servant, pointing to the clay jars on the floor as if to explain what has just taken place, offers the bridal pair a goblet of the transformed liquid.

That the artist has absorbed the traditions of fifteenth-century Flemish painting is evident in his mastery of the oil technique and his meticulous rendering of texture and minute detail. Combined with these elements are purely Spanish ones such as the solemn faces with downturned mouths and the recognizably Spanish costumes.

The unidentified artist's name is derived from his principal work, *The Altarpiece of the Catholic Kings,* of which this panel is a part. Visible among the heraldic devices are the insignia of provinces united by the marriage of Ferdinand and Isabella. The additional presence of the Holy Roman Emperor's coat-of-arms implies that *The Marriage at Cana* also alludes to two contemporary weddings significant in European history – those of Ferdinand and Isabella's daughter Juana in 1496 and son Juan in 1497 to the son and daughter of the Holy Roman Emperor Maximilian I of Austria.

Although the original reference to the wise men, or magi, in the Gospel of Matthew is minimal, churchmen eventually elevated them to the status of kings, gave them names – Balthasar, Caspar, and Melchior – and invested their gifts of gold, frankincense, and myrrh with specific meanings. The royal status and foreign origins of the three travelers inspired medieval and Renaissance artists, who gave free reign to their imaginations in treating the colorful subject.

Juan de Flandes (John of Flanders) took the opportunity to paint a fanciful scene replete with opulent costumes, gleaming gold and jewels, and varied racial types. All wear exotic headgear and carry ornate vessels containing their gifts. Visible in the distance, on horseback, are several smaller figures, members of the kings' retinue.

Although there are numerous references to this presumably northern painter in the records of his Spanish patrons, nothing is known of his early years. His reputation as an artist derives entirely from the works he produced in Spain, where he served as court painter to Queen Isabella until her death in 1504. Later, he painted this panel and its three companion pieces, also in the National Gallery; together, they once formed part of a large altarpiece in the Church of San Lázaro in Palencia.

JUAN DE FLANDES
(Hispano-Flemish, active 1496–1519)
The Adoration of the Magi, c.1508/19

Wood. 126.1 × 82.6 cm.
(49⅝ × 32¼ in.)

Samuel H. Kress Collection
1961.9.24

MICHEL SITTOW
(Netherlandish,
c.1469–1525/26)

*Portrait of Diego de
Guevara (?)*, c.1515/18

Wood. 33.6 × 23.7 cm.
(13¼ × 9⁵⁄₁₆ in.)

Andrew W. Mellon Collection
1937.1.46

Michel Sittow, a northern painter who was born in Estonia on the Baltic Sea but apprenticed in Bruges, was an acclaimed portraitist at the Spanish court. After Queen Isabella's death in 1504, his peripatetic career took him to several northern European centers, including Burgundy, where he probably painted this portrait.

The sitter gazes with serious mien, not at the viewer, but at an unseen point beyond the picture's frame. The ornate carpet covering the stone parapet on which his hand rests provided scholars with an important clue that led to the discovery of the object of his concentration – a painting of the Madonna and Child, of similar dimensions, in the Gemäldegalerie in Berlin. In that panel a larger portion of the parapet, covered by the same carpet, appears as a support for the Christ Child. It seems certain that the Berlin and Washington panels were originally hinged together to form a devotional diptych.

Circumstantial evidence suggests that the National Gallery's portrait represents Diego de Guevara, a nobleman whose family came from Santander in northern Spain. For forty years Don Diego was a valued member of the Habsburg court in Burgundy. Supporting this identity is the embroidered cross of the Spanish Order of Calatrava on his golden doublet; after serving in numerous positions of trust in the households of Philip the Fair and Charles V, Don Diego was appointed to the wardenship of that order.

In this tempestuous scene, El Greco depicted an angry Christ driving the moneychangers from the Temple. An uncommon theme, it became increasingly popular in the latter half of the sixteenth century, promoted by the Council of Trent as a symbol of the Catholic church's attempt to purify itself after the Protestant Reformation. Here El Greco portrayed partially draped women and bare-chested men writhing and twisting to escape the blows of Christ's scourge, emphasizing the agitation of the participants and exaggerating their irreverence. The setting is one of classical grandeur, more reminiscent of an Italian Renaissance palace than of the sacred precincts of the Temple in Jerusalem.

This panel was painted in Venice before El Greco made his way to Spain. The illusionistic space and voluptuous figures in this early work are vastly different from the flattened space and stylized forms of Byzantine art, which continued to dominate painting in El Greco's native Crete. El Greco's arrival in Venice, in about 1567, coincided with a high point in that city's artistic achievement. That the Cretan artist had absorbed the influence of the Venetian masters and taught himself a new way of painting is evident in the movement and drama, solidly modeled figures, and boldly brushed colors of this panel. The influence of the Venetians is equally evident in the elaborate architectural setting with its complicated perspective.

EL GRECO (Domenikos Theotokopoulos) (1541–1614)

Christ Cleansing the Temple, probably before 1570

Wood. 65.4 × 83.2 cm. (25¾ × 32¾ in.)

Samuel H. Kress Collection 1957.14.4

EL GRECO (Domenikos
Theotokopoulos)
(1541–1614)

*Saint Martin and the
Beggar*, 1597/99

Canvas. 193.5 × 103 cm.
(76¼ × 40½ in.)

Widener Collection
1942.9.25

Commissioned for the Chapel of San José in Toledo by Martín Ramírez, a namesake of the saint and donor of the chapel, *Saint Martin and the Beggar* was part of one of the artist's most successful ensembles.

The saint, who lived during the reign of Constantine the Great, was a member of the imperial cavalry stationed near Amiens, in Gaul. Coming upon a shivering beggar near the city gates on a cold winter day, the young soldier divided his cloak with his sword and shared it with him. Tradition has it that Christ later appeared to Martin in a dream, saying, "What thou hast done for that poor man, thou hast done for me."

El Greco portrayed the fourth-century saint as a young nobleman, clad in elegant gold-damascened armor, astride a white Arabian horse. Seen from a low vantage point, the figures seem monumental, looming over the landscape with its distant view of Toledo and the River Tagus. The saint's relatively naturalistic proportions contrast with the attenuated form of the nearly nude beggar. The obvious distortion of the beggar's form suggests that he is not of this world and hints at the later revelation of his true identity in Martin's dream.

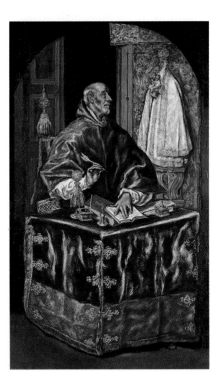

Ildefonso, whose name is more familiar in its Castilian form, Alfonso, was appointed archbishop of Toledo in 657 and later became that city's patron saint. He was especially famed for his book defending the purity of the Virgin, which he was said to have written at her dictation.

El Greco represented the saint in a richly decorated room, seated at a writing table furnished with costly silver desk ornaments consistent with the style of the artist's own time. The contemporary setting notwithstanding, an otherworldly aura pervades the room as the saint pauses in his writing and, as though awaiting the next word, gazes attentively at the source of his inspiration, a statuette of the Madonna. The combination of strangely compacted space, the chalky highlights that play over the saint's sleeves and the velvet tablecover, and, not least, Ildefonso's fervent expression, remove the scene to a spiritual realm.

El Greco's image of the Virgin resembles an actual wooden figure that Ildefonso is said to have kept in his oratory until it was given by him to the church of the Hospital of Charity in the small Spanish town of Illescas, near Toledo. The statuette is preserved there today together with El Greco's larger version of *Saint Ildefonso*.

EL GRECO (Domenikos Theotokopoulos) (1541–1614)

*Saint Ildefonso, c.*1605/14

Canvas. 112 × 65.8 cm. (44⅛ × 25⅞ in.)

Andrew W. Mellon Collection 1937.1.83

EL GRECO (Domenikos
Theotokopoulos)
(1541–1614)

Laocoön, c.1610/14

Canvas. 137.5 × 172.5 cm.
(54⅛ × 67⅞ in.)

Samuel H. Kress Collection
1946.18.1

Widespread interest in the story of Laocoön, a mythical priest of Troy, developed after an ancient, monumental sculpture representing him and his two sons was unearthed in 1506 in Rome. Suspecting trickery, Laocoön had warned his countrymen not to accept the wooden horse left outside Troy by the Greeks and had hurled his spear at it to prove that it was hollow. Thus the priest incurred the wrath of the gods, for desecrating an object dedicated to the goddess Athena. El Greco depicted serpents, sent by the angry gods, engaging Laocoön and one son in a mortal struggle, while a second son lies already dead at his father's side. The identity of the unfinished figures on the right continues to be debated; perhaps they represent the gods themselves supervising their vengeance.

Utilizing every available means – writhing line, lurid color, and illogically conceived space – the artist projected an unrelieved sense of doom. The figures seem incorporeal; sinuous outlines and anti-natural flesh tones contribute to their specterlike appearance. The striking setting carries this visionary late work of El Greco to an apocalyptic extreme.

Did El Greco intend to relate this mythical theme of conflict and divine retribution to the Inquisition then raging in Toledo? Whatever the case, the story of Laocoön is the only classical theme he is known to have painted.

C anvases like this one earned Van der Hamen his reputation as the greatest Spanish still-life painter of the seventeenth century, when that form was revived as a worthy subject in and of itself rather than as an adjunct to a symbolic or narrative work. Concerned simply with the harmonious arrangement of objects and the accurate representation of texture and light, Van der Hamen established the ringlike stoneware bottle as the center of the composition around which other circles and spheres play. Marzipan boxes foreshortened into ovals, spherical jars of honey and preserved cherries, a circular tray of round, sugared donuts, serpentine cakes, and plump, glazed figs – delicacies found on the refined tables of the aristocracy in Spain – contrast with the geometric severity of the setting. The artist arranged the objects on stepped stone ledges, thus varying their distances from the light source. Braided straw, wood, terra cotta, and crystal are masterfully described. These carefully rendered textures reach a pinnacle in the water-filled glass finger bowl that casts a shadow and, at the same time, reflects the light. The calculated distribution of a single color, red in various tones, weaves the forms into a harmonious whole whose simplicity, at first glance, belies its careful structure.

Juan van der
Hamen y León
(1596–1631)

*Still Life with Sweets and
Pottery*, 1627

Canvas. 84.2 × 112.8 cm.
(33⅛ × 44¾ in.)

Samuel H. Kress Collection
1961.9.75

S.LVCÍA.

FRANCISCO DE
ZURBARÁN
(1598–1664)

Saint Lucy, c. 1625/30

Canvas. 105 × 77 cm.
(41⅜ × 30¼ in.)

Chester Dale Collection
1943.7.11

Few images of saints show women as gorgeously attired as Francisco de Zurbarán's. His *Saint Lucy* portrays the young martyr as a contemporary woman of Seville. Bejeweled and carefully coiffed, she presents her startling attribute, a pair of naturalistically painted eyeballs on a pewter dish.

Multiple versions of the legend of Saint Lucy, the daughter of an aristocratic family in fourth-century Syracuse, arose during the Counter-Reformation. One popular interpretation, inspired by her unusual attribute, maintained that Lucy, determined to dedicate her life to Christ, had plucked out her eyes and sent them to a tenacious suitor after he insisted that their beauty allowed him no peace. Astounded by her devotion to her faith, the admirer converted to Christianity, and Lucy, the legend continues, later found her eyesight miraculously restored one day during prayer. It is possible that the young saint's connection with eyes originated in the Latin source for her name, *Lux* or "light," which is inextricably linked with vision.

The success of Zurbarán's many images of virgin martyrs derived not only from their inherently pleasing theme – beautiful, splendidly dressed women – but also from the artist's gifts as a colorist and his talent for combining the spiritual and material.

D iego Velázquez ranks among the greatest masters of seventeenth-century Europe. By 1623, the twenty-four-year-old artist was established as court painter to Philip IV in Madrid. For nearly forty years, he was primarily occupied with painting remarkably innovative portraits of the monarch and the royal family. But in his spare hours, Velázquez turned to subjects that interested him personally; *The Needlewoman* is among those works.

His observation of the optical effects of light on the forms he painted caused Velázquez to abandon the tenebrism – or extreme contrast of lights and darks – that characterized his earlier works in favor of a softer style. Here, no area is obscured by darkness. The artist used a gentle light and deep, but translucent, shadow to reveal each plane of the face, to sculpt the swelling bosom, and to suggest the repetitive motion of the hand.

Because the painting remains unfinished, the steps in the artist's process are visible. He began by priming the canvas with a gray-green base. Next, he indicated the main forms of the composition, sketching them in with darker paint, then brushing them in with broad areas of opaque color, and finally, building up the face – the only area that appears to be finished – with transparent layers of glaze, giving it the effect of flesh seen through softly diffused light.

DIEGO VELÁZQUEZ
(1599–1660)

The Needlewoman,
*c.*1640/50

Canvas. 74 × 60 cm.
(29⅛ × 23⅝ in.)

Andrew W. Mellon Collection
1937.1.81

BARTOLOMÉ ESTEBAN
MURILLO
(1617–82)

*Two Women at a
Window, c.* 1655/60

Canvas. 125.1 × 104.5 cm.
(49¼ × 41⅛ in.)

Widener Collection
1942.9.46

Seville's most popular painter in the later seventeenth century was Bartolomé Esteban Murillo.

While Murillo is best known for works with religious themes, he also produced a number of genre paintings of figures from contemporary life engaged in ordinary pursuits. These pictures often possess a wistful charm; *Two Women at a Window* is a striking example. A standing woman attempts to hide a smile with her shawl as she peeks from behind a partially opened shutter, while a younger woman leans on the window ledge, gazing out at the viewer with amusement. The difference in their ages might indicate a chaperone and her charge, a familiar duo in upper-class Spanish households. Covering one's smile or laugh was considered good etiquette among the aristocracy. An engraving made one hundred years after the painting suggested, however, an entirely different interpretation of the women. Its title, *Las Gallegas (The Galician Women),* implied that the women were prostitutes, because Galicia, a poor province in western Spain, provided many of Seville's courtesans. Today, scholars tend toward the first explanation of these two casually attired ladies.

The convincingly modeled, life-size figures, framed within an illusionistically painted window, derive from Dutch paintings that were meant to fool the eye.

M urillo's great talent for dramatic painting is apparent in this monumental depiction of the familiar parable of the prodigal son, an allegory of repentance and divine forgiveness. With players and props effectively placed to underscore the drama, it is reminiscent of a well-staged theater piece.

The artist selected the essential elements of the story's climax: the penitent son welcomed home by his forgiving father; the rich garments and ring that signify the errant son's restoration to his former position in the family; and the fatted calf being led to the slaughter for the celebratory banquet. The larger-than-life, central, pyramidal grouping of father and son dominates the picture, while the richest color is reserved for the servant bearing the new garments. Murillo may have chosen to emphasize that aspect of the parable – symbolic of charity – because of the nature of the commission. *The Return of the Prodigal Son* was one of eight huge canvases painted for the Church of the Hospital of Saint George in Seville, a hospice for the homeless and hungry.

Murillo's model was the life around him; part of the appeal of this canvas lies in its human touches – the realism of the prodigal's dirty feet, the puppy jumping up to greet his master, and perhaps most of all, the ingenuous smile of the little urchin leading the calf.

BARTOLOMÉ ESTEBAN
MURILLO
(1617–82)

*The Return of the
Prodigal Son*, 1667/70

Canvas. 236.3 × 261 cm.
(93 × 102¾ in.)

Gift of the Avalon Foundation
1948.12.1

87

JUSEPE DE RIBERA
(1591–1652)

The Martyrdom of Saint Bartholomew, 1634

Canvas. 104 × 113 cm.
(41 × 44½ in.)

Gift of the 50th Anniversary Gift
Committee 1990.137.1

Apopular subject in Counter-Reformation Italy and Spain, Ribera's profoundly moving work portrays the apostle's final moments before he is to be flayed alive. The viewer is meant to empathize with Bartholomew, whose body seemingly bursts through the surface of the canvas, and whose outstretched arms embrace a mystical light that illuminates his flesh. His piercing eyes, open mouth, and petitioning left hand bespeak an intense communion with the divine; yet this same hand draws our attention to the instruments of his torture, symbolically positioned in the shape of a cross. Transfixed by Bartholomew's active faith, the executioner seems to have stopped short in his actions, and his furrowed brow and partially illuminated face suggest a moment of doubt, with the possibility of conversion.

The use of sharp light-dark contrasts and extreme naturalism reveal the influence of Caravaggio, whose work Ribera would have seen both in Rome and in Naples, where he lived from 1616 until the end of his life. Yet unlike Caravaggio, Ribera has enlivened the canvas with a variety of brushstrokes and textures, allowing the viewer to become further involved with this psychologically charged painting.

L uis Meléndez was the greatest still-life painter of eighteenth-century Spain, and one of the finest painters of the genre in Europe. His father was a well-known artist instrumental in founding the Spanish Royal Academy of Fine Arts and Luis was admitted as a member with much promise. However, the father's difficult character – which the son unfortunately shared – proved to be their undoing. Both were dismissed from the Academy, and Luis' career was irrevocably damaged. He nevertheless studied in Italy before returning to Madrid.

Much of what is known of Meléndez comes from his writings. A letter of 1772 to the future Charles IV centers on still-life painting. Meléndez writes of painting "the four Seasons . . . with the aim of composing an amusing cabinet with every species of food produced by the Spanish climate." Meléndez delivered forty-four canvases to the royal residency. Although he was appreciated by his patrons, the desired salaried position of royal painter forever eluded him.

Meléndez' *Still Life with Figs and Bread* contains elements characteristic of the painter's greatest works. His talent for rendering everyday kitchen objects with exacting detail is evident, as are his marvelous effects of color, light, and texture. The smooth bone knife handle, the subtle variations in the skin and hues of the figs, the crusty bread, the wood grain of the bucket, the rubbery cork, and the shiny glass and copper surfaces show his mastery at portraying texture through the skillful manipulation of the fluid properties of oil.

LUIS MELÉNDEZ
(1716–80)

Still Life with Figs and Bread, 1760s

Canvas. 47.6 × 34 cm.
(18¾ × 13⅜ in.)

Patrons' Permanent Fund
2000.6.1

89

FRANCISCO DE GOYA
(1746–1828)

*The Marquesa de
Pontejos*, c.1786

Canvas. 210.8 × 126.4 cm.
(83 × 49¾ in.)

Andrew W. Mellon Collection
1937.1.85

Trees, grass, and shrubbery, simplified almost to abstraction, set off the fragile, wasp-waisted figure of María Ana de Pontejos y Sandoval, the Marquesa de Pontejos. Splendidly attired, she typifies those ladies of the Spanish aristocracy who affected the "shepherdess" style of Marie Antoinette, so popular in pre-revolutionary France.

The eighteenth century's sentimental fondness for nature, influenced by the writings of Jean-Jacques Rousseau, is alluded to in the parklike setting, the roses arranged around the bodice of the gown and tucked into the folds of the voluminous overskirt, and in the carnation that the marquesa holds with self-conscious elegance. Framing her artfully arranged coiffure, the broad-brimmed picture hat again bespeaks high fashion, perhaps imported from England; such hats were often seen in contemporary portraits by Gainsborough and other British painters. While the painting's pale tones reflect the last stages of the rococo in Spanish art, the overall silvery gray-green tonality is equally reminiscent of the earlier Spanish master, Velázquez, whose paintings Goya had studied and copied.

Goya probably painted this portrait on the occasion of the marquesa's first marriage, to Francisco de Monino y Redondo, brother of the all-powerful Count of Floridablanca, another of Goya's noble patrons.

FRANCISCO DE GOYA
(1746–1828)

*Bartolomé Sureda y
Miserol, c.*1803/04

Canvas. 119.7 × 79.4 cm.
(47⅛ × 31¼ in.)

Gift of Mr. and Mrs. P. H. B.
Frelinghuysen in memory of her
father and mother, Mr. and
Mrs. H. O. Havemeyer
1941.10.1

This is one of Goya's liveliest male portraits. The sitter's relaxed stance reflects the painter's intimate response to a friend, a young liberal whose disheveled hair and garb in the mode of revolutionary France speaks not only of his affinity for contemporary French fashion, but also of his sympathy for current French politics.

Goya's life spanned a period of political upheaval and military turmoil. In the early years of the nineteenth century, before he witnessed the horror of the Peninsular wars, Goya welcomed the idea of a Napoleonic invasion, believing the ideals of the French revolution to be the only antidote to the abuses of the Spanish monarchy. Bartolomé Sureda was one of a group of like-minded liberal intellectuals.

A clever young industrialist, Sureda studied cotton spinning in England in order to introduce the technique into Spain. Later he went to France to learn the secrets of Sèvres porcelain manufacture and in 1802 became director of the Spanish royal porcelain factory at Buen Retiro. During the French invasion of Spain, Napoleon considered him so important to Spanish industry that he detained him in France.

Since this portrait predates many of the sitter's illustrious achievements, Goya presented him, not as a brilliant industrialist, but simply as an urbane young man.

The years between Goya's appointment as first painter to the court of Charles IV and the Napoleonic invasion of 1808 were a time of great activity and financial security for the artist. He painted some of his finest portraits at that time, *Señora Sabasa García* and several others in the National Gallery's collection among them.

In contrast with his earlier work – *The Marquesa de Pontejos*, for example – Goya dispensed with the setting entirely and treated the costume much more impressionistically. Eliminating unessential details, he gave life to the figure with the greatest technical economy, his vibrant brushwork merely suggesting the gossamer qualities of the señora's mantilla rather than defining its details.

Señora Sabasa García was the niece of Evaristo Pérez de Castro, Spain's minister of foreign affairs, for whom Goya was painting an official portrait when, according to a perhaps legendary anecdote, the young woman appeared. The artist, struck by her beauty, stopped work and asked permission to paint her portrait. With images like this, spotlighting the restrained fire and beauty of the subject, Goya created the visual vocabulary that embodies the words "Spanish beauty," just as his earlier tapestry cartoons and genre paintings of popular pastimes distilled the essence of Spanish life.

FRANCISCO DE GOYA
(1746–1828)

Señora Sabasa García,
*c.*1806/11

Canvas. 71.1 × 58.4 cm.
(28 × 23 in.)

Andrew W. Mellon Collection
1937.1.88

Italian Painting
OF THE XVI–XVIII CENTURIES

The glorious era of the High Renaissance drew to a close in the 1520s with the death of Raphael and the Sack of Rome. At the same moment, new ideas were ripening elsewhere in Italy as Raphael's gifted Roman pupils dispersed, while, in Venice, brilliant painters issued forth at a phenomenal rate. A repertoire of new subjects for painting was devised – landscapes and cityscapes, still lifes, ecstatic visions of saints, and genre scenes of everyday life – and artists greatly expanded the expressive potential of the relatively new medium of oil paint.

The mastery of drawing combined with an idealization of nature found in the works of Leonardo, Raphael, and Michelangelo established a norm which would be reassessed constantly by subsequent generations of artists. A group of central Italian painters, including Perino del Vaga and Pontormo, devised self-consciously elegant poses and frequently used markedly unnatural colors. The style of these "mannerists" was not fully accepted by Venetian artists, however, who were more interested in effects of color, light, atmosphere, and texture. Titian instilled a new sensuality in his art while Tintoretto's scenes are boldly sketched and highly dramatic in mood.

During the later sixteenth century, one family of artists in Bologna, the Carracci, set about reinvigorating the grand tradition of Italian painting. Their efforts to combine central Italian skill in drawing with the lifelike warmth and coloristic richness of the Venetians led to a new synthesis of nature and the ideal, which came to be called the baroque style. If the Carracci's was a spirit of reform, the attitude of Caravaggio might be called revolutionary. His dramatic naturalism was imitated by dozens of artists all over Europe.

Fueled by the wealth of the Vatican and the spate of construction of new buildings, seventeenth-century Rome offered great opportunities for artists. The eighteenth century was the age of the Grand Tour; a brisk trade in painted views of Venice and Rome grew up in response to the tourists' demands for souvenirs, with Canaletto, Bellotto, Guardi, and Pannini at the forefront of production. Italian painters were also commissioned by foreign princes to decorate their palaces. It is a mark of the times that Tiepolo, perhaps the most celebrated Italian painter of the eighteenth century, died in Spain after completing the most ambitious mural program of his career, for the Royal Palace in Madrid.

Detail:
CANALETTO,
Entrance to the Grand Canal from the Molo, Venice

MORETTO DA BRESCIA
(Brescian, 1498–1554)

Pietà, 1520s

Wood. 175.8 × 98.5 cm.
(69⅛ × 38¾ in.)

Samuel H. Kress Collection
1952.2.10

The *Pietà* or lamentation over the dead Christ is not a scene from the Gospels. Rather, it was a medieval invention that translated the pathos of the Passion into a picture, an image to elicit an emotional response from the worshipper.

The Virgin, Saint John the Evangelist, and Mary Magdalene have assembled at Christ's tomb and hold up his gray, lifeless body against the marble sarcophagus. Behind them is the dark mouth of the rock-cut tomb, and beyond it opens a verdant river landscape. Moretto has frozen the mourners in their awkward poses, their strain fueling the anguished pitch of the image. By contrast, the disposition of Christ's body is almost balletic. It stands out pale against the deep colors of the mourners' robes. Moretto's palette is rich but acerbic, darkening to iron-gray in the shadows.

Although Moretto had absorbed the styles of the Venetians, especially their brilliant experiments with color and light, this intensely emotional *Pietà*, which must have been intended as an altarpiece, could only have been created in the sincere religious atmosphere of a provincial site like Brescia, so distant in spirit from the secular, cosmopolitan city of Venice.

The theological virtue of Charity is traditionally represented by a woman with several small children, one of whom she is shown nursing. Here, those figures appear hard and solid amidst a smoky, undefined setting. Sharp colors, like the pink and turquoise of the garments or the burnt orange and purple stripes of the tablecloth, heighten this contrast of tangible form and indeterminate space. It is, above all, in the ideal grace of slowly revolving poses that the real expressive force of the picture is conveyed.

That the subject is subservient to the style in this painting is underlined by the fact that the panel was first planned as a *Holy Family*, but with a few changes in details, del Sarto transformed it into a *Charity*.

Andrea d'Agnolo was called "del Sarto" from his father's trade as a tailor. He had a successful and productive career in Florence and was particularly celebrated for the beauty and originality of his color. Sarto worked briefly at the court of Francis I at Fontainebleau in 1518. This *Charity*, probably painted shortly before the artist's death, was also commissioned for the French king.

ANDREA DEL SARTO
(Florentine, 1486–1530)

Charity, before 1530

Wood. 120 × 92.7 cm.
(47¼ × 36½ in.)

Samuel H. Kress Collection
1957.14.5

PERINO DEL VAGA
(central Italian, 1501–47)

The Nativity, 1534

Transferred from wood to
canvas. 274.4 × 221.1 cm.
(108¼ × 87⅛ in.)

Samuel H. Kress Collection
1961.9.31

Although called a nativity, this painting lacks the manger, ox, and ass traditionally found in scenes of Christ's birth. It would be better interpreted as a mystical adoration of saints. John the Baptist, Catherine of Alexandria, and the Virgin are in the foreground. From left to right standing behind them are Sebastian, pierced with arrows, the pilgrim James Major; Joseph, the husband of Mary; and the pilgrim Roch. Soaring through the heavens is God the Father accompanied by a phalanx of putti.

Commissioned by a member of the Baciadonne family of Genoa, this large altarpiece is the most important religious painting by Perino del Vaga to survive. Perino had been a pupil of Raphael in Rome, and his indebtedness to his master is evident here in the idealization of the figures and the grace of the postures. Like others of his generation, however, Perino departed from Raphael's serene harmonies to instill in his works a greater degree of tension and artifice. In this altarpiece the studied gestures hang in the air as if to function in the place of speech. Poses seem choreographed and, in several instances, tipped off balance. Rich colors glow phosphorescently with a stained-glass intensity out of the oddly dark morning.

G iovanni della Casa, who is in all likelihood the subject of this portrait, belonged to a wealthy Tuscan family and rose to prominence in the service of the church. As poet, humanist, and political theorist, he circulated at the highest levels of Italian intellectual life. Della Casa also wrote a book on manners, and in this portrait of the early 1540s displays the sober self-possession espoused in that work. When Pontormo painted this image, della Casa was in his early thirties and acting in Florence as Apostolic Commissioner of taxes. Pontormo shows the monsignor in a dim interior, and although the architectural details are few, they suggest that the building is Santa Maria del Fiore, the cathedral of Florence.

Pontormo's mannerist style was a brilliantly expressive synthesis of fantasy and acute observation of nature. Here the balance is tilted in favor of visible reality, but a reality intensified by plausible exaggerations. For example, the monsignor's small head is made to look even smaller by the huge conical bulk of his caped torso looming so close to the picture plane and brushing the sides of the frame.

PONTORMO
(Florentine, 1494–1556/57)

Monsignor della Casa,
probably 1541/44

Wood. 102.1 × 78.8 cm.
(40⅛ × 31 in.)

Samuel H. Kress Collection
1961.9.83

99

Who is this elegant lady? A noblewoman surely, and most likely a member of the court of Cosimo I de' Medici, Duke of Florence in the mid-sixteenth century. Her ornate and costly attire establish her as an aristocrat. She holds herself rigidly with the controlled demeanor that distinguishes portraits of members of Cosimo's court. Bronzino was the principal portraitist to the court, and one wonders how much his own coldly idealized, polished style of painting may, itself, have contributed to the taste for the marble-hard perfection and chilly hauteur of his models.

Tucked in the corner of the panel, the small blond boy was an afterthought, added by Bronzino in a second campaign of painting. X-radiography has revealed that the woman had first stood alone with her proper right hand placed against her dress. Not only did Bronzino insert the ivory-skinned child, but he also brought the woman's apparel up to date: her headdress grew larger and more elaborate; the puffed sleeves of her dress were broadened (a change evident in the darker silhouette of the contours that were painted over the green background); the gloves were added and, probably, the damask pattern on the bodice as well.

R anuccio Farnese was twelve years old when Titian painted his portrait. The boy had been sent to Venice by his grandfather, Pope Paul III, to become prior of an important property belonging to the Knights of Malta. As a member of the powerful and aristocratic Farnese family, Ranuccio went on to an illustrious ecclesiastical career. He was made Archbishop of Naples at the age of fourteen, and he later served as Bishop of Bologna, Archbishop of Milan and Ravenna, and Cardinal Sant'Angelo, dying when he was only thirty-five years old.

Adult responsibility came to Ranuccio when still a child, as Titian so brilliantly conveyed through the cloak of office, too large and heavy, sliding off the youth's small shoulders. The boy in the role of the man is what gives this characterization such poignancy.

Portraits by Titian were in great demand, distinguished as they were for their remarkable insight into character and their brilliant technique. Nowhere is the painter's genius more in evidence than in this image. Limiting his palette to black, white, and rose, Titian enlivened the surface with light: the dull gleam rippling over the sleeves of the velvet cloak; the fitful pattern flickering across the slashed doublet; and the hanging reflections on the satin Maltese Cross.

TITIAN
(Venetian, *c*.1490–1576)

Ranuccio Farnese, 1542

Canvas. 89.7 × 73.6 cm.
(35¼ × 29 in.)

Samuel H. Kress Collection
1952.2.11

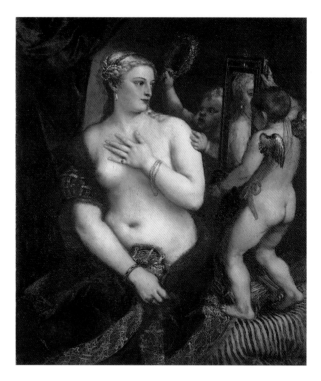

TITIAN
(Venetian, c.1490–1576)

Venus with a Mirror,
c.1555

Canvas. 124.5 × 105.5 cm.
(49 × 41½ in.)

Andrew W. Mellon Collection
1937.1.34

At the core of Renaissance art is the revival of the classical past, and in his *Venus with a Mirror*, Titian revealed both his appreciation of antiquity and his remarkable modernity. During a sojourn in Rome he wrote that he was "learning from the marvelous ancient stones" that were being unearthed daily in the city. Indeed, he based the gesture of the goddess, her hands held to her breast and lap, on a famous Roman statue of Venus that later belonged to the Medici.

Yet Titian breathed a warmth and life into these remote sources to conjure a startlingly immediate and sensual modern Venus. Her pliant flesh seems to melt at the touch of the cupid who strains to bestow on her the crown of love. While she pulls about her a wrap of wine-colored velvet lined in fur, soft and opulent and evoking the sense of touch, Venus reveals her body as much as she conceals it. The beautiful woman gazing at her reflection is a favorite theme of Renaissance love poetry in which the writer envies the fortunate mirror that enjoys his lady's splendid image.

Few artists could match Moroni's skill in depicting the appearance of his sitters, far less his ability to conjure the inner workings of their minds. The identity of the gentleman in this penetrating portrait is a mystery. For a long time the painting was thought to be by Titian and to represent that artist's ideal of a schoolmaster. But according to another tradition, the picture got its name because Titian admired it and learned so much from it. Whether or not the older master ever saw this painting, Moroni's strong, simple composition and trenchant characterization did impress two later specialists in portraiture: Anthony van Dyck and Joshua Reynolds both made copies of it.

The subject, dressed all in black, sits in a Savanarola chair that is seen – unexpectedly – in profile. He rests one beautifully drawn hand on the arm of the chair and turns as if to regard the spectator. With his other hand he holds his place in a book, thoughts of which, judging from his absorbed gaze, still occupy his mind. The white, embroidered collar sets off the face, and the asymmetrical points echo the man's uneven features. Even the bristly textures of the trimmed whiskers and clipped, grizzled hair command attention.

GIOVANNI BATTISTA MORONI
(Brescian, c.1525–78)

"Titian's Schoolmaster,"
c.1575

Canvas. 96.8 × 74.3 cm.
(38¼ × 29¼ in.)

Widener Collection
1942.9.45

JACOPO TINTORETTO
(Venetian, 1518–94)

*Christ at the Sea of
Galilee*, c.1575/80

Canvas. 117 × 168.5 cm.
(46 × 66¼ in.)

Samuel H. Kress Collection
1952.5.27

The Venetian master Tintoretto marshaled the unstable forces of nature to heighten the drama of this scene from John's Gospel; the wind that fills the sail and bends the mast also agitates the sea and sky, and the rocky waves meet the low clouds that blow onto the land. Christ's outstretched arm draws Peter like a magnet, the charge between them creating a dynamic link between the center of the picture and the left foreground. Tintoretto has broken all forms into multiple planes, splintering the light, and frosting the edges with a brush loaded with dry, lead-white oil paint. This use of a thick, white impasto to accent the highlights and as a ghostly shorthand, as in the grassy shore at Christ's feet, is a hallmark of Tintoretto's bravura style.

Too wild and improvisatory to find a real following among his compatriots in Venice, Tintoretto's bold expressions instead fired the imagination of one kindred temperament: El Greco, who studied there before moving to Spain. So close in style and spirit was El Greco's art that, earlier in this century, some experts believed that he, and not Tintoretto, had painted the *Christ at the Sea of Galilee*.

W hile exposing her breast to the thrust of the dagger that will kill her, Saint Lucy turns her head to accept communion from a priest. This unconventional addition of the sacrament to the scene of Lucy's martyrdom is a reminder of the Counter-Reformation climate that shadowed Veronese's career. Twice, the artist had defended himself against allegations of impropriety in his treatment of religious subjects.

Sketchily rendered in the background is a team of oxen; these are the beasts who had failed to drag the chaste Lucy – made miraculously immobile – to the brothel where she had been condemned for her Christian faith. A glimpse of fire behind Lucy alludes to another failed attempt to martyr this third-century saint.

Veronese's own Venice, and not Lucy's ancient Syracuse, is made the backdrop to this scene. A brilliant decorator, Veronese was celebrated for his sumptuous histories and mythologies which he translated into opulent present-day surroundings and dress. If the artist was best known for the sparkling blond harmonies of his mature work, the *Martyrdom of Saint Lucy* is a masterpiece of his late style and reveals a different aspect of his temperament. Here, cast in evening light, the colors have deepened and acquired a muted glow.

VERONESE
(Venetian, 1528–88)

The Martyrdom and Last Communion of Saint Lucy, c.1582

Canvas. 139.7 × 173.4 cm.
(55 × 68¼ in.)

The Morris and Gwendolyn Cafritz Foundation and Ailsa Mellon Bruce Fund
1984.28.1

LODOVICO CARRACCI
(Bolognese, 1555–1619)

*The Dream of Saint
Catherine of Alexandria,*
c. 1593

Canvas. 138.8 × 110.5 cm.
(54⅝ × 43½ in.)

Samuel H. Kress Collection
1952.5.59

We recognize this sleeping figure as Saint Catherine by the fragment of spiked wheel in the lower left corner, which was the instrument of an attempted martyrdom. Here Lodovico Carracci represented her legendary dream in which Mary and the infant Christ, accompanied by angels, appeared to her. Plighting his troth, Christ placed a ring on Catherine's finger, and through this mystic marriage she became his bride. To cast the event as a dream, rather than having Saint Catherine receive the ring while awake, is Lodovico's innovation.

Two angels at the left look on with protective tenderness, while others barely emerge amid the vaporous bronze radiance at the right – spirit becoming matter. The figures, solid and robust, bask in an indeterminate setting. A languorous warmth pervades the scene and slows the composition. At the same time, the quirky folds and pleats cascading down Catherine's garments impart a vertiginous sensation – the dizziness of sleep.

Lodovico was the eldest of the three Carracci, the family of Bolognese artists who inaugurated the age of the baroque. His depictions of saints in states of visionary ecstasy were highly prized in an age when the purpose of religious art was to arouse intensely pious emotions in the spectator.

Procaccini was one of the most gifted artists working in Lombardy in the early seventeenth century. His art was influenced by a variety of painters, from Raphael to Correggio, Parmigianino, and Rubens. His work was also affected by the reformist teachings of the powerful Milanese Cardinal Federico Borromeo. Procaccini primarily painted devotional subjects with great fervor that are nevertheless full of sensuality and drama.

His elegant *Ecstasy of the Magdalen* was probably painted for the prominent Doria family in Genoa, for whom he painted no fewer than sixty pictures. Mary Magdalen swoons in ecstasy as she is supported by winged putti below a group of refined celestial music-making angels. The two figure groups are united through gesture, glance, and expression to form one of Procaccini's most successful compositions.

An early follower of Christ, Mary Magdalen was present at the Crucifixion, and may be the woman who anointed his feet in the house of Simon. She has been called a prostitute, a sinner, or simply a woman who abandoned herself to a life of luxury before devoting herself to Jesus and his teachings. Earlier depictions of Mary Magdalen usually focused on her meditative or tearful penitence for her sins, with the identifying ointment jar nearby. As was common to later depictions, Procaccini's Magdalen is shown in uninhibited ecstasy moments before she is borne aloft to heaven, a dramatic scene that allowed the artist to best show off his virtuoso painting technique.

GIULIO CESARE
PROCACCINI
(Lombard, 1574–1625)

The Ecstasy of the Magdalen, 1616/20

Canvas. 215.9 × 146.1 cm.
(85 × 57½ in.)

Patrons' Permanent Fund
2002.12.1

ORAZIO GENTILESCHI
(Florentine,
1563–1639)

The Lute Player,
probably *c.* 1612/20

Canvas. 143.5 × 128.8 cm.
(56½ × 50⅝ in.)

Ailsa Mellon Bruce Fund
1962.8.1

Orazio Genitileschi was one of the earliest and most gifted painters to be inspired by the genre scenes of Caravaggio in Rome. Here, he must have had in mind Caravaggio's famous picture on the same theme. Orazio's young woman listens intently to a note as it resonates in the pear-shaped body of the instrument. She may be tuning her lute in anticipation of the concert promised by the assortment of recorders, a cornetto and violin, and the song books lying open on the table before her.

The graceful musician and her lute are seen, unexpectedly, from the back, turned three-quarters away from the spectator. Orazio's meticulous attention to detail is such that every surface is described with a precision of focus that gives pleasure to the eye. Dutch painters, famous for their amazingly illusionistic renderings of fabrics, improved their craft by studying Orazio's works. His gift for conveying the textures of fine cloth is shown off here in the sharp gold of the dress, the dull gleam of the scarlet velvet on the stool, and the matte softness of the dark-green cloth covering the table.

It might be said that with paintings like this one, Annibale Carracci invented the landscape as a subject for Italian baroque painting. Nature here is appreciated first and foremost for herself and not as the backdrop for a story. A mellow sunlight dapples the land and picks out the ripples disturbing the surface of the river. The gold in the treetops suggests a day in early autumn. Brightly clad in red and white, a boatman poles his craft through the shallow water.

In the company of his brother Agostino and his cousin Lodovico Carracci, Annibale made excursions into the country in order to sketch the landscape. From these quick studies made on the spot he worked up his paintings in the studio. The resulting composition is an artful balancing of forms. As the river wends its way through the countryside towards the foreground, the spits of land that chart its course are made to recede and project in an alternating rhythm of triangles. Trees, like signposts, mark the progress of recession into the distance. At the same time the bold strokes of dark trees in the foreground form a dramatic pattern on the surface to snap the spectator's attention back from the hazy blue of the distant horizon.

ANNIBALE CARRACCI
(Bolognese, 1560–1609)
River Landscape,
c. 1590

Canvas. 88.5 × 148.2 cm.
(34¾ × 58¼ in.)

Samuel H. Kress Collection
1952.5.58

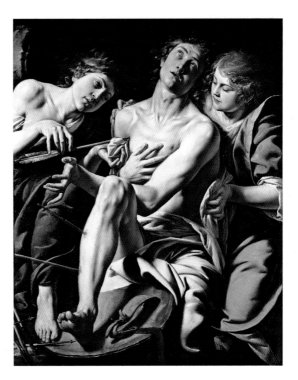

A fevered intensity in this portrayal of Saint Sebastian marks it as a characteristic work by Tanzio, whose native village of Varallo in the mountains north of Milan was a major center of popular piety. The painter has shown Sebastian, who was persecuted as a Christian under Diocletian, being rescued by angels after the assault on him by the Emperor's archers. The thickset figure at the right who tenderly steadies Sebastian's body for the angel's ministrations may be Saint Irene, who nursed the martyr back to health.

The visual excitement of Tanzio's portrayal serves to convey Sebastian's state of emotional transport and transcendence of bodily pain. Contributing to the fervid drama is the extreme compression of the composition. Tanzio's large, solid forms are crowded by the frame, seeming to twist and strain to fit its confines. If the vivid illusionism and sharp contrasts of light and dark – pulsating in the drapery across Sebastian's lap and in the spiky patterns of expressively tapering fingers – reveal a study of Caravaggio's art, Tanzio's use of discordant colors is uniquely his own.

Throughout his career Tiepolo painted small pictures of mythological themes, which proved extremely popular. The subjects of these works came from the best-known episodes from ancient literature, but his conception of the stories was varied and original. His depiction of Apollo and Daphne comes directly from Ovid's *Metamorphoses*. Daphne, the beautiful nymph and follower of the chaste goddess Diana, was pursued by the sun god Apollo, who had been struck by Cupid's golden arrow of love. Fleeing Apollo, Daphne reached her father, the river god Peneus, seen here at left. To avoid Apollo's unwanted advances, she was turned into a laurel tree. The transformation takes place before us as her leg turns into a trunk and her arms sprout branches.

The *Apollo and Daphne* is unique among interpretations of the theme. Apollo's forward thrust seems to propel Daphne backward in a composition of excited movement. Cupid takes cover from the wrath of Apollo that will shortly ensue, and Peneus remains firmly rooted in an effort to stop the ardent pursuer. The off-center composition, typical of Venetian art, was used by Tiepolo elsewhere but never in such a dramatic and emotionally intense manner.

GIOVANNI BATTISTA
TIEPOLO
(Venetian, 1696–1770)

Apollo Pursuing Daphne,
c. 1755/60)

Canvas. 68.5 × 87 cm.
(27 × 34¼ in.)

Samuel H. Kress Collection
1952.5.78

CORRADO GIAQUINTO
(Roman, 1703–66)

Autumn, c. 1740/50

Canvas. 108.4 × 151.5 cm.
(42¹¹⁄₁₆ × 59⅝ in.)

Gift of the Rizik Family
2001.123.1

A leading exponent of the rococo school that flourished in Rome during the first half of the eighteenth century, Corrado Giaquinto – a kind of "Italian Boucher" – was trained in Naples. The baroque style that Giaquinto formed there took on a lighter tone after he moved to Rome in 1727, where he specialized in painting altarpieces and large decorative ensembles. In Rome his style also became more classicizing, and the kind of elegant sophistication that marks Giaquinto's mature works soon established his international reputation. Accordingly, he was invited to become court painter to King Ferdinand VI in Madrid, where he remained until returning to Italy in 1762 four years before his death. In Madrid Giaquinto painted decorative cycles glorifying the Spanish monarchy that are a direct precedent for those of his successor, Giovanni Battista Tiepolo (whose 1762 *Wealth and Benefits of the Spanish Monarchy* is in the Gallery's collection).

Autumn represents the god Bacchus and other mythological figures lounging in a lush landscape. Dating from the artist's mature period, the 1740s, this work is in almost perfect condition. The painting forms part of a series of four allegories of the seasons: *Winter* also belongs to the Gallery's Italian baroque collection, while the canvases representing spring and summer are known today only through photographs. Both Gallery paintings, particularly *Autumn*, with its air of overripe, languid elegance, are superb examples of Giaquinto's art

A woman in a powder-pink gown seems to be at the center of a domestic crisis as she sinks back, deathly pale, into a chair. The explanation for her indisposition is not hard to discover. A table has been tipped over at the left, spilling cards, an open purse, and coins on to the floor. The lady has been gambling. Dealt an unfortunate hand of cards, she pretended to faint, conveniently upsetting the table as she swooned. Her servants and companions rush to her aid, while the man on the right may be a doctor, or a gambling partner who had been winning.

Longhi's fame rested on such intimate glimpses of Venetian upper-class life in a period of refined decadence. His aristocratic subjects were also his patrons, and they would have appreciated this accurate portrayal of an elegant interior with a chinoiserie card table and moss-green damask on the walls. The realistic comedy of Longhi's playwright friend Carlo Goldoni may have been a source of inspiration, but Longhi's vignettes lack Goldoni's satirical bite. The feathery touch of Longhi's brush and the filtered light soften the scene, as do the pastel colors and the diminutive, doll-like actors.

PIETRO LONGHI
(Venetian, 1702–85)

The Faint, c. 1745

Canvas. 48.9 × 61 cm.
(19¼ × 24 in.)

Samuel H. Kress Collection
1939.1.63

CANALETTO
(Venetian, 1697–1768)

*Entrance to the Grand
Canal from the Molo,
Venice,* 1742/44

Canvas. 115.2 × 153.6 cm.
(45⅜ × 60⅜ in.)

Gift of Mrs. Barbara Hutton
1945.15.4

The most avid customers for Canaletto's views of Venice were the English gentlemen who flocked to the city as tourists during the eighteenth century. The buyer of the *Entrance to the Grand Canal from the Molo, Venice* (and its pendent, *The Square of Saint Mark's,* also in the National Gallery) was, in fact, the Earl of Carlisle, who incorporated them into the decor of his country house, Castle Howard.

It was Canaletto's loving transcription, detail by detail, of his native city that made his paintings so popular: each view vividly calls to mind a particular time and place. Here it is morning activity on the quay near St. Mark's Square that Canaletto recreated with such specificity. Groups of people idle along the landing dock while a fishmonger shows the day's catch of eels to a bewigged pair of gentlemen. Gondolas and ocean-going vessels ply the waterways. Canaletto conveyed the sunlight that drenches Venice in fair weather, sparkling off the canals and revealing fine-etched details of the tiles on distant rooftops or the bricks beneath peeling stucco. Across the lagoon toward the Island of San Giorgio appear (left) the domed church of the Redentore by the sixteenth-century architect Palladio, the double-domed church of Santa Maria della Salute, designed by Longhena in the seventeenth century, and (center) the Customs House.

The painting is one of five large views of an ancient fortress near Dresden commissioned from Bellotto by Augustus III, King of Poland and Elector of Saxony. The panorama encompasses a broad expanse of the picturesque, craggy landscape known as "Saxonian Switzerland," which Bellotto invested with a monumental quality rarely seen in eighteenth-century Italian painting. The great castle sits atop a mountain that rises precipitously from the Elbe River Valley, hundreds of feet below. In the distance on the left is the Lilienstein, one of the prominent sandstone formations scattered across the countryside.

Bellotto began working at Königstein in the spring of 1756. He was commissioned to paint five views of the interior and exterior of the fortress that were intended to complete the twenty-five views of Dresden and Pirna he previously painted for the royal collection. His work was interrupted when Frederick II of Prussia opened hostilities in the Seven Years War by invading Saxony in August 1756. It is thought that Bellotto completed the canvases by 1758, but none were delivered to the court and all five paintings were recorded later in the century in England where two remain in a private collection and in two the City Art Gallery, Manchester.

BERNARDO BELLOTTO
(Venetian, 1721-80)

The Fortress of Königstein,
1756-1758

Canvas, 133 x 235.7 cm.
(52½ x 93¾ in.)

Patrons' Permanent Fund
1993.8.1

Giovanni Battista
Tiepolo
(Venetian, 1696–1770)

*Wealth and Benefits of the
Spanish Monarchy under
Charles III,* 1762

Canvas. 181 × 104.5 cm.
(71½ × 41⅛ in.)

Samuel H. Kress Collection
1943.4.39

Famed as a decorator, Tiepolo made this small sketch as his model for a vast ceiling fresco in the throne room of the Royal Palace of Madrid, a project that was the climax of his illustrious career. Taking its cue from the room's function, Tiepolo's design has as its central feature the allegorical figure of Spain enthroned and flanked by Herculean statues. Just above is the trumpeting figure of Fame. The borders are packed with lively figures representing the provinces of Spain and the continents where she held colonies. At the upper left, Christopher Columbus stands with outstretched arms on the deck of his ship. Nearby are Neptune, god of the sea, who guides the expedition, and an American Indian in a feathered headdress.

One must think of this as a design to be seen overhead in a large high-ceilinged room. With his legendary facility, Tiepolo resolved the difficulties of foreshortening forms seen from sharply below, of deploying the figures in coherent groups, and, in turn, incorporating the groups into an effective overall design. The result is an airy sweep that seems to open directly to the heavens with all its buoyant and extravagant population paying homage to Spain.

In Pannini's day, as in our own, the Pantheon was one of the great tourist attractions of Rome. Built under Hadrian in the second century, this monumental domed temple has survived intact, owing to its consecration as a Christian church – Santa Maria Rotunda - in AD 609. Pannini's depiction is populated with foreign visitors and a lively mix of Romans from all social strata who congregate in the Pantheon to pray, to chat, and to admire the wondrous architecture.

Trained in architecture and theatrical design, Pannini manipulated the perspective to show a larger view of the interior than is actually possible from any single place. The viewpoint is deep within the building, facing the entrance. The portals open to the colossal columns of the porch and a glimpse of the obelisk in the piazza before the church. Through the oculus in the center of the dome, Pannini revealed the bright blue sky flecked with clouds.

As Canaletto was to Venice, so Pannini was to Rome. Both artists documented with exacting skill and vibrancy the monuments of their cities and the daily comings and goings of the inhabitants. In this case, Pannini depicted the classical landmark that inspired the design of the Rotunda in the National Gallery's West Building.

For several decades after Canaletto painted his *Quay of the Piazzetta,* Francesco Guardi continued producing picturesque cityscapes for the tourist trade. Although the artist was little-known in his own day, his views of Venice are now highly prized for their atmospheric qualities and broad, sketchy brushwork.

The Rialto Bridge, built in 1592 as the first stone bridge to span the Grand Canal, is the focal point of Guardi's composition, one of several versions of this popular attraction. Lined with market stalls and shops, it formed the hub of an important commercial center. Just beyond the bridge at the right is the Fondaco dei Tedeschi, the warehouse of the German merchants – now a post office – that became famous in the Renaissance when Giorgione and Titian frescoed its facade.

People poke their heads out of windows and gather on the balconies to watch the spectacle of daily life on the Rialto. The artist must have taken his view from a similar perch, looking down on the bustling scene. Market barges draped in canvas canopies are tied up at the quayside. Energetic gondoliers pole their boats up the crowded canal.

FRANCESCO GUARDI
(Venetian, 1712–93)

Grand Canal with Bridge, Venice,
probably *c.* 1780

Canvas. 68.5 × 91.5 cm.
(27 × 36 in.)

Widener Collection
1942.9.27

Dutch Painting

The emergence of the Dutch school of painting in the early seventeenth century is one of the most remarkable phenomena in the history of the visual arts. The Netherlands, a small country that had only become a political entity in 1579 and was still suffering from the effects of a long and arduous war against Spain, would hardly seem to have had the resources to nourish and sustain its artistic traditions. Nonetheless, in every respect, the Dutch seem to have drawn strength from adversity; they profited in terms of trade, political awareness, religious tolerance, wealth, and above all, self-esteem. They were proud of their achievements and were determined to provide for themselves a broad and lasting foundation that would define their unique social and cultural heritage.

The political and religious attitudes of the period are not readily apparent in the paintings, drawings and etchings produced by Dutch artists. The still lifes, portraits, landscapes, seascapes, and genre scenes that characterize this school of painting are surprisingly devoid of information on the major occurrences of the day. Nevertheless, the philosophical bases from which artists worked are clearly the same as those governing decision in contemporary political, military, and religious spheres of activity. This ideology was essentially threefold; that God's work is evident in the world itself; that, although things in this world are mortal and transitory, no facet of God's creation is too insubstantial to be noticed, valued, or represented; and that the Dutch, like the ancient Israelites, were a chosen people, favored and blessed by God's protection.

Underlying the essential realism of Dutch art, thus, is an allegorical view of nature that provided a means for conveying various messages to contemporary viewers. The Dutch, with their ingrained Calvinist beliefs, were a moralizing people. While they thoroughly enjoyed the sensual pleasures of life, they were aware of the consequences of yielding to its temptations. Paintings, even those representing everyday objects and events, often provide reminders about the transitoriness of life and the need for moderation and temperance in one's conduct. Subjects drawn from the Bible, mythology, and ancient history, likewise, were often chosen for their moralizing messages, or for establishing parallels between the Dutch experience and great historical, literary, and political events of the past.

The Dutch paintings included here are some of the highlights of the Gallery's collection, but they also represent the range of subject matter and stylistic approaches so characteristic of this important school of painting.

Detail:
JAN VAN GOYEN,
View of Dordrecht from the Dordtse Kil

JOACHIM WTEWAEL
(c.1566–1638)

Moses Striking the Rock,
1624

Wood. 44.5 × 66.5 cm.
(17½ × 26¼ in.)

Ailsa Mellon Bruce Fund
1972.11.1

Wtewael's lifelong commitment to mannerism is apparent in this depiction of *Moses Striking the Rock*. This miraculous event, drawn from the Old Testament Book of Numbers, occurred during the Israelites' journey out of Egypt. While in the wilderness, the Israelites suffered from a critical lack of water. God miraculously granted them relief through the actions of Moses who, accompanied by his brother Aaron, struck the rock and produced water.

The mannerists' use of alternating patterns of light and dark, elongated figures, contorted poses, and pastel colors created elegant, yet extremely artificial, scenes. Wtewael here depicts many figures who feverishly use pots, pans, and other drinking utensils to capture the precious water.

This religious subject was a favorite one for mannerist artists. Such paintings were often produced in cooperation with humanist scholars and had allegorical implications. Moses, in his role as leader of the Israelites, was often seen as a forerunner of Christ; more specifically for the Dutch, however, were the parallels that could be drawn between Moses and their national hero William the Silent. Both led their people against an oppressive foreign rule, but neither of them lived to witness the formation of the new nation they had foreseen.

The strength and vitality of the people who helped establish the new Dutch Republic are nowhere better captured than in paintings by Frans Hals. Hals was the preeminent portrait painter in Haarlem, the most important Dutch city in the early part of the seventeenth century. This mercantile, intellectual, and artistic center attracted many immigrants from Flanders, including Hals' parents.

Although the name of this sitter is not known, Hals inscribed her age, sixty, and the date of the painting, 1633, in the background on the left. The prayer book she holds in her right hand and her conservative black costume with its white ruff clearly indicate her pious nature, yet Hals tells us far more about her through her face and hands than through her costume and book. With firm yet broad strokes of his brush he conveys her lively, robust personality. Her self-confidence is felt in the twinkle of her eyes, in the firm grasp of her hand on the arm of the chair, and by the strong silhouette of her form against the gray background.

FRANS HALS
(c.1580–1666)

Portrait of an Elderly Lady, 1633

Canvas. 103 × 86.4 cm.
(40¼ × 34 in.)

Andrew W. Mellon Collection
1937.1.67

REMBRANDT VAN RIJN
(1606–69)

A Polish Nobleman, 1637

Wood. 97 × 66 cm.
(38¼ × 26 in.)

Andrew W. Mellon Collection
1937.1.78

Rembrandt van Rijn began his career in his native city of Leiden, but moved to Amsterdam around 1631. He immediately established himself as the foremost artist in the city and was sought after as a portrait painter as well as for his depictions of biblical and mythological subjects.

A Polish Nobleman is not an actual portrait, but a fanciful one of a type Rembrandt favored during the decade of the 1630s. He often dressed models in unusual costumes because of their exotic associations. The bear's-skin cap, dark fur cloak, and massive gold chain and tassel have suggested to many that the sitter was Slavic, but the painting's title has no factual basis.

These paintings allowed Rembrandt to expand the limits of portraiture because he was not constrained by traditional conventions. He often used these fanciful portraits as a means of evoking aspects of human psychology. Through his dramatic accents of light and dark on the sitter's face, his bold brushwork, and dense application of paint, he created a powerful, almost sculptural presence; but by emphasizing the sitter's furrowed brow and by shading his heavy, forlorn eyes, Rembrandt suggested a deeply pensive personality.

The Netherlands was a great trading nation that depended on shipping as a basis for wealth and power. Whether on the open sea or through the network of rivers and canals that spread across the low-lying land, Dutch ships carried goods for trade and commerce. Cities and towns grew up along the inland waterways so that transport of goods by barges and passengers by ferries could be facilitated.

Depictions of such water views were extremely popular in the first half of the seventeenth century. One of the greatest early landscape artists, Jan van Goyen was particularly adept at suggesting the various moods of the land in different seasons of the year or weather conditions. In this view of Dordrecht, the sky is overcast and the water calm, the atmosphere carefully created through Van Goyen's subtle range of ochers and grays.

Figures animate the scene; a fisherman works his traps on the left and behind him a sailboat takes on more travelers from a smaller transport boat. Another rowboat in the center foreground has already taken on passengers from the ferry boat and is transporting them to the harbor of Dordrecht.

JAN VAN GOYEN
(1596–1656)

View of Dordrecht from the Dordtse Kil, 1644

Wood. 64.7 × 95.9 cm.
(25½ × 37¾ in.)

Ailsa Mellon Bruce Fund
1978.11.1

ISACK VAN OSTADE
(1621–49)

The Halt at the Inn,
*c.*1645

Panel. 49.5 × 66 cm.
(19½ × 26 in.)

Widener Collection
1942.9.49

One of the most delightful aspects of seventeenth-century Dutch art is that it conveys a vivid sense of daily life. In this painting, for example, we see the bustle of activity outside a village inn as two well-dressed travelers arrive and dismount from their horses. A beggar woman with a child strapped to her back stands to watch while other figures converse with one of the travelers. The main street of the village is filled with other groups, among them men smoking pipes at a bench before the inn, a child playing with a mother's apron, and a man talking to a woman spinning yarn. Van Ostade creates a sense of conviviality by the apparent informality of these human contacts, and by including an array of animals within the scene. He also was careful to suggest the picturesque character of the buildings, trees and vines, and depicted the aged brick and mortar construction of the inn.

Isack van Ostade was the most important of a number of Haarlem artists who painted such subjects in the early seventeenth century. A student of his more famous, older brother, Adriaen van Ostade, Isack tragically died at the age of twenty-eight. Despite his short artistic career, he had an extensive influence on his contemporaries, including Jan Steen, with whom he occasionally collaborated.

The still life was developed as a separate category of painting in the seventeenth century. Dutch artists worked in a variety of still-life traditions that ranged from banquet pieces to paintings focused solely on fruit, shells, books, or flowers. De Heem was one of the most gifted and versatile of these artists, and one of the most influential. His consummate technique allowed him to portray a great variety of textures in a convincing manner. In this flower painting we can delight in his realistic depiction of tulip petals, long bent reeds of wheat, minute animals including butterflies, ants, snails, caterpillars, and finally, reflections on the transparent glass vase.

De Heem also had great compositional sensitivity. Over twenty types of flowers, vegetables, and grains have been brought together here in a way that permits their colors and shapes to balance in an harmonious arrangement. Despite De Heem's realistic depiction, this floral arrangement never actually could have existed. The flowers represented grow at different seasons of the year. In many of his paintings De Heem chose to include specific animals and flowers because of their symbolic meanings; the butterfly, for example, is often a symbol for the Resurrection.

JAN DAVIDSZ. DE HEEM
(1606–83/84)

*Vase of Flowers, c.*1660

Canvas. 69.6 × 56.5 cm.
(27⅜ × 22¼ in.)

Andrew W. Mellon Fund
1961.6.1

PIETER JANSZ.
SAENREDAM
(1597–1665)

*Cathedral of Saint John at
's-Hertogenbosch*, 1646

Wood. 128.8 × 87 cm.
(50⅝ × 34¼ in.)

Samuel H. Kress Collection
1961.9.3

Saenredam's paintings are almost always church interiors in which the luminous and balanced treatment of the architecture has the elegance of an abstract design. In this painting Saenredam not only gives an apparently accurate portrayal of the details of the Cathedral of Saint John, but creates a unified feeling of spaciousness and light. The town of 's-Hertogenbosch, near the Dutch-Flemish border, became part of the United Provinces in 1629, only three years before Saenredam visited it. Thus the cathedral, unlike other Dutch churches, still retained the decorations associated with Catholic ceremony, notably the elaborate black and white baroque altar with its statues of the Virgin and Child and Saint John, and the memorial tablets to the Habsburg rulers Philip II and Albert of Austria that hang above the altar.

Saenredam subtly changed proportions of columns and arches to enhance our sense of the soaring quality of the architecture. The painting of the *Adoration of the Magi* on the high altar had been made for another church in Utrecht by Abraham Bloemaert. Saenredam had depicted it because the altarpiece in the cathedral had been removed before Saenredam visited Utrecht in 1632. In Saenredam's drawing of the apse one sees that a curtain hung over the altar at that time. Saenredam's portrayal of 1646 is thus an imaginative reconstruction of the church.

uyp's masterful depiction of Dordrecht differs extensively from Van Goyen's calm and serene view of this island city (p.125). Here the river Maas is the focus of great activity; in the foreground a dignitary dressed in a black jacket with an orange sash has just arrived at a large sailing ship. He is greeted by a distinguished looking gentleman who stands among numerous other figures, including a man beating a drum. On the left a second rowboat approaches, carrying other dignitaries and a trumpeter who signals their impending arrival. Most of the ships of the large fleet anchored near the city have their sails raised and flags flying as though they are about to embark. The early morning light, which floods the tower of the great church and creates striking patterns on the clouds and sails, adds to the dramatic character of the scene.

Cuyp was probably commissioned to represent an event that occurred during the summer of 1646. At that time an enormous fleet of ships carrying thirty thousand soldiers was anchored at Dordrecht; presumably for symbolic purposes rather than for specific military ones as peace was finally at hand. The Treaty of Münster, which ended all hostilities with Spain, was signed only two years later.

AELBERT CUYP
(1620–91)

The Maas at Dordrecht,
*c.*1650

Canvas. 115 × 170 cm.
(45¼ × 67 in.)

Andrew W. Mellon Collection
1940.2.1

REMBRANDT VAN RIJN
(1606–69)

*The Mill, c.*1645/50

Canvas. 87.5 × 105.5 cm.
(34½ × 41½ in.)

Widener Collection
1942.9.62

The Mill is one of those few paintings that are significant not only because they are beautiful but because they have profoundly influenced the history of taste. As part of important eighteenth- and nineteenth-century collections, *The Mill* was well known to connoisseurs and artists who valued it as one of Rembrandt's greatest creations. The romantic aura of the scene, with the dramatic silhouette of the mill seen against the stormy sky, captured their imagination. Many stories and myths circulated about the painting, among them that this was a picture of Rembrandt's father's mill. The dark, threatening sky seemed to others to portend the severe financial difficulties that Rembrandt had in the mid-1650s.

While we may find such interpretations unfounded today, particularly after the blue sky that had been obscured by the discolored varnish was revealed in a recent restoration, the painting still speaks to us as a powerfully expressive work. Rembrandt evokes a feeling of the forces of nature in the dramatic confrontation of the mill against the sweep of the sky. At the same time, the figures within the landscape give it a human element that we can respond to on a personal basis.

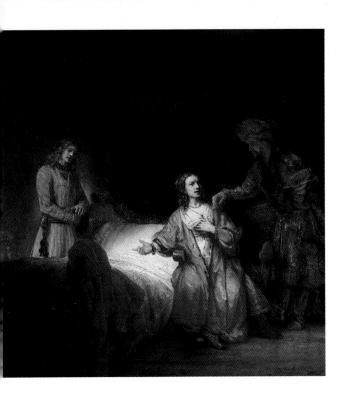

Rembrandt's primary aspiration as an artist was to become a great history painter. In the seventeenth century, history painting, which meant the depiction of biblical, mythological, and allegorical scenes, stood at the highest echelon of art. Theorists placed it before other subjects like landscape, portraiture, or still life because the role of the artist's imagination was so crucial to the successful interpretation of the story and its moral.

Rembrandt drew his interpretations of his subjects from three basic sources: written texts, earlier pictorial images of the scenes, and careful study of human emotions as he saw them in daily life. He then gave his scenes special meaning through a suggestive use of light and dark accents, rich colors, and bold application of paint.

Rembrandt was particularly fond of the story of Joseph. This scene, drawn from the Book of Genesis, chapter 39, depicts the moment when Potiphar's wife falsely accused Joseph of trying to violate her. While speaking to her husband, Potiphar's wife here points to Joseph's red robe to support her accusation. In the biblical account, Joseph, who stands quietly on the far side of the bed in Rembrandt's painting, was not present at the moment of the accusation. Rembrandt, however, included him to give added poignance to the scene.

REMBRANDT VAN RIJN
(1606–69)

Joseph Accused by Potiphar's Wife, 1655

Canvas. 106 × 98 cm.
(41⅝ × 38½ in.)

Andrew W. Mellon Collection
1937.1.79

PIETER DE HOOCH
(1629–84)

A Dutch Courtyard,
c.1658/60

Canvas. 68 × 59 cm.
(26¾ × 23 in.)

Andrew W. Mellon Collection
1937.1.56

The serenity and self-confidence characteristic of Dutch art of the mid-seventeenth century are admirably expressed in this representation of a middle-class courtyard in Delft. The woman takes time from her round of chores to share a drink with two men relaxing in the pale sunlight; the little girl brings coals for their pipes.

De Hooch worked in Delft from 1652 to about 1660 when he moved to Amsterdam. In the 1650s, together with other artists active in that small and relatively quiet city, notably Carel Fabritius and Johannes Vermeer, he painted everyday scenes remarkable for their clarity of perspective and harmony of light. De Hooch gave order to his compositions by carefully determining how his architectural elements should be placed. The position of doors, windows and their shutters, floor tiles, or bricks were all carefully calculated and painted. As in this example, he often suggested a sequence of ordered spaces by showing distant views through windows or doors.

Despite the realistic appearance of the scene, this courtyard view is a distillation of typical elements found in many of De Hooch's courtyard paintings. Thus, even though the tower of the Nieuwe Kerk appears in the left background, it is unlikely that this view ever existed or that the exact location of the courtyard could be found.

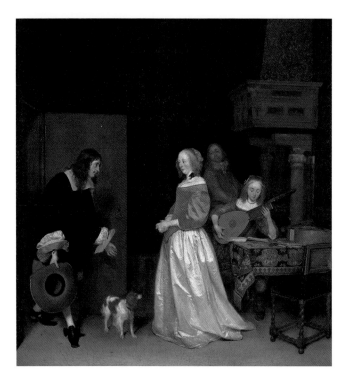

Dutch seventeenth-century artists drew their subject matter from all elements of society. The artist who best captured the refinement of the wealthy bourgeoisie in the second half of the century was Gerard Terborch. In this example, an elegant gentleman bows gracefully as he enters the room. A young woman wearing a beautiful satin dress with an orange-red jacket stands to greet him while another woman sits at a table playing a theorbo, a musical instrument. Behind this group a man warms his hands at a fireplace. The costumes, instruments, imposing mantelpiece, and gilded wallpaper all attest to the high social status of the figures.

Terborch's exquisite painting technique, which consisted of delicate touches with the brush and the use of thin glazes to suggest transparencies, allowed him to create realistic textural effects, whether of lace, satin, or the pile of a wool tablecloth. His main focus was the psychological interaction of the two protagonists, the suitor and the standing woman. These two figures are clearly communicating through their glances and gestures. Seen in the context of the musical instruments and dog, both of which have associations of love, their meeting has strong sexual overtones.

GERARD TERBORCH II
(1617–81)

The Suitor's Visit,
*c.*1658/60

Canvas. 80 × 75 cm.
(31½ × 29⅝ in.)

Andrew W. Mellon Collection
1937.1.58

WILLEM VAN AELST
(1627–83)

*Still Life with Dead
Game*, 1661

Canvas. 84.7 × 67.3 cm.
(33⅜ × 26½ in.)

Pepita Milmore Memorial Fund
1982.36.1

Still lifes with hunting motifs became popular in Dutch art in the latter part of the seventeenth century, at a time when Dutch society grew wealthier and more refined. One of the most important artists in this tradition was Willem van Aelst, who came from Delft but trained and worked for a number of years in France and Italy.

Van Aelst depicted a number of dead animals hanging above and resting upon a stone ledge on which a blue and gold hunter's game pouch lies. The animals were painted very precisely, and most of them can be identified. Aside from the large European hare and roosters are a partridge, kingfisher, and common wheatear. Also visible are two falconer's hoods, perhaps to indicate the nature of the hunt.

That Van Aelst's painting was intended to represent the general theme of the hunt rather than the spoils of a specific hunt is evident from the relief depicting Diana and Actaeon on the front of the stone ledge. This popular story from Ovid's *Metamorphoses* describes how Actaeon, a mortal hunter, accidentally disturbs Diana, the goddess of the hunt, at her bath; Diana transforms him into a stag as punishment.

The mood and subject matter in Steen's paintings range enormously, from intimate moments when a family says grace before a meal to festive celebrations of Twelfth Night. But in all of his paintings we respond in a warm and compassionate way to the ordinary figures he represents.

The Dancing Couple is characteristic of many of his paintings for it shows people celebrating a festive occasion; perhaps, judging from the tents in the background, a village *kermis*. Two figures dance while musicians play, people eat, drink or smoke, couples flirt, and children play with their toys. Steen even portrayed himself in the scene; he is the grinning figure on the left touching the chin of the woman who drinks from a wine glass.

Despite the apparent frivolity of the scene, the painting has a rather sobering message. Steen was a moralist who often used emblematic references in his paintings to warn the viewer about the transitoriness of life. The cut flowers and broken eggshells on the floor, and the young boy blowing bubbles on the right have symbolic meanings attached to them. Earthly pleasures are short-lived and, as Steen seems to suggest, we should contemplate more lasting values, symbolized here by the church tower in the background.

JAN STEEN
(*c.*1626–79)

The Dancing Couple,
1663

Canvas. 102.5 × 142.5 cm.
(40⅜ × 56⅛ in.)

Widener Collection
1942.9.81

JACOB VAN RUISDAEL
(1628/29–82)

*Forest Scene, c.*1660/65

Canvas. 105.5 × 131 cm.
(41½ × 51½ in.)

Widener Collection
1942.9.80

The culmination of Dutch landscape painting occurs in the work of Jacob van Ruisdael. This great painter began his career in Haarlem but moved to Amsterdam around 1656. Throughout his long and productive professional life he portrayed many types of scenes, but his most characteristic paintings are those in which massive oak trees with craggy branches tower above the rugged countryside.

Ruisdael had a vision of the grandeur and forces of nature quite different from that of his pupil Meindert Hobbema. Figures in his paintings seem dwarfed by the elements of nature. In this scene a man and a woman walk along a path near some grazing sheep in the middle distance, but they are almost inconsequential in comparison to the broad waterfall, the rocks, and the huge fallen birch tree in the foreground.

The mood in Ruisdael's paintings is somber. The clouds are heavy and gray, and the greens of the grass and foliage are dark. Trees do not grow easily for their twisted roots need to grasp onto rocky outcroppings for support and nourishment. Death is also part of Ruisdael's world. The massive broken trees in the foreground are not just compositional devices, they are conscious reminders of the transitoriness of life and the inevitability of death.

A woman dressed in a blue jacket with fur trim stands alone before a table in a corner of a room. She holds a balance in her right hand and with lowered eyes waits for it to come to rest. Behind her, on the back wall of the room, is a large painting of *The Last Judgment* framed in black. On the side wall is a mirror. A blue cloth, some open boxes, two strands of pearls, and a gold chain lie on the table. A soft light, which passes through a window and its orange-yellow curtain, illuminates the scene. While the woman is psychologically removed from us, her graceful figure and serene face suggest an inner peace that one often experiences at unexpected and fleeting moments in one's life.

Woman Holding a Balance is an allegorical scene that urges us to conduct our lives with temperance and moderation. The painting within the painting offers an important clue in that Christ's Last Judgment is echoed by the woman's own actions. Before her are earthly treasures; behind her is the symbol of the eternal consequences of her actions here on earth. In waiting for the balance to rest at equilibrium she acknowledges the importance of judgment in weighing her own actions in anticipation of the life to come.

JOHANNES VERMEER
(1632–75)

Woman Holding a Balance, c.1664

Canvas. 42.5 × 38 cm.
(16¾ × 15 in.)

Widener Collection
1942.9.97

MEINDERT HOBBEMA
(1638–1709)

A View on a High Road,
1665

Canvas. 93 × 128 cm.
(36¾ × 50½ in.)

Andrew W. Mellon Collection
1937.1.62

Hobbema often painted rural scenes where a road meanders past houses and farms nestled among trees. One senses the soft winds of a summer day as clouds billow in the sky. Pools of sunlight accent buildings and fields as well as the leaves and branches of distant trees. Figures strolling along the road or resting beside it are integrated harmoniously into this peaceful and idyllic setting.

Hobbema, who studied for a short while in Amsterdam with Jacob van Ruisdael, was a prolific painter, particularly during the 1660s when this work was done. He frequently painted variants of his scenes by slightly changing the position of buildings, trees, and figures. In this instance the elegant foreground couple may have been painted by a specialist in depicting such figures. Hobbema often collaborated with other artists in this manner when completing his works.

The idyllic qualities of his scenes, combined with the realistic effects of light and atmosphere, appealed tremendously to English collectors. This painting, along with another that Hobbema may have painted as its pendant, belonged to the collection of the Duke of Westminster in the nineteenth century.

The Dutch Republic differed in both its political structure and religious orientation from the Catholic monarchies that ruled most other seventeenth-century European nations. Dutch culture was, however, open to many influences; one of the most pervasive of these was the introduction of classical ideals, specifically in architecture.

A number of Dutch architects designed and built large homes, palaces, and town halls in classical styles similar to that of the château in this painting. Although this particular château and the formal gardens surrounding it are fanciful creations of the artist, the image of refined elegance and wealth that the scene conveys reflects the social aspirations of the Dutch landed gentry at that time.

Van der Heyden was an inventor as well as an artist. In 1669 he devised a plan for lighting the city streets of Amsterdam. He later developed a vacuum pump that permitted the use of hoses for fire-fighting. As a painter he specialized in depicting views of cities and country estates. He worked in such a precise style that it seems he delineated every brick and course of mortar on his buildings. Surprisingly, despite such a devotion to detail, most of his views are imaginary creations.

JAN VAN DER HEYDEN
(1637–1712)

An Architectural Fantasy,
*c.*1670

Wood. 49.6 × 70.5 cm.
(19½ × 27¾ in.)

Ailsa Mellon Bruce Fund
1968.13.1

British Painting

The history of British painting is intimately linked with the broader traditions of European painting. Kings and queens commissioned portraits from German, Dutch, and Flemish artists, and British painters found inspiration and guidance from their journeys abroad, in Italy especially. Not until the early eighteenth century, in the work of William Hogarth, does one sense the evolution of a new and inherently British idiom.

By far the most predominant genre of painting in the sixteenth and seventeenth centuries was portraiture of royalty, aristocracy, clergy, and gentry. Van Dyck and other eminent foreign portraitists imparted an aura of perfection, even to the most insipid of their sitters. Eventually English artists were able to create their own styles in marine and allegorical painting, and William Hogarth began depicting satirical and moralizing scenes of contemporary life.

Emphatically propounding the Englishness of his art, Hogarth promoted an academy for the arts, the predecessor of the Royal Academy of Arts. The latter was founded by Sir Joshua Reynolds, whose influential *Discourses* stressed the preeminence of history painting. Ironically, perhaps the key figure in the development of English history painting was the American-born Benjamin West, who became the second president of the Royal Academy after Reynolds' death. Other American painters followed West's example and relocated to London, such as John Singleton Copley, who became one of the most celebrated artists of the day and painter to the king.

The late eighteenth century also saw a growing interest in landscape painting. Some artists, such as Richard Wilson, painted idealized scenes imbued with the spirit of the classical past, while others, such as Joseph Wright of Derby, pursued more individual and personal visions of the natural world. Thomas Gainsborough, although best known for his fashionable portraits, painted highly imaginative landscapes (and seascapes) that relate to no specific time or place.

The great flourishing of English landscape painting came during the first half of the nineteenth century, primarily in the works of two masters, John Constable and J. M. W. Turner. Constable's true-to-life views of the English countryside expressed romantic ideals about the essential harmony and purity of nature. Turner, on the other hand, was a romantic who sought to project the way in which sun, fire, smoke, wind, and water affected and transformed the physical world. With their fresh vision and powerfully original styles, Constable and Turner profoundly influenced the works not only of many subsequent British painters, but of countless American and European artists as well.

Detail:
SIR JOSHUA REYNOLDS,
*Lady Elizabeth Delmé
and Her Children*

WILLIAM HOGARTH
(1697–1764)

*A Scene from the Beggar's
Opera, c.*1728/29

Canvas. 51.1 × 61.2 cm.
(20⅛ × 24⅛ in.)

Paul Mellon Collection
1983.1.42

Hogarth represents an important watershed in British art, marking the end of the century-long predominance of Dutch and Flemish painters in England and the beginning of a native school. Although his style was influenced by French rococo artists, Hogarth was a realist and social critic whose subjects came from the London middle classes as he observed them in the streets, in coffee houses, or at the theater.

This vivid scene is a small version of Hogarth's earliest dated painting, now in the Tate Gallery, London. The subject was based on John Gay's popular and long-playing ballad-opera. With its open buffooning of Italian grand opera and its more subtle attacks on the British ruling class and Walpole government, the story was a ready medium for Hogarth's incisive pictorial satire.

The setting (act 3, scene II) is in Newgate prison where Macheath, a highwayman and antihero of sorts, has been brought after his arrest for robbery. He stands in the middle of the stage, shackled, legs astride, a dominant figure in brilliant red. To the left is Lucy, Macheath's lover, the daughter of the jailer Lockit. To the right is Macheath's wife, Polly, who kneels by her father, Peachum, the fence who betrayed Macheath and in doing so brought about the present crisis. Both wife and lover plead for Macheath's life to be spared.

The British demand for portraiture increased rapidly in the eighteenth century as members of the wealthy middle class became art patrons in their own right. Arthur Devis was a provincial artist who came to live in London, where sophisticated portraitists of the upper class such as Reynolds and Gainsborough dominated the art world. Devis received commissions from the middle-class landowning families, merchants, and officials who lived in smaller cities outside London.

This informal portrait is a conversation piece, a genre favored by Devis. The figures, while full-length, are relatively small and are placed somewhat back in the landscape; the background is larger and more detailed than in traditional portraiture and describes the subjects' personal and social context.

Devis devised a repertoire of postures and gestures that he used to express the social status of his sitter. Arthur Holdsworth, governor of Dartmouth Castle, is shown seated, an alert, attentive expression on his face. The ship sailing into the mouth of the River Dart in the background may be a reference to the Holdsworth family's trading business. Holdsworth's brother-in-law, Thomas Taylor, stands behind him in riding clothes. The third man is Captain Stancombe.

ARTHUR DEVIS
(1712–87)

Arthur Holdsworth Conversing with Thomas Taylor and Captain Stancombe by the River Dart, 1757

Canvas. 127.6 × 102.1 cm. (50¼ × 40¼ in.)

Paul Mellon Collection
1983.1.40

GEORGE STUBBS
(1724–1806)

*Captain Samuel Sharpe
Pocklington with His
Wife Pleasance, and (?)
His Sister Frances,* 1769

Canvas. 100.2 × 126.6 cm.
(39⅜ × 49¾ in.)

Gift of Mrs. Charles S. Carstairs in
memory of her husband,
Charles Stewart Carstairs
1952.9.4

Captain Pocklington, who wears the uniform of the Scots Guard retired from the third regiment in 1769, the same year that Stubb painted this group portrait. Seated on the bench is the captain's wife Pleasance, who is probably wearing bridal clothes. The woma standing behind Pleasance is presumably Pocklington's sister, Frances

Stubbs' fame is based on his precise and naturalistic depictions of animals, primarily horses, even in paintings such as this that ar ostensibly about human matters. Stubbs lived in a world fascinate with scientific inquiry; he himself actually performed dissections of animals to fully understand their anatomy.

Stubbs' interest in the structure and complexity of living things le him to adopt a working style in which he first painted the individual figures and then completed the background and secondary details. Th subjects are arranged in a friezelike pattern against the darker, mor muted shades of the massive tree and fanciful landscape. Stubbs was no invited to exhibit at the Royal Academy because he had been labeled a a horse painter, and his popularity sank even lower during th romantic era. Now in an age that looks back on pioneers such as Stubb with fascination and respect, his stature as an artist has greatl increased.

144

W heatley's portrait style has much in common with the traditional conversation pieces of artists such as Arthur Devis. While the figures in Wheatley's portraits are larger in proportion to the background than in Devis' works, both artists employed the same formula of presenting middle-class families engaged together in some pleasant activity, often with one member of the group looking out at the viewer.

The figures of this group are arranged in a parklike setting, silhouetted against a backdrop of dark-green foliage. Wheatley suggested the psychological relationships of the subjects through their physical arrangement in the group. Despite the difference in size, the mother and daughter are, in effect, mirror images of each other, brought together by similarity of their forms and postures. The daughter's intimate relationship with each parent balances and unifies the composition.

Wheatley portrayed sitters' faces with great sensitivity, but his artistic talents are best seen in drapery and costume details. Moving easily from broad, suggestive brushstrokes to ones that are fine and precise, he achieved a variety of techniques that stimulate and delight the eye.

FRANCIS WHEATLEY
(1747–1801)

Family Group, c. 1775/80

Canvas. 91.7 × 71.4 cm.
(36⅛ × 28⅛ in.)

Paul Mellon Collection
1983.1.43

HENRY FUSELI
(1741–1825)

*Oedipus Cursing His Son,
Polynices*, 1786

Canvas. 149.8 × 165.4 cm.
(59 × 65⅛ in.)

Paul Mellon Collection
1983.1.41

Fuseli, a native of Switzerland, began his career in England as a history painter. He developed an expressionistic style composed of a unique blend of influences – German romanticism, the monumental vision of Michelangelo, and the physical and psychological exaggerations of the sixteenth-century Italian mannerists.

Fuseli's own pessimism and fascination with the extremes of human passion are evident. He heightened the intensity of this scene from Sophocles' *Oedipus at Colonus* by placing Oedipus and his children in a dark, shallow space. The tragedy of the father's curse is played out through the gestures of the four figures. Polynices, who had expelled his blind father from Thebes and left him to live as a beggar, has come to ask his father's support in overthrowing his brother. Oedipus, enraged at his son's request, stretches out his accusing arms and levies his dreadful curse, by which each son would die at the hands of the other. Ismene, weak and despairing, kneels with her head on her father's knee. Antigone, whose strength and determination have kept her father alive, is highlighted above the terrible drama as she reaches out to protect her brother with one hand and restrain Oedipus with the other. Her gesture, however heroic, is futile.

Lady Caroline Howard, daughter of Frederick, the fifth Earl of Carlisle, and Margaret Caroline Howard, and niece of Lady Delmé (opposite), was portrayed by Reynolds at the age of seven.

Reynolds deliberately imposed on his compositions certain formal artistic qualities that would give them the solidity and nobility of Greek, Roman, and Renaissance art. He also liked to suggest associations in his portraits that elevate them to some level beyond the merely descriptive. Roses are symbolically related to Venus and the Three Graces, and Reynolds may well have intended to allude to their attributes, Chastity, Beauty, and Love, as ideals to which Lady Caroline should aspire.

Lady Caroline's father affectionately described his daughter as a determined, strong-minded child whose need for discipline he met fairly but reluctantly. He wrote that she was "always a great favorite," suggesting that her spirited personality made her faults tolerable. Reynolds captured some of Lady Caroline's complexity in the serious, intent expression of her attractive face, her averted gaze, and the tension implied in her closed left hand.

SIR JOSHUA REYNOLDS
(1723–92)

Lady Caroline Howard,
1778

Canvas. 142.9 × 113 cm.
(56¼ × 44½ in.)

Andrew W. Mellon Collection
1937.1.106

SIR JOSHUA REYNOLDS
(1723–92)

Lady Elizabeth Delmé and Her Children, 1777/79

Canvas. 239.2 × 147.8 cm.
(94 × 58⅛ in.)

Andrew W. Mellon Collection
1937.1.95

Reynolds sought to elevate British painting, including portraiture, to the lofty realms of classical expression. After traveling to Rome, Florence, Bologna, and Venice, Reynolds became the first president of the Royal Academy, which had been founded in 1768. Through his teaching at the Academy and the publication of his annual lectures, the *Discourses*, he urged the adoption of grand classical values and the study of Greek and Roman sculpture and Renaissance painting.

In *Lady Delmé*, Reynolds created an image of idealized, majestic feminine grace that has many precedents in Renaissance art. The pyramidal composition of the sitters, Lady Delmé's encircling arms and quiet manner, and the regal folds of the deep-rose drapery across her knees are reminiscent of Madonna and Child compositions by Raphael.

The rich, warm colors of the informal landscape and the beautifully controlled movement of light into the deep reaches of the background owe much to Titian. Finally, Reynolds' sensitive use of everyday, intimate details prevents the portrait from becoming remote and unapproachable. The tenderness with which Lady Delmé holds her son and daughter, the nuances of personality in the three faces, the realistic costumes of the children, and the attentive posture of the Skye terrier give the painting a worldly, familiar context.

Gainsborough's landscapes are highly personal statements that evolved from ideas and images he developed in his studio, either directly on canvas or in scale models. In this work he focused on the physical exertions of fishermen as they confront strong winds and pounding surf. Even the massive cliff on the far side of the cove, its thrusting diagonal posed against the wind, seems to echo the efforts of the men struggling to launch their boat into the waves.

Gainsborough owned works by Dutch marine painters, and their influence is evident here. His own free and suggestive painting technique, however, gives the scene a unique degree of freshness and spontaneity. He applied his paint in thin, translucent layers that are accented by deft touches of impasto, particularly in the fishermen's clothing and on the white foam of the waves. A restrained palette of browns and creams suggests the shore and rocks; gray-greens, gray-blues, and white highlights describe the sun-filled expanse of the sea, while the sky is colored with delicate hints of purple, blue, and pink.

THOMAS GAINSBOROUGH
(1727–88)

Seashore with Fishermen,
c. 1781/82

Canvas. 102.2 × 127.9 cm.
(40¼ × 50⅜ in.)

Ailsa Mellon Bruce Collection
1970.17.121

GEORGE ROMNEY
(1734–1802)

Miss Juliana Willoughby,
1781/83

Canvas. 92.1 × 71.5 cm.
(36¼ × 28⅛ in.)

Andrew W. Mellon Collection
1937.1.104

Juliana Willoughby stands quietly but alertly, engaging the viewer with her direct, slightly questioning gaze. The blended harmonies of the pinks, whites, and creams of her skin tones, her dress, and her shining wisps of fine hair evoke not just Juliana, but the essence of all little girls of this age. The dramatic diagonals of the landscape, the energetic brushwork of the trees at the right, and the strong coloration of the sky provide a dynamic backdrop for the young subject.

Romney's sure sense of formal values is evident here in the effective balance of figure and landscape. In this portrait Romney successfully adapted his composition to a change in the sitter's costume, X-rays show that Juliana originally wore a small, brimless cap. During the two years it took Romney to complete the portrait, Juliana, who was by then almost six years old, had outgrown her mobcap and wore, instead, this broad-brimmed bonnet.

Like many of his contemporaries, Romney traveled to Italy, where he spent two years studying the work of Renaissance masters, in particular paintings by Titian and Raphael. The impact of these artists on his work can be seen in the simply expressed folds of Juliana's dress, the ease and certainty of his outlines, and the artful balance of broad areas of color.

Elizabeth Linley's beauty and exceptional soprano voice brought her professional success in concerts and festivals in Bath and London. After marrying Sheridan in 1773 she left her career to support and participate in her husband's activities as politician, playwright, and orator. Sheridan's work was immensely popular, and his witty plays, *A School for Scandal* and *The Rivals*, are a beloved part of today's theatrical repertoire.

Mrs. Sheridan is shown here at the age of thirty-one, a mature and elegant woman. Merged into the landscape, her gracious form bends to the curve of the trees behind her. Light plays as quickly and freely across her dress as it does across the clouds and the sky. The distinct textures of rocks, foliage, silk, and hair are unified by the strong, animated rhythms of Gainsborough's brush.

The freely painted, impressionistic style of Mrs. Sheridan's costume and the windblown landscape reflect the strong romantic component in Gainsborough's artistic temperament. However, his primary focus remains on his sitter's face and on her personality. Her chin and mouth are firm, definite, and sculptural, and her heavily drawn eyebrows give her a steady, composed, and dignified expression. There is a hint of romantic melancholy in her eyes, with their slightly indirect gaze.

THOMAS GAINSBOROUGH
(1727–88)

Mrs. Richard Brinsley Sheridan, 1785/87

Canvas. 219.7 × 153.7 cm.
(86½ × 60½ in.)

Andrew W. Mellon Collection
1937.1.92

151

JOSEPH WRIGHT
OF DERBY
(1734–97)

Italian Landscape, 1790

Canvas. 103.5 × 130.4 cm.
(40¾ × 51⅜ in.)

Paul Mellon Collection
1983.1.47

Wright's artistic interests varied widely, ranging from portraiture and scientific topics in his early "candlelight" period to popular subjects, romantic history, literature, and landscapes in later years. This painting dates from the end of Wright's career. It is a romantic and fantastic blend of his memories of Italy and the countryside of his native Derby.

In the foreground, a rustic figure sits by the side of a rock-strewn path; he is a small, lonely human presence in this broad and arresting view of nature. A path winds above him to the villas in the hills, while to the right the land gives way to a rolling meadow, a still lake, and a distant mountain. In the background great masses of earth rise dramatically, culminating in a long silhouette against the pale blue sky.

Wright's unorthodox use of color in the cliffs has an expressionistic quality that seems to foreshadow the works of later artists. At a distance from the painting the sharp contrast between the colors emphasizes the geometry of the forms. Viewed closer, the forms begin to flatten out into abstract patterns. While Wright's vision of nature is romantic in its use of light and color and in its pervasive nostalgic mood, it is also classical in its purity of line and form and in its controlled and balanced composition.

Like Reynolds and Romney before him, Lawrence preferred the "higher" genre of history painting but, through talent and necessity, became a portraitist. He was enormously successful in his own lifetime, was knighted in 1815, and elected president of the Royal Academy in 1820.

Although unschooled, Lawrence had a great natural gift for fluent linear rhythms and for the dramatic uses of light and color. Composed, gentle, and serene, Lady Templetown is a woodland goddess of otherworldly proportions. The purity and simplicity of the sitters' costumes draw the pair into a sympathetic unity that is further enhanced by the surrounding darker tones of the broadly rendered landscape. Lawrence animated the paint surface with accents of vibrant red in Lady Templetown's earrings and necklace, her son's cheeks, and in the landscape.

Lawrence's idealized presentation of his sitters in an expressive, theatrical landscape epitomizes the romantic style of portraiture. But Lawrence, like Reynolds, was also a passionate student of the classical past. His ideas on beauty were adapted from Aristotle's *Poetics*. He participated in the project that brought the Parthenon sculptures – the Elgin marbles – to England and owned a vast collection of old master prints.

SIR THOMAS LAWRENCE
(1769–1830)

Lady Templetown and Her Eldest Son, 1802

Canvas. 215.3 × 148.9 cm.
(84¾ × 58⅝ in.)

Andrew W. Mellon Collection
1937.1.96

JOHN CONSTABLE
(1776–1837)

Wivenhoe Park, Essex,
1816

Canvas. 56.1 × 101.2 cm.
(22⅛ × 39⅞ in.)

A pleasant sense of ease and harmony pervades this landscape of almost photographic clarity. The large areas of brilliant sunshine and cool shade, the rambling line of the fence, and the beautiful balance of trees, meadow, and river are evidence of the artist's creative synthesis of the actual site. The precision of Constable's brushwork, seen in the animals, birds, and people, lends importance to these smaller details.

Constable was a native of Suffolk, the county just north of Essex. His deep, consuming attachment to the landscape of this rural area is a constant factor in his works. His studies and sketchbooks reveal his complete absorption in the pictorial elements of his native countryside the movement of cloud masses, the feel of the lowlands crossed by rivers and streams, and the dramatic play of light over all.

The commission for this painting came from Major General Francis Slater-Rebow, owner of Wivenhoe Park, who had been a close friend of Constable's father and was the artist's first important patron. This was not the first work Constable had done for the Rebows; in 1812 he had painted a full-length portrait of the couple's daughter, then aged seven. She can be seen in this painting riding in a donkey cart at the left.

During his brief career Richard Bonington painted a variety of subjects, including landscapes, seascapes, and genre and historial scenes. Working primarily in Paris and London, he also regularly ade sketching trips elsewhere; in 1826 he spent almost a year in aly, including a month in Venice. While there Bonington painted any small sketches that he later used in his studio to create finished orks such as this exquisite small painting.

Bonington was greatly admired in his own day for his exceptionl ability to capture effects of light and atmosphere with unerring ssurance. The French painter Eugene Delacroix, an especially devotd admirer, admitted that he never ceased to wonder at Bonington's marvelous understanding of effects, and the facility of his execuon. . . . that lightness of touch which . . . makes his pictures as it were ke diamonds that delight the eye." Here the lovely play of light on he building facades, the delicate reflections on the water, and the weep of the clouds across the sky are clear evidence of what elacroix so greatly admired.

RICHARD PARKES
BONINGTON
(1802–28)

The Grand Canal,
1826/27

Canvas. 23 × 33 cm.
(9 1/16 × 13 in.)

Gift of Roger and Victoria Sant
2001.87.1

JOSEPH MALLORD
WILLIAM TURNER
(1775–1851)

*Mortlake Terrace, c.*1826

Canvas. 92.1 × 122.2 cm.
(36¼ × 48¼ in.)

Andrew W. Mellon Collection
1937.1.109

This painting, one of two views of Mortlake Terrace painted by Turner, is a view from the house, looking directly west into the luminous glow of the setting sun. Turner established the quiet mood of the late-afternoon scene with two ivy-covered elm trees, whose soft feathery leaves and curving limbs frame the painting. Long shadows create elegant patterns on the lawn that almost obscure the human element in the scene. Scattered about are a gardener's ladder, a hoop, a doll on a red chair, and an open portfolio of pictures that have been just left behind by figures watching the Lord Mayor's ceremonial barge.

The painting was done about eight years after Turner's first stay in Venice, where his perception of nature and the physical world was profoundly changed by the city's unique light and atmosphere. Light immobilizes the river and gives its surface a dreamlike shimmer. The stable mass of the classical gazebo, the delicate linear clarity of its architectural details, and the carefully depicted windows in the buildings on the left bank of the river coexist in Turner's vision with the heavy impasto of the sun's forceful rays that spill over the top of the embankment wall and dissolve the stone's very substance.

Here Turner brings the great force of his romantic genius to a common scene of working-class men at hard labor. Although the subject of the painting is rooted in the grim realities of the industrial revolution, in Turner's hands it transcends the specifics of time and place and becomes an image of startling visual poetry.

An almost palpable flood of moonlight breaks through the clouds in a great vault that spans the banks of the channel and illuminates the sky and the water. The heavy impasto of the moon's reflection on the unbroken expanse of water rivals the radiance of the sky, where gradations of light create a powerful, swirling vortex.

To the right, the keelmen and the dark, flat-bottomed keels that carried the coal from Northumberland and Durham down the River Tyne are silhouetted against the orange and white flames from the torches, as the coal is transferred to the sailing ships. To the left, square-riggers wait to sail out on the morning tide. Behind these ships Turner suggested the distant cluster of factories and ships with touches of gray paint and a few thin lines. Through the shadowy atmosphere ships' riggings, keels and keelmen, fiery torches, and reflections on the water merge into a richly textured surface pattern.

JOSEPH MALLORD
WILLIAM TURNER
(1775–1851)

*Keelmen Heaving in
Coals by Moonlight*, 1835

Canvas. 92.3 × 122.8 cm.
(36¼ × 48¼ in.)

Widener Collection
1942.9.86

French Painting
OF THE XVI–EARLY XIX CENTURIES

The French state from the sixteenth to the nineteenth centuries witnessed the solidification of a form of government based on the rule of an absolute monarch which reached its apogee under the reign of the Sun King, Louis XIV. This same period gave birth to the French Revolution, and ten years later, the rise to power of Napoleon Bonaparte. The history of French painting for these three centuries has been divided into distinct styles – baroque, rococo, neoclassical, and romantic.

The reign of Louis XIV (1643–1715) brought France to the center of the European stage both culturally and politically. Paris rivaled Rome as the art center of Europe, and a distinctly French style rivaled the more exuberant Italian baroque. The history and landscape paintings of Poussin and Claude Lorrain are characterized by symmetry and clarity of form; the artist's organization of his composition was to demonstrate the power of reason which pervaded seventeenth-century French culture.

On the death of Louis XIV, the center of French society moved from the court at Versailles to Paris, where wealthy patrons built fashionable *hôtels*. These became the setting for sophisticated salons, for gossip and the discussion of politics and the arts. Their interiors were decorated with motifs called *rocailles*, sinuous curves and arabesques. The S curve of the rococo style was incorporated in paintings such as the *fêtes-galantes* of Antoine Watteau, which showed fashionable ladies and gentlemen socializing in a pastoral setting. François Boucher, who started his career as an engraver copying Watteau's paintings, indicated the taste of the mid-eighteenth century in his idealized depictions of courtly beauty.

In the closing decades of the century, the curvilinear and sensual shapes of the rococo were supplanted by a surge of interest in archaeology and a rediscovery of the straight lines and regularized proportions of Greek and Roman art. The French Revolution (1789–99) profoundly changed the entire political system and subsequently the structure which had supported the arts since the reign of Louis XIV. Jacques-Louis David created new motifs suited to the political needs of the Revolution and also for the Emperor Napoleon, reinterpreting the principles of classicism.

Nineteenth-century painting was dominated by Ingres and Delacroix, the first continuing in the neoclassical tradition in his emphasis of linear purity, and the second championing the expressive, romantic use of color as opposed to line. Both significantly influenced a new generation of painters who sought to communicate their own personal responses to the tumultuous political events of their time.

Detail:
ANTOINE WATTEAU,
Italian Comedians

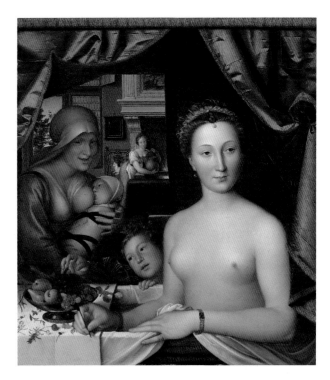

FRANÇOIS CLOUET
(c.1522–72)

"Diane de Poitiers,"
c.1571

Wood. 92.1 × 81.3 cm.
(36¼ × 32 in.)

Samuel H. Kress Collection
1961.9.13

François Clouet, the son of a Netherlandish artist, became court painter to the French kings Francis I, Henry II and Charles IX. In this Renaissance portrait Clouet has depicted a female nude, whose identity is unknown, at her bath. The bather is seated in her tub, which is lined with a white cloth and hung on both sides with regal crimson curtains to ward off the cold. Her left hand draws back the bath sheet revealing the artist's name inscribed below, while her right hand rests on a covered board that displays a sumptuously rendered still life. Slightly behind the bather a young boy reaches for some grapes as a smiling wet nurse suckles a baby. In the background, a maid is seen holding a metal pitcher of bath water as more water is heated in the fireplace. The allusion is to a happy, healthy home.

The mask-like symmetry of the bather's face makes exact identification difficult; scholars have suggested that her aristocratic features indicate that she is one of several royal mistresses, most notable among them Diane de Poitiers, the mistress of Henry II. It is possible that the nude, a Venus type, represents ideal beauty rather than a specific individual. The contrast of the smoothly rendered nude figure to the intricate surface details of the fruit, draperies, and jewelry, presents a union of Flemish and Italian motifs that characterized French courtly art of the sixteenth century.

According to the tenets of the seventeenth-century Catholic church, Mary Magdalene was an example of the repentant sinner and consequently a symbol of the Sacrament of Penance. According to legend, Mary led a dissolute life until her sister Martha persuaded her to listen to Jesus Christ. She became one of Christ's most devoted followers and he absolved her of her former sins.

In Georges de La Tour's somber canvas Mary is shown in profile seated at a table. A candle is the source of light in the composition, but the light also carries a spiritual meaning as it casts a golden glow on the saint's face and the objects assembled on the table. The candle-light silhouettes Mary's left hand which rests on a skull that is placed on a book. The skull is reflected in a mirror. The skull and mirror are emblems of *vanitas*, implying the transience of life.

The simplification of forms, reduced palette, and attention to details evoke a haunting silence that is unique to La Tour's work. La Tour's intense naturalism rendered religious allegory accessible to every viewer. Although his work is deeply spiritual in tone, the solidity and massing of the forms reveal the same emphasis on clarity and symmetry that pervaded contemporary history painting and was a hallmark of French baroque art.

GEORGES DU MESNIL DE LA TOUR (1593–1652)

*The Repentant Magdalene, c.*1640

Canvas. 113 × 92.7 cm. (44½ × 36½ in.)

Ailsa Mellon Bruce Fund 1974.52.1

LOUIS LE NAIN
(1593–1648)

Landscape with Peasants,
*c.*1640

Canvas. 46.5 × 57 cm.
(18¾ × 22½ in.)

Samuel H. Kress Collection
1946.7.11

Louis Le Nain lived in a region to the north of Paris known for its open fields that produced cereals and grain. Although he settled in Paris with his two brothers, who were also painters, he produced a series of rural images that recall the landscape of his youth.

In the *Landscape with Peasants*, an old woman regards three children: a little girl dressed in white collar and cap, a small boy who plays the pipe, and a boy dressed in a cloak and hat who plays a hurdy-gurdy. In the middle ground several shepherds guard their sheep while the background is dominated by a townscape and rolling hills. The clear spacing of the figures and the interlocked planes of space linking land and sky reveal how precisely Le Nain organized his composition.

Their fitted clothes and shoes suggest that the children were not peasants but perhaps members of an emerging class of farmers acquiring land in the early decades of the century. Le Nain's emphasis on the land in this composition implies that the rich soil holds potential profits for these new landowners. The Le Nains' rural subjects were very popular, suggesting their patrons appreciated the agricultural messages encoded in the structure of the paintings.

Although Nicolas Poussin's work exerted an enormous influence on the development of French seventeenth-century painting, the artist perfected his style in Rome, incorporating the lessons of Renaissance and contemporary Italian painters into his own idiom. Poussin's *Baptism of Christ* is one of a series of canvases illustrating the Seven Sacraments executed from 1638–42 for his friend and patron Cassiano dal Pozzo.

In Poussin's composition, the river Jordan winds through the foreground plane where he has placed thirteen figures. Christ is located to the right of the canvas; on his left side – which represents paradise – two figures, probably wingless angels, kneel to help him. To his right, on the earthly side of the Jordan, Saint John holds a vessel over Christ's head.

The reactions of the figures to the right of Christ demonstrate why mastery of the human form was essential to history painting. The row of figures behind Saint John have anguished expressions and contorted poses. Poussin has depicted the specific moment when the voice of the Lord proclaimed: "This is my beloved son, in whom I am well pleased" (Matthew 3:17). By presenting complex poses and physiognomies, Poussin has evoked a very human reaction – the fear of those present as they acknowledge Christ as the son of God – thereby encouraging the viewer to identify with this significant moment.

NICOLAS POUSSIN
(1594–1665)

The Baptism of Christ,
1641/42

Canvas. 95.5 × 121 cm.
(37⅝ × 47⅝ in.)

Samuel H. Kress Collection
1946.7.14

163

CLAUDE LORRAIN
(1600–c.82)

The Judgment of Paris,
1645/46

Canvas. 112 × 149.5 cm.
(44¼ × 58⅞ in.)

Ailsa Mellon Bruce Fund
1969.1.1

Like his compatriot Nicolas Poussin, Claude Lorrain forged hi career in Rome. Claude's vision of the Roman countryside i grounded in a careful observation of nature, but he transformed the landscape into a timeless, idealized world through his masterfu rendering of sunlight and strict structuring of space.

The Judgment of Paris is one of the best known Greek myths. The goddess Strife threw a golden apple marked "to the fairest" amidst the gods and Jupiter selected Paris, a Trojan shepherd, to award it. Each goddess tried to influence Paris with a special gift. Minerva, depicted here with a spear at her side, offered him victory in war. Juno, attended by her regal peacock, offered to make him ruler of the world, while Venus, accompanied by Cupid, proposed the most beautiful woman in the world. Paris chose Venus who then led him to Helen of Sparta which precipitated the Trojan War.

Although the subject is suitable to history painting, the figures are relegated to the left-hand corner of the composition, making it clea that Claude's real interest was the landscape. The viewer's eye slowly moves from the tree in the extreme right foreground to the massive green trees in the middle ground. A winding river leads through the background until the mountains disappear in an atmospheric haze Like Poussin, Claude has ordered nature – here through paralle interlocked planes of space.

Sébastien Bourdon was one of the twelve founding members of the Royal Academy of Painting and his *Finding of Moses* embodies the principles of seventeenth-century academic art, which showed the influence of Poussin.

The book of Exodus (2:5) recounts how a Hebrew woman saved her infant son from Pharoah's massacre of Hebrew children by placing him in a basket on the Nile. Pharoah's daughter, while bathing on the banks of the river, found the child, adopted him, and named him Moses. In Bourdon's composition, Pharoah's daughter, dressed in yellow, occupies the central vertical axis of the painting, supported on her left by her ladies in waiting. The figures form a frieze, like antique sculptures, across the foreground plane. They are dressed according to the seventeenth-century concept of ancient costume and placed in a fanciful setting with Egyptian palm trees.

The careful division of the composition into three parallel planes of space recalls the principles of symmetry and order propounded by the Academy. The dignified gestures – especially that of the princess – and expressions of the figures tell the story in a way considered appropriate to the event, but the work is also enlivened by vivid color and clarifying light. Bourdon based his composition on earlier works of the same subject by Poussin.

SÉBASTIEN BOURDON
(1616–71)

The Finding of Moses,
*c.*1650

Canvas. 119.6 × 172.8 cm.
(47 × 68 in.)

Samuel H. Kress Collection
1961.9.65

ANTOINE WATTEAU
(1684–1721)

*Italian Comedians, c.*1720

Canvas. 64 × 76 cm.
(25⅛ × 30 in.)

Samuel H. Kress Collection
1946.7.9

Antoine Watteau's *Italian Comedians* presents fifteen figures arranged on stone steps, dressed in costumes typical of the *commedia dell'arte* theater. The Italian comedians were extremely popular performers whose fame rested on the audience's recognition of stock characters. Their plays were often greatly exaggerated by pantomime, gesture, and innuendo. Watteau, who spent his early years in the studio of a scene painter, often depicted the *commedia dell'arte* actors in his *fêtes-galantes*.

Pierrot, dressed in shimmering white satin, stands in the center of the composition. Pierrot was a naïve clown whose declarations of love were rejected by Flaminia, the heroine, placed to his left. Other well-known characters are Scaramouche, dressed in yellow and black, whose sweeping arm gesture presents Pierrot to the audience; on the left, Mezzetin, another clown, who flirts with Sylvia, the *ingénue*; and Harlequin, the adventurer, shown with a black face in his red and green diamond-cut costume.

The garland of flowers strewn across the foreground steps implies the actors are taking a bow after a stage performance, but it appears that the members united here were Watteau's own invention, and do not represent a specific play or troupe. This tension between illusion and reality is typical of Watteau and influenced a generation of his followers to explore the relationships between painting and theater.

Nicolas Lancret was one of Antoine Watteau's most talented followers and helped to disseminate the taste for *fête-galante* subjects in the eighteenth century. On the far left musicians are hidden amidst the trees, while across the canvas from left to right, arranged on an exaggerated S curve, stylishly dressed spectators have assembled in intimate groups to watch a couple perform a *pas de deux*. Lancret, like Watteau, was often inspired by the stage, and the female dancer depicted here is Marie-Anne de Cupis de Camargo, a ballet star of the Paris Opéra.

La Camargo is dressed in a white gown embroidered with flowers, suggesting a pastoral opera. She is gracefully poised and her partner's gestures subtly mirror her movements. Camargo, who was immensely talented, expanded the repertoire of eighteenth-century ballet with new steps that encouraged active footwork. To facilitate her movements, she shortened her skirts and may have been one of the first dancers to wear ballet slippers.

Lancret's weaving of figure and landscape into an intricate curvilinear design epitomizes the rococo style. The color scheme imbues the composition with a magical quality where the idea of nature and the fantasy of the theater are merged to create an idyllic setting for La Camargo's fashionable audience – who were also Lancret's patrons.

NICOLAS LANCRET
(1690–1743)

La Camargo Dancing,
*c.*1730

Canvas. 76 × 107 cm.
(30 × 42 in.)

Andrew W. Mellon Collection
1937.1.89

JEAN-SIMÉON CHARDIN
(1699–1779)

Soap Bubbles, probably
1733/34

Canvas. 93 × 74.6 cm.
(36⅝ × 29¾ in.)

Gift of Mrs. John W. Simpson
1942.5.1

Jean-Siméon Chardin was celebrated by his contemporaries for his still lifes painted with thick strokes of paint and great attention to detail. In this composition a boy poised on a window sill is blowing a soap bubble. Both he and the younger boy next to him are fully absorbed in the amusing activity; however, for the eighteenth-century viewer, bubbles were not only a form of entertainment, but symbols of the transience of life. The subject was popular in seventeenth-century Dutch prints which were widely disseminated in France, and Chardin made at least three and probably four versions of this painting. The monumentality of his figure here gives a twist to the *vanitas* theme: the suggestion that the boy is lazy and wasting his time.

Although Chardin gives the illusion he has caught two youths in an unsuspected moment, he has rigorously constructed his composition. The two boys are framed by a rectangular stone window, the sharp rectangles offset by the hunched youth whose arms and head form a triangle. This triangular shape is echoed in the hat of the younger boy. The focus of the composition, however, is the circular translucent bubble, which glistens when set against the muted warm brown tones of the canvas.

In Enlightenment France the dedicated search to define truth engendered a re-evaluation of the natural. The belief that it was right to follow nature, and that the pursuit of pleasure was natural, influenced the prevailing conception of the nude. François Boucher, who became the first painter to Louis XV, fully explored his century's interest in the relationship between the rational and the sensual.

In *Venus Consoling Love*, the mythological goddess has lost any allusions to classical history painting and is offered up to the viewer as an object of physical beauty. Venus, located in a lush garden setting, coyly attempts to restrain a pouting Cupid as two putti point to the scene in mocking disapproval. Boucher's success in communicating the charm and sensuality of the nude lies in his mastery of color and fluid brushstrokes. Venus is rendered in porcelain tones, delicately accented in pink, her body highlighted against luscious blue velvet and silk. The two white doves at her feet contrast a thick impasto surface with the transparent water and cool greens and blues of the foliage. The painting exemplifies the rococo love of asymmetric lines and sinuous curves, artfully arranged to seduce both the eye and the mind of the beholder.

FRANÇOIS BOUCHER
(1703–70)
Venus Consoling Love,
1751
Canvas. 107 × 85 cm.
(42$\frac{1}{8}$ × 33$\frac{3}{8}$ in.)
Chester Dale Collection 1943.7.2

François-Hubert Drouais dated his life-size informal family portrait 1 April 1756, thereby revealing a hidden meaning. In the medieval calendar New Year's Day coincided with the vernal equinox of 25 March, and 1 April, which marked the beginning of Spring, was celebrated with festivities and gift-giving. After the Gregorian calendar of 1582 proclaimed 1 January as New Year's Day, the tradition of exchanging springtime gifts on 1 April continued and is still celebrated today, albeit in a rather distilled form as April Fool's Day. The springtime exchange of gifts is elaborately displayed in Drouais' work: the little girl presents flowers to her mother, the husband reads a letter or sonnet to his wife, and the wife, while arranging flowers in her daughter's hair, also points to their child as a symbolic gift to her husband.

Drouais does not provide enough specific information for us to identify his sitters, but he does give an intimate view into the boudoir. Neither husband nor wife are fully dressed; she wears a smock to prevent powder from spoiling her dress, and he wears a silken housecoat embroidered with fashionable oriental motifs. Like his master Boucher, Drouais relishes in the display of contrasting tones and sumptuous colors.

Like Jacques Onésime de Bergeret, Lalive de Jully (1725–79) was an influential collector, amateur, and painter in the Parisian art world of the 1750s and 1760s. One of Jean-Baptiste Greuze's first patrons, Lalive is depicted seated on a chair he had commissioned as part of a suite of furniture *à la grecque*. This furniture subtly reveals Lalive's avant-garde taste in rejecting the curvilinear forms of the rococo in favor of rectilinear shapes and archaeological decor before the full flowering of the neoclassical style.

Greuze placed Lalive in the center of the canvas; his torso twists toward the harp, as his head, shown in three-quarter pose, turns to the viewer. He is casually attired in a white silk dressing gown, a scarf around his neck, and his britches unbuttoned at the knees. The captivating expression, a faint smile and slightly raised eyebrows, further enhances the contrived informality of the portrait. The emphasis on the face and hands counterbalances the rigid series of parallel vertical lines that define the space.

The prominent display of the harp, accompanied by the furniture with the portfolio of drawings and statue of the Erythrean Sibyl in the background, suggests that Greuze has depicted Lalive as a new Apollo, alluding to his patronage of the arts.

JEAN-BAPTISTE GREUZE
(1725–1805)

Ange-Laurent de Lalive de Jully, c. 1759

Canvas. 117 × 88.5 cm.
(46 × 34⅞ in.)

Samuel H. Kress Collection 1946.7.8

CLAUDE-JOSEPH VERNET
(1714–89)

The Shipwreck, 1772

Canvas. 113.5 × 162.9 cm.
(44¹¹⁄₁₆ × 64⅛ in.)

Patrons' Permanent Fund
and Chester Dale Fund
2000.22.1

Claude-Joseph Vernet was one of the most famous marine painters in eighteenth-century Europe. In 1734, he traveled to Italy where he soon established his reputation. He sketched in and around Rome and along the Mediterranean coast, capturing scenes that provided the basic repertoire of his art for the rest of his career. His paintings were much sought after by Roman collectors and an international community of French diplomats and wealthy travelers, especially the British making their Grand Tour. For these patrons Vernet painted views of Rome and Naples, and imaginary landscapes and coastal scenes that evoke, rather than describe, an idyllic Italian countryside and coastline.

The Shipwreck epitomizes the type of subject for which Vernet was best known. Commissioned in November 1771 by Lord Arundell, *The Shipwreck* formed a dramatic contrast with its more tranquil pendant, *Mediterranean Coast by Moonlight* (location unknown since about 1955): the first work illustrates the "Sublime" (eliciting a sensation of horror in the spectator) and the second, the "Beautiful" (an agreeable and reposeful sensation), concepts that were much discussed in aesthetic discourse of the day. Here, desperate survivors slide down a rope in an attempt to gain the land as their ship, caught in a storm, lurches against the rocks. Such dramatic narratives were greatly admired by contemporaries who responded with genuine emotion to Vernet's depiction of man's plight in the face of an unrelenting nature.

Perhaps more than the work of his two teachers, Boucher and Chardin, Jean-Honoré Fragonard's bravura handling of brushwork and color embodies eighteenth-century painting aesthetics. In *A Young Girl Reading*, the subject is shown in profile holding a book in her right hand and completely absorbed in her reading. She appears to be sitting in a window as light illuminates her face and body, casting a faint shadow against the wall. She wears a lemon-yellow dress with a white collar and cuffs accented with lilac ribbons at her bodice, neck, and hair. She is resting on fluffy pillows rendered in warm brown tones and highlighted in light purple. Each texture is rendered in a different brushstroke: her dress a thick weave of yellow and white, the pillows more loosely sketched, and her collar edged with the handle of the brush.

As in Chardin's *Soap Bubbles* (p. 168), the viewer has the illusion he is privy to an intimate moment. However, in Fragonard's work, the bright yellow of the girl's dress and the agitated strokes clash with the solitude associated with reading.

JEAN-HONORÉ
FRAGONARD
(1732–1806)

A Young Girl Reading,
c.1776

Canvas. 81.1 × 64.8 cm.
(32 × 25½ in.)

HUBERT ROBERT
(1733–1808)

*The Old Bridge, c.*1775

Canvas. 91.3 × 121 cm.
(35⅞ × 47⅝ in.)

Samuel H. Kress Collection
1952.5.50

Hubert Robert, known as "Robert of the Ruins," spent eleven years as a student in Rome from 1754 until 1765. During his sojourn he studied at the French Academy, but dedicated most of his energy to sketching the Eternal City and the Roman *campagna*. He reworked the ideas recorded in his sketchbooks, in drawings, and paintings throughout his career.

In the *Old Bridge*, Robert used an ancient monument as the basis for his modern composition. The Ponte Salario, which was built in the sixth century, is shown from below. The arch of the bridge, illuminated by a soft pink glow, separates foreground from background space. Through the bridge we see the Roman countryside in the distance. The crumbling pier on the far left has been converted into a contemporary barn.

Robert has combined the grandeur of ancient Rome with the anecdotal. For example, the young man on the right bank admires the washerwoman opposite, while the old woman on the pier entices her cat to return. Robert, by linking present and past under the warm light of the Italian sun, reminds us that bridges are emblems of the passage of time, thus evoking a nostalgia for the glory of ancient Rome.

Politics played an important role in the career of Madame Vigée-Lebrun. A painter to Marie Antoinette since 1779, she was elected to the Royal Academy of Painting by the queen's decree in 1783. Her close ties to the royal family put her life in danger during the Revolution and she fled France in 1789, not to return until the first Bourbon Restoration of 1812–14. Therefore, it is not surprising that her portraits of society ladies reveal graceful poses, finished surfaces, and sweet, but controlled expressions, that both mask and betray the charged political climate surrounding her sitters.

This young woman's elaborate costume displays three different foreign cultures. Her turban and jacket recall a Turkish harem outfit. The allusions to the exotic Orient signal an escape from the present as well as an Enlightenment acceptance of non-western ideas. Her flowing white gown recalls the costumes of ancient Greece and Rome, meant to inspire republican virtues. The prominent Wedgwood cameo at her sash is English; at this time British imports represented products of another political system, a parliamentary monarchy, that was considered as a potential model for France. In rigorously detailing the costume, Vigée-Lebrun shows how deeply contemporary politics had penetrated daily life. The unknown subject's engaging expression conveys the nascent tensions of the period.

ELISABETH
VIGÉE-LEBRUN
(1755–1842)

Portrait of a Lady, 1789

Wood. 107 × 83.2 cm.
(42⅛ × 32¾ in.)

Samuel H. Kress Collection
1946.7.16

JACQUES-LOUIS DAVID
(1748–1825)

Napoleon in His Study,
1812

Canvas. 203.9 × 125.1 cm.
(80¼ × 49¼ in.)

Samuel H. Kress Collection
1961.9.15

Careful examination of the details embedded in this portrait reveal the key to David's success as a painter during the time of Louis XVI, Robespierre, and Napoleon: the artist's ability to transform his subjects into politically powerful icons.

Napoleon is placed in the center of a vertical canvas dressed in his uniform as a colonel of the Foot Grenadiers of the Imperial Guard. His pose – the slightly hunched shoulders and hand inserted into his vest – contrasts to the formality of his costume. In addition, his cuffs are unbuttoned, his leggings wrinkled, and his hair disheveled. David, in a letter to the patron of this portrait, Alexander Douglas, the tenth Duke of Hamilton, explained that his appearance was designed to show that Napoleon had spent the night in his study composing the Napoleonic Code, an impression enforced by details, such as the flickering candles that are almost extinguished, the quill pen and papers scattered on the desk, and the clock on the wall which points to 4.13 a.m.

David strategically placed the sword on the chair to allude to Napoleon's military success, while the prominent display of the word "Code" in his papers, suggests his administrative achievements. Other decorative details – the heraldic bees and the fleurs-de-lys – are symbols of French absolutism, and imply Napoleon's power as ruler.

Between 1812 and 1814, while Napoleon's armies waged war across Europe, Théodore Géricault began a series of small canvases depicting Napoleonic cavalry officers. These paintings provided Géricault with the opportunity to explore two of the subjects that he loved best: the horse and the pomp of military life.

The *Trumpeters of Napoleon's Imperial Guard* is part of this series. Géricault does not portray an individual, but rather a romantic ideal of the dashing soldier. Though the depiction of the officers suggests actual portraits, the painting is an invention. The painting's composition is based upon strong visual contrasts. Géricault used short, rapid brushstrokes to define the central figures in the foreground while using broader, more sweeping strokes to create a neutral background. He further distinguished the figures from the background through his use of color. The background is in dark tones, while the figures are in warm, vibrant tones, that cause them to advance toward the viewer. The brightly colored parade uniform gives the painting a sensuous appeal and provides visual unity as it is repeated across the canvas. Produced during the height of war, the artist makes no reference to its hardships or defeat; instead he creates a romantic image of military grandeur.

THÉODORE GÉRICAULT
(1791–1824)

Trumpeters of Napoleon's Imperial Guard,
1812/1814

Canvas. 60.4 × 49.6 cm.
(23¾ × 19½ in.)

Chester Dale Fund
1972.25.1

Jean-Auguste-Dominique Ingres, a student of David, promulgated his master's neoclassical aesthetic throughout his long and very successful career. Ingres espoused the supremacy of line over color, the study of antique sculpture, and the value of drawing after the live model, principles he perfected in his expressive use of line to define form.

Madame Moitessier, the daughter of a wealthy government official and wife of a lace merchant, is shown in three-quarter length against a magenta damask background. She wears a black velvet evening dress with a white lace band at the top which is overlaid with a black lace shawl. The black dress and her skin offset her glistening jewels. The surface is finely finished, and the brushstroke almost invisible.

Ingres has simplified Madame Moitessier's features, recalling a Greco-Roman ideal. Her hairstyle and the decorative halo of roses further accentuate the fact that her face is perfectly oval and her features symmetrical. The sitter's body is rather flat, thus emphasizing that the figure-ground relationship is a play between lines and shapes. Ingres, by exploiting the curvilinear possibilities of the female form, has transformed Madame Moitessier into a monumental vision of ideal beauty.

The foremost romantic painter of the first half of the nineteenth century in France, Eugène Delacroix advocated the opposite aesthetic of Ingres. In contrast to Ingres' controlled images that are characterized by his interests in linear purity and a finished surface, Delacroix championed the primacy of color and quick execution as expressive of the artist's imagination.

The *Arabs Skirmishing in the Mountains* was painted a few months before the artist's death and recalls an entry from his diary of a visit to North Africa in 1832. The figures and horses are placed on a diagonal that traverses the lower right foreground plane: the action then shifts to the middle ground as a horse and rider charge towards battling Arabs in the center. The background abruptly rises into a craggy landscape, with a fortified castle and a line of mountains blending with the clouds.

The fluidity of Delacroix's brushstroke animates the composition, heightening the violence of the scene and the moment when the rider is thrown off his horse. The brilliant use of red, blue and white forces the eye to stop at each grouping, accenting the rhythm of the battle itself. Delacroix has created a fictive battle, his work not only recalling an earlier personal experience but stimulating the imagination of his viewers.

EUGÈNE DELACROIX
(1798–1863)

Arabs Skirmishing in the Mountains, 1863

Canvas. 92.5 × 74.6 cm.
(36¾ × 29¾ in.)

Chester Dale Collection
1966.12.1

French Painting
OF THE LATER XIX CENTURY

Painting in France during the nineteenth century was not a logical progression from one -ism to another leading toward expressionism, cubism, and subsequent twentieth-century movements, but impressionism was a deliberate attempt to break from the past. During the seventeenth century the Academy, the School of Fine Arts, and the Salon, the official exhibition, were instituted to foster a national artistic tradition. By the middle of the nineteenth century the academic system had degenerated, and the principal innovations now associated with the era were breaches of its moribund practices and rigid standards.

During the 1860s and 1870s, the impressionists concluded that the smoothly idealized presentation of academic art was formulaic and artificial. Their relatively loose, open brushwork underscored their freedom from the meticulously detailed academic manner. They chose subjects devoid of overtly didactic content, landscape and ordinary activities of daily life, subjects considered trivial or degenerate by the Academy.

The impressionists thought that if their works were exhibited fairly, they would gain acceptance. Favorable viewing conditions – good lighting and ample space between paintings – were considered essential, and the impressionists also wanted to exhibit more works than the two allowed by Salon rules. Often juries, dominated by academic attitudes, rejected the young artists' paintings altogether.

In 1874 Monet, Renoir, Pissarro, Degas, Morisot, and Sisley led a number of friends to form an association and publicly presented the first group exhibition independent of the official Salon. They called themselves "Artists, Painters, Sculptors, Printmakers, etc., Inc." to avoid descriptive titles and pejorative epithets. Nonetheless critics noted their unorthodox style and especially a work exhibited by Monet with the title *Impression, Sunrise* (Musée Marmottan, Paris) and sarcastically dubbed them impressionists. The group, which presented eight exhibitions in all, survived until 1886. By then the core impressionists were beginning to attain a degree of popular success; the group exhibition strategy which had been essential to their enterprise was no longer necessary and the group disbanded.

The audacious impressionist venture had overturned contemporary artistic institutions and freed artists to explore new forms of expression. A variety of styles arose as the impressionist movement concluded. Usually associated with Seurat, Cézanne, Gauguin, and Van Gogh, postimpressionism was neither a style nor a movement. With postimpressionism the naturalist and realist impulses that had shaped impressionism were supplanted by largely symbolic and imaginary sources of inspiration.

Detail:
CLAUDE MONET,
Woman with a Parasol – Madame Monet and Her Son

181

JEAN-BAPTISTE-CAMILLE
COROT
(1796–1875)

Forest of Fontainebleau,
*c.*1830

Canvas. 175.6 × 242.6 cm.
(69⅛ × 95½ in.)

Chester Dale Collection
1963.10.109

The impressionist style developed as a method to render more accurately the appearance of the natural world, and was principally a technique for landscape painting. Corot, whose career began in the late 1820s when the academic tradition of landscape painting was being revived, was one of the most prolific and influential exponents of the genre. *Forest of Fontainebleau,* painted for and exhibited at the Salon of 1831, is a historic landscape, the hybrid category devised to elevate the status of landscape painting by combining with it the subjects of history painting. Although Corot's principal subject here was landscape, contemporaries readily identified the reclining woman in the foreground as Mary Magdalene. Her unbound hair and peasant costume, the deer in the background, and her solitude in the wilderness are traditional attributes of the saint.

In accord with academic training, *Forest of Fontainebleau* was created in the studio on the basis of sketches and studies that had been painted outdoors. The artist's humble attitude toward nature, unostentatious compositions, responsive paint handling, and conscientious clarity and freshness of vision distinguish his work from the formulaic landscapes of academic contemporaries. Corot declined to participate in the first impressionist exhibition, but his pervasive influence was manifest in works by pupils and followers including Pissarro, Morisot, Renoir, Monet, and Sisley.

Courbet painted events and scenery primarily from his native Ornans, a village in the remote Franche-Comté region. A proponent of realism, he challenged traditional ideas about art by depicting simple peasants and rustic scenery with dignity and on the grand scale usually reserved for history paintings.

Overhanging trees and lush green undergrowth surround a narrow waterway in the forest interior shown in *The Stream*. The primitive site, seemingly undisturbed by civilization, evokes a yearning popular during the nineteenth century, a romantic desire for a peaceful, restorative retreat from the rigors of modern life. Courbet used an unorthodox palette knife technique to apply irregular layers of pigments, creating a roughly worked surface imitating the textures of foliage, water, and chalky rocks to evoke the physical presence of the terrain.

When he exhibited this painting at the Exposition Universelle in 1855, Courbet specifically identified the wooded gorge in *The Stream* as *Le ruisseau du Puits-noir, vallée de la Loue* (Stream of the Black Well, Valley of the Loue), a famous site near Ornans. Long interested in the natural history of his region, including its geology, Courbet was scrupulously acccurate in depicting the setting. Freshly observed details and subtle paint manipulation place the National Gallery painting as the first of several depictions of the site.

GUSTAVE COURBET
(1819–77)

The Stream (Le ruisseau du Puits-noir, vallée de la Loue), 1855

Canvas. 104.1 × 137.1 cm. (41 × 54 in.)

Gift of Mr. and Mrs. P.H.B. Frelinghuysen in memory of her father and mother, Mr. and Mrs. H.O. Havemeyer 1943.15.2

B est known for political cartoons and humorous caricatures satirizing contemporary life, Daumier's paintings reveal a more serious examination of the human condition. The itinerant street musicians and acrobats in *Wandering Saltimbanques* are depicted without ridicule, the artist sympathetically revealing the poverty and isolation of their offstage lives.

Daumier may have felt a personal affinity with the entertainers. The little boy carrying a chair could be a recollection of Daumier's childhood, when his family, destitute and living in Paris, endured numerous displacements to progressively worse lodgings. Further, it has been suggested that the older clown clad in traditional costume and leading his family in this painting may be associated with the artist's father, a failed poet and playwright committed to the insane asylum at Charenton in 1851, where he died.

Daumier was self-taught as a painter, and his style has many characteristics of the graphic media in which he trained. The blunt silhouettes of the figures and the simplified space they occupy are stylistic elements that originated in his lithographs. The unspecific, indefinite appearance thus produced endows them with more universal meaning. Personal associations aside, the saltimbanques here are artists struggling to make their way in a world that, as Daumier depicts it, is a bleak, anonymous place.

In a review of the 1846 Salon, poet and critic Charles Baudelaire urged artists to depict "the Heroism of Modern Life." Manet embodied Baudelaire's urbane painter of contemporary Paris. Emperor Napoleon III ordered the renovation of Paris under the direction of Baron Haussmann, and early in the 1860s the slum where Manet located his studio was being razed to accommodate the planned broad, tree-lined boulevards which still characterize the city. In the painting, Manet represented a strolling musician flanked by a gypsy girl and infant, an acrobat, an urchin, a drunkard, and a ragpicker – individuals the artist might have observed near his studio. The seemingly casual gathering is composed of the urban poor, all dispossessed by Haussmann. Neither anecdotal nor sentimental, Manet studied them with the careful neutrality of an unbiased onlooker, and the distinctly modern ambiguity and detachment of *The Old Musician* are characteristic of all Manet's work.

By placing pigments side by side rather than blending tones, Manet could preserve the immediacy and directness of preliminary oil studies in his finished works. Effects produced by this technique were sharper and crisper than those obtained with academic method. When they first encountered Manet's work early in the 1860s, future impressionists such as Monet and Renoir admired his manner of painting and emulated Manet as they forged the style known as impressionism.

EDOUARD MANET
(1832–83)

The Old Musician, 1862

Canvas. 187.4 × 248.3 cm.
(73¾ × 97¾ in.)

Chester Dale Collection
1963.10.162

PAUL CÉZANNE
(1839–1906)

The Artist's Father, 1866

Canvas. 198.5 × 119.3 cm.
(78¼ × 47 in.)

Collection of Mr. and
Mrs. Paul Mellon
1970.5.1

In *The Artist's Father* Cézanne explored his emotionally charged relationship with his banker father. Tension is particularly evident in the energetic, expressive paint handling, an exaggeration of Courbet's palette knife technique. The unyielding figure of Louis-Auguste Cézanne, the newspaper he is reading, his chair, and the room are described with obtrusively thick slabs of pigment.

The Artist's Father can be interpreted as an assertion of Cézanne's independence. During the early 1860s, Cézanne rejected the legal and banking careers advocated by his father and instead studied art, a profession his father considered grossly impractical. In this calculated composition, he seated his father precariouly near the edge of the chair and tilted the perspectival slope of the floor as though trying to tip his father out of the picture, an effect heightened by the contrast between his father's heavy legs and shoes and the delicate feet of the chair supporting him. The framed painting displayed on the back wall is a still life that Cézanne painted shortly before *The Artist's Father*, a statement of his artistic accomplishment. The newspaper *L'Evénement* refers to novelist Emile Zola, the childhood friend who championed Cézanne's bid to study art in Paris and who became art critic for the paper in 1866. Cézanne's father customarily read another journal.

In an 1876 review, a sarcastic critic referred to participants in the second impressionist exhibition as "five or six lunatics – among them a woman – a group of unfortunate creatures." Berthe Morisot is the woman to whom he alluded. Morisot, an original member of the group, showed in seven of its eight exhibitions and contributed financially to sustain the impressionist movement. *The Mother and Sister of the Artist*, one of Morisot's largest works, was exhibited at the Salon of 1870 and perhaps again in 1874 at the first impressionist exhibition.

The painting, a family portrait and an intimate domestic genre scene, was begun when Morisot's sister Edma Pontillon stayed with her family in the winter of 1869–70 to await the birth of her first child, a pregnancy discreetly disguised by Edma's loose white morning robe. Anxious about sending the painting to the Salon, Morisot solicited Manet's advice, and on the last day for submissions he visited the Morisot home. Morisot's correspondence reveals that, rather than offer verbal suggestions, Manet extensively repainted the figure of the artist's mother. Manet's suave shorthand, seen in the mother's features and black dress, differs obviously from the nervous refinement of Morisot's touch in her sister's features, the floral upholstery, and the reflections in the mirror over Edma's head.

BERTHE MORISOT
(1841–95)

The Mother and Sister of the Artist, 1869/70

Canvas. 101 × 81.8 cm.
(39½ × 32¼ in.)

Chester Dale Collection
1963.10.186

In 1862 Bazille arrived in Paris to study both medicine, at his parents' insistence, and art, his preference. He joined the academic teaching studio run by Charles Gleyre, where he met Monet, Renoir, and Sisley. Attracted by the modernist tendencies of avant-garde art, the four abandoned the studio in favor of direct observation of nature. Working in close harmony, they gradually invented impressionism. Unlike his cohorts, Bazille has remained relatively obscure. Bazille's output was limited and the artist died in 1870 during battle in the Franco-Prussian War.

Early in the summer of 1870, before the outbreak of war, Bazille painted two similar works depicting a black woman with a lush array of flowers. Avoiding anecdotal specificity, the woman in the National Gallery painting is posed as a vendor extending a clutch of peonies chosen from her basket laden with seasonal blooms. The proffered peonies, flowers cultivated by Manet and subject of a series of still lifes he painted in 1864–65, are firmly described in a manner reminiscent of Manet. Extending his modest tribute to the debonair leader of the avant-garde, Bazille's composition also alludes to one of Manet's most celebrated and notorious works, *Olympia* (Musée d'Orsay, Paris), in which a black servant offers a floral tribute to a naked prostitute.

Camille Pissarro, one of the creators of the impressionist style, was the only impressionist to participate in each of the eight group exhibitions. He sent five paintings to the first show in 1874. Its modest scale and simple subject notwithstanding, *Orchard in Bloom, Louveciennes* headed the list of Pissarro's works in the catalogue, perhaps for personal associations. Fleeing with his family to London during the Franco-Prussian War, the artist waited until late 1871, after the suppression of the Commune, to return to his home in Louveciennes. His house had been occupied and many of the paintings he had left behind had been destroyed. As France began to rebuild, the artist also gradually recovered from the disaster. In *Orchard in Bloom, Louveciennes*, painted the next spring, abundant white blossoms and freshly plowed soil are tokens of hope and renewal.

Early in his career Pissarro designated himself a pupil of Corot, and in this 1872 painting Pissarro's broad method of composing and choice of a tranquil rural setting inhabited by a few small peasant figures still recall the older artist. Pissarro was able to sell the painting in July 1872, soon after its completion. It was bought by a new and important patron, Paul Durand-Ruel, one of the earliest impressionist purchases by the dealer remembered for his courageous and sustained support of the avant-garde artists.

CAMILLE PISSARRO
(1830–1903)

Orchard in Bloom,
Louveciennes, 1872

Canvas. 45.1 × 54.9 cm.
(17¾ × 21⅝ in.)

Ailsa Mellon Bruce Collection
1970.17.51

AUGUSTE RENOIR
(1841–1919)

Pont Neuf, Paris, 1872

Canvas. 75.3 × 93.7 cm.
(29⅝ × 36⅞ in.)

Ailsa Mellon Bruce Collection
1970.17.58

While his figure paintings are better known, Renoir's landscapes resonate with a vigor and freshness of vision central to the development of impressionism, most apparent here in his transcription of the effects of sunlight. Midday sun suffuses the panorama, its intensity heightening the artist's palette and suppressing incidental detail to clarify the crowded scene.

Edmond Renoir, the artist's younger brother and a novice journalist in 1872, later recounted the inception of this painting in an interview. Renoir secured an owner's permission to occupy an upper floor of a café for one day to depict the view of the famous bridge. Edmond periodically descended to the street to delay passersby long enough for the artist to record their appearance. Renoir even noted Edmond's presence, walking stick in hand and straw boater on his head, in two locations.

If, as Edmond indicated, *Pont Neuf, Paris* was painted during a single day, it was preceded by careful preparations, possibly including preliminary delineation of the permanent architectural features. The painting seems more richly nuanced and the subject laden with broader meaning than Edmond's anecdote would suggest. Painted in the wake of the Franco-Prussian War and ensuing civil strife that had devastated France in 1870 and 1871, Renoir's 1872 image depicts a representative sampling of French citizenry crossing the oldest bridge in Paris, the intact heart of the recovering country.

Flooding early in the spring of 1872 drew Sisley to Port-Marly, a village on the Seine near Louveciennes, the artist's home. The water here is calm and human activity is minimal. Rather than dramatic or picturesque incident, the artist's attention was engaged by purely visual effects of rain-laden clouds and water-covered streets. The tranquility of the painting and the directness and simplicity of Sisley's observation are qualities derived from Corot, whom Sisley had met in the 1860s.

The composition is traditional. The Restaurant à Saint Nicolas at the left and the erect pylon on the right and its reflection establish a stable foreground and frame an opening at the center toward a stand of trees and distant hillside. The artist's handling, however, distinguishes *Flood at Port-Marly* as an impressionist work. Painted quickly on the scene, probably in a single session, Sisley used muted tones of a wide spectrum of hues, applying them in a thin layer of supple brushstrokes which Sisley varied in response to individual components of the landscape. The distinctive nuanced tonality and animated surface of this painting are hallmarks of the best of Sisley's mature work.

Sisley painted the floods at Port-Marly again in 1876, echoing this 1872 composition in two virtually identical works. Such repetition was unusual for Sisley and suggests that he found the motif congenial and this painting successful.

ALFRED SISLEY
(1839–99)

Flood at Port-Marly,
1872

Canvas. 46.4 × 61 cm.
(18¼ × 24 in.)

Collection of Mr. and
Mrs. Paul Mellon
1985.64.38

EDOUARD MANET
(1832–83)

Gare Saint-Lazare, 1873

Canvas. 93.3 × 111.5 cm.
(36¼ × 45⅛ in.)

Gift of Horace Havemeyer in
memory of his mother,
Lousine W. Havemeyer
1956.10.1

The Gare Saint-Lazare, in 1873 the largest and busiest train station in Paris, is unseen in this painting. Advances in industrial technology and train travel, intrinsic to most contemporary depictions of the site, are in Manet's painting the almost invisible background for a genre depiction of a woman and child. Confined to a narrow space backed by the black bars of an iron fence and isolated by clouds of steam sent up from a train passing below, Manet's two models are inactive and enigmatic presences. The woman is Victorine Meurent, Manet's favorite model in the 1860s, and the child was the daughter of the painter friend who allowed Manet to use his garden to paint *Gare Saint-Lazare*. The composition is a complex contrapuntal apposition of the two figures: one clad in a white dress trimmed with blue bow and the other dressed in dark blue trimmed with white, one with hair bound by a narrow black ribbon and the other with flowing tresses under a black hat, one a child standing and looking to anonymous trains and buildings in the background and the other a seated adult staring forward to confront viewers directly.

As the impressionists were opening their first exhibition, Manet was instead preparing for the 1874 Salon. Of the four works he submitted to the jury only two were accepted, *Gare Saint-Lazare* and a watercolor. Critical of the painting's unfinished appearance and disturbed by its title, reviewers nonetheless identified Manet as leader of the impressionists.

The impressionist style was incompatible with Degas' meticulous paint handling and premeditated method of composing, and he preferred "independent" or "realist" to "impressionist" as the name of the movement. Degas did help establish and direct the impressionist organization, however, and participated in seven of the eight exhibitions. He selected insistently modern themes – ballet dancers, laundresses, prostitutes, cafés and café-concerts, and race tracks – and depicted them in numerous variations. One other recurring genre was portraiture. Degas selected family and friends as models rather than paint commissioned portraits, and his portraits are often unconventional characterizations. This portrait of Estelle Musson Balfour de Gas, the artist's first cousin and sister-in-law, was painted during Degas' 1872–73 visit to New Orleans.

The 1871 discovery of the deterioration of his own vision sensitized the artist to Estelle's near-blindness when he visited the next year. Posture, gesture, accessories, and activities were often used by Degas to characterize the models in his portraits. Such incidental details were deliberately omitted here, a similarly informative decision. The soft focus of the painting, subdued and nearly monochromatic color harmonies, and Estelle's unfocused gaze parallel her limited visual capacity and indicate the artist's respect for Estelle and compassionate understanding of her situation.

EDGAR DEGAS
(1834–1917)

Madame René de Gas,
1872/73

Canvas. 72.9 × 92 cm.
(28¾ × 36¼ in.)

Chester Dale Collection
1963.10.124

CLAUDE MONET
(1840–1926)

*Woman with a Parasol –
Madame Monet and Her
Son*, 1875

Canvas. 100 × 81 cm.
(39⅜ × 31⅞ in.)

Collection of Mr. and
Mrs. Paul Mellon
1983.1.29

With Manet's assistance, Monet found lodging in suburban Argenteuil in late 1871, a move that initiated one of the most fertile phases of his career. Impressionism evolved in the late 1860s from a desire to create full-scale, multi-figure depictions of ordinary people in casual outdoor situations. At its purest, impressionism was attuned to landscape painting, a subject Monet favored. In *Woman with a Parasol – Madame Monet and Her Son* his skill as a figure painter is equally evident. Contrary to the artificial conventions of academic portraiture, Monet delineated the features of his sitters as freely as their surroundings. The spontaneity and naturalness of the resulting image were praised when it appeared in the second impressionist exhibition in 1876.

Woman with a Parasol was painted outdoors, probably in a single session of several hours' duration. The artist intended this to look like a casual family outing rather than an artificially arranged portrait, using pose and placement to suggest that his wife and son interrupted their stroll while he captured their likenesses. The brevity of the fictional moment portrayed here is conveyed by a repertory of animated brushstrokes of vibrant color, hallmarks of the style Monet was instrumental in forming. Bright sunlight shines from behind Camille to whiten the top of her parasol and the flowing cloth at her back, while colored reflections from the wildflowers below touch her front with yellow.

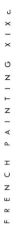

The harsh reception of the first impressionist group exhibition and disastrous results of an auction that Renoir optimistically organized in 1875 placed him in dire financial straits. Perhaps as a remedy, within the year he began to paint anecdotal depictions of women and children, subjects in which he excelled. *A Girl with a Watering Can*, typical of these works, displays a mature impressionist style attuned to the specific requirements of figure painting. Renoir's colors reflect the freshness and radiance of the impressionist palette, while his handling is more controlled and regular than in his landscapes, with even brushstrokes applied in delicate touches, especially in the face. Brilliant prismatic hues envelope the little girl in an atmosphere of warm light and charmingly convey her innocent appeal.

Specific identifications have been proposed for the girl, but none is convincing. More probably Renoir depicted a neighborhood child whose pretty features pleased the artist. A girl with similar curly blond hair, sparkling blue eyes, plump pink cheeks, and smiling red lips appears, similarly clad, in a painting of about five years later. Further recurrence suggests that she became a commercially viable stock figure in Renoir's repertory. *A Girl with a Watering Can*, designed to attract portrait commissions, is a showcase of the grace and charm of the artist's work.

AUGUSTE RENOIR
(1841–1919)

A Girl with a Watering Can, 1876

Canvas. 100.3 × 73.2 cm.
(39½ × 28¾ in.)

Chester Dale Collection
1963.10.206

JAMES JACQUES JOSEPH
TISSOT
(1836–1902)

Hide and Seek, c.1877

Wood. 73.4 × 53.9 cm.
(28⅞ × 21¼ in.)

Chester Dale Fund
1978.47.1

In early 1874 Degas wrote, "Look here, my dear Tissot. . . you positively must exhibit at the Boulevard [in the first impressionist exhibition]. . . Exhibit. Be of your country and with your friends." Degas and Tissot, who met as students during the late 1850s, stayed in close communication even after Tissot fled to London in 1871 to avoid punishment for activities in the abortive Commune. Arguing that the benefits of declaring his allegiance to French art outweighed the potential harm it might cause among Tissot's London audience, Degas urged Tissot to show with the impressionists and thereby affirm his ties to France and more particularly to Degas and realism.

Although he chose not to accept the invitation, Tissot, like Degas, worked in a realist vein. *Hide and Seek* depicts a modern, opulently cluttered Victorian room, Tissot's studio. After Kathleen Newton entered his home in about 1876, Tissot focused almost exclusively on intimate, anecdotal descriptions of the activities of the secluded suburban household, depicting an idyllic world tinged by a melancholy awareness of the illness that would lead to her death in 1882. The artist's companion reads in a corner as her nieces and daughter amuse themselves. The artist injected an atmosphere of unease into this tranquil scene by comparing the three lively faces peering toward the infant in the foreground at the left with an ashen Japanese mask hanging near Mrs. Newton in the entry to the conservatory.

Seurat's *Sunday Afternoon on the Island of La Grande-Jatte* (The Art Institute of Chicago), the most controversial work shown in 1886 at the eighth and last impressionist exhibition, established him as a leading modernist. Based on new theories about optical characteristics of light and color, Seurat invented a technique called neoimpressionism, or divisionism, as a scientifically objective form of impressionism. Seurat juxtaposed minute touches of unmixed pigments in hues corresponding to the perceived local color, the color of light, the complement of the local color for shadow, and reflected color of nearby areas, which in principle will combine visually when viewed at the proper distance. This meticulous technique, less random than impressionism, enabled Seurat to record appearances more accurately while preserving the fresh, natural qualities he admired in impressionist works.

Following the intensive studio campaign leading to the exhibition of *La Grande-Jatte*, Seurat spent the summer at Honfleur, a coastal resort near Le Havre. He relaxed by painting local landmarks such as the hospice and lighthouse in *The Lighthouse at Honfleur*. Balancing warm blond tones in the sand and lighthouse with cool blues in the sky and water and constructing a stable composition around the horizontals of the jetty and horizon crossed by the vertical tower, Seurat created a work of majestic serenity.

GEORGES SEURAT
(1859–91)

The Lighthouse at Honfleur, 1886

Canvas. 66.7 × 81.9 cm. (26¼ × 32¼ in.)

Collection of Mr. and Mrs. Paul Mellon
1983.1.33

VINCENT VAN GOGH
(1853–90)

La Mousmé, 1888

Canvas. 73.3 × 60.3 cm.
(28⅞ × 23¾ in.)

Chester Dale Collection
1963.10.151

The intention and determination that inform Van Gogh's art can be obscured by the sensational legends that have arisen about his life. The artist's correspondence, particularly from his brief mature period of 1888 to 1890, contradicts popular lore and attests to the deliberateness, sensitivity, and integrity of his work.

On about 25 July 1888, Van Gogh wrote his younger brother Theo, a dealer in a Parisian art gallery, to announce, "And now, if you know what a 'mousmé' is (you will know when you have read Loti's *Madame Chrysanthème*), I have just painted one. It took me a whole week . . . but I had to reserve my mental energy to do the mousmé well. A mousmé is a Japanese girl – Provençal in this case – twelve to fourteen years old." The carefully modeled face and the vigorous linear patterns of bold complementary colors that describe the girl are stylistic devices that express Van Gogh's sympathetic response to his young sitter. In several descriptions of the painting Van Gogh mentioned the oleander buds in her hand. The significance of the flowers is unclear but may be related to the artist's pantheistic beliefs in natural cycles of birth and renewal.

La Mousmé was one of a group of portrait studies which, Vincent wrote, were, "the only thing in painting that excites me to the depths of my soul, and which makes me feel the infinite more than anything else."

*B*oy in a Red Waistcoat is one of a group of works – two watercolors and four paintings – depicting the Italian model Michelangelo di Rosa dressed in the distinctive titular waistcoat. The use of a professional model was a departure for Cézanne who, until this time, had relied upon family and friends as subjects. Little is known about this sitter beyond his name and nationality, but the painting is less a portrait than a study in style and composition.

The model's pose is conventional, reminiscent of academic nude studies produced in life-drawing classes. However, it also hearkens back to other more elegant antecedents from the High Renaissance, such as the aristocratic portraits of Agnolo Bronzino, notably in the slender, languid figure, the sinuous line of his torso, and the three-quarter-length format. Cézanne seems to have paid homage to the past even as he transformed its traditions through the introduction of a bolder visual language.

In this painting, Cézanne achieved a complex balance of contrasts: between the languor of the young man's pose and the vigorous brushwork, between the subtle palette of blues, grays, and mauves in the drapery and the boy's shirt and the vivid red of the waistcoat. What appears to be a straightforward depiction of a single figure reveals itself, upon closer examination, to be a sophisticated marriage of line and muted tonal harmonies that is almost musical.

PAUL CÉZANNE
(1839–1906)

Boy in a Red Waistcoat,
1888–90

Canvas. 89.5 × 72.4 cm.
(35¼ × 28½ in.)

Collection of Mr. and Mrs. Paul
Mellon, in Honor of the 50th
Anniversary of the National
Gallery of Art
1995.47.5

PAUL GAUGUIN
(1848–1903)

Self-Portrait, 1889
Wood. 79.2 × 51.3 cm.
(31¼ × 20¼ in.)

Chester Dale Collection
1963.10.150

Self-portraiture constituted a significant element of Gauguin's production, particularly in 1888 and 1889. Gauguin's interest was prompted in part by Van Gogh's 1888 portrait series including *La Mousmé* (p. 198), which he knew from Van Gogh's letters. In addition, Van Gogh hoped to establish an artists' colony in the south that could be analogous to Gauguin's circle in Brittany, and proposed an exchange of self-portraits. Gauguin's only known statements about his self-portraiture concern one he painted in response to Van Gogh. He described manipulating his image to accord with a predetermined symbolic program, a program somewhat similar to the Gallery *Self-Portrait* and referring to the 1888 depiction as "the face of an outlaw . . . with an inner nobility and gentleness," a face that is "symbol of the contemporary impressionist painter" and "a portrait of all wretched victims of society."

The Gallery *Self-Portrait*, painted on a cupboard door in the dining room of an inn in the Breton hamlet Le Pouldu, is one of Gauguin's most important and radical paintings. His haloed head and disembodied right hand, a snake inserted between the fingers, float on amorphous zones of yellow and red. Elements of caricature add an ironic and aggressively ambivalent inflection to this painted assertion of Gauguin's artistic superiority and make him the sardonic hero of his new aesthetic system.

L ured to Tahiti in 1891 by reports of its unspoiled culture, Gauguin was disappointed by its civilized capital and moved to the countryside, where he found an approximation of the tropical paradise he had expected. The Tahiti of his depictions was derived from native folklore supplemented by material culled from books written by earlier European visitors and overlaid with allusions to western culture. The pose of the standing nude, for instance, is derived from a medieval statue of the biblical Eve and more distantly from the Venus Pudica of classical sculpture. The artist placed this rich combination of references to original sin, the loss of virginity, and occidental standards of beauty and art within the context of his Tahitian mythology and primitive, non-European aesthetics.

The meaning of the title *Parau na te Varua ino* is unclear. The phrase *varua ino*, evil spirit or devil, refers to the masked kneeling figure and *parau* means words, suggesting the interpretation "Words of the Devil." The meaning of many of Gauguin's Tahitian paintings remains elusive. There is little likelihood that Gauguin's original audience would have been able to interpret the Tahitian legends that Gauguin carefully inscribed on most of the sixty-six paintings he took back to Paris in 1892.

PAUL GAUGUIN
(1848–1903)

*Parau na te Varua ino
(Words of the Devil),*
1892

Canvas. 91.7 × 68.5 cm.
(36⅛ × 27 in.)

Gift of the W. Averell Harriman
Foundation in memory of
Marie N. Harriman
1972.9.12

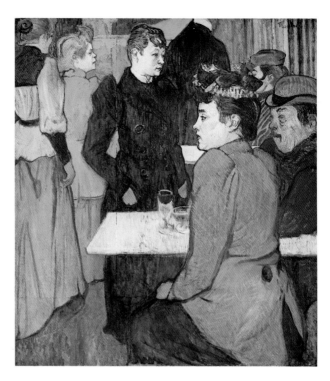

The seamy underside of the Parisian demimonde, the singers, dancers, and patrons of Montmartre nightclubs, the notorious whores of the district and their clients were Toulouse-Lautrec's principal subjects. Scion of one of France's great aristocratic families, Lautrec was afflicted in youth by injuries that stunted his growth. He was encouraged to draw during his long convalescence and permitted professional training in an academic studio, which he deserted to embrace modernism. Lautrec particularly admired Degas and emulated his unusual perspectives and gritty social realism. He mastered the new medium of color lithography and produced an impressive body of posters and printed illustrations which share the incisive linear quality of the design of this painting.

Isolated by his painful physical deformity, Lautrec became an alcoholic and a denizen of dance halls and nightclubs in Montmartre, a poor working class neighborhood untouched by Baron Haussmann's renovations of Paris. Insight gained from his handicap and his emotional remoteness from his subjects gave his depictions special force, bitterness, and sympathy, while the artifice of his preferred settings and the disguised role playing of his subjects could alter reality amusingly or grotesquely in his work. Lautrec was an observer, a voyeur rather than a participant, and alienation is endemic even in the crowded *Corner of the Moulin de la Galette*.

Toward the middle of the 1880s, a number of artists became disaffected with impressionism. Monet began to explore a new kind of painting, serial imagery. The series paintings were a break from impressionism in two critical respects: the works, based on campaigns in front of the motif, were usually extensively reworked in the studio and lacked the spontaneity integral to impressionism, and the motif itself was secondary to effects of light and weather.

The new qualities of Monet's series paintings were given concentrated expression in the *Rouen Cathedrals*, in which the stone façade fills the canvases. Monet showed twenty of the thirty extant *Cathedrals*, among them these two works, as a group in an 1895 exhibition. Individual paintings, named according to the view and weather conditions depicted, are chiefly distinguished by color, which assumes the principal role in the series. The cumulative impression reported by visitors extended beyond the impact of individual works. The rich surfaces of the paintings seem to imitate the cathedral's fabric of the carved stone. Individually the paintings depict a religious edifice, but collectively the series becomes a denial of the solidity of Rouen Cathedral as an entity, and gives precedence to artistic concerns of light, color and mood.

CLAUDE MONET
(1840–1926)

Rouen Cathedral, West Façade, Sunlight, 1894

Canvas. 100.2 × 66 cm.
(39½ × 26 in.)

Chester Dale Collection
1963.10.179

Rouen Cathedral, West Façade, 1894

Canvas. 100.4 × 66 cm.
(39½ × 26 in.)

Chester Dale Collection
1963.10.49

Vuillard belonged to a quasi-mystical group of young artists that arose in about 1890 and called themselves the Nabi, a Hebrew word for prophet. The Nabi rejected impressionism and considered simple transcription of the appearance of the natural world unthinking and unartistic. Inspired by Gauguin's work and symbolist poetry, their paintings evoke rather than specify, suggest rather than describe. Recognizing that the physical components of painting – colored pigments arranged on a flat surface – were artificial, they considered as false the traditional convention of regarding paintings as re-creations of the natural world.

Woman in a Striped Dress is one of five decorations Vuillard painted in 1895 for Thadée Natanson, publisher of the avant-garde journal *La Revue Blanche*, and his wife Misia Godebska, an accomplished pianist. The five, which differ in size and orientation, are intimate, self-contained interiors, Vuillard's principal subject. All display rich harmonies in a restricted range of color and densely arranged in intricate patterns. The introspective woman arranging flowers here perhaps represents the red-haired Misia, whom Vuillard admired greatly. Vuillard adopted the symbolist idea of synesthesia, whereby one sense can evoke another, and in *Woman in a Striped Dress* the sumptuous visual qualities of Vuillard's reds may suggest the lush chords of music that Misia performed.

Degas studied his preferred subject, ballet performers, in hundreds of works. *Four Dancers*, one of the largest and most ambitious of his late works, exists in several variants that show different kinds and degrees of modification. While Degas suppressed descriptive detail elsewhere in the painting, emphatic dark lines shape the heads and arms, underlining the artist's formal concerns. Theatrical lighting over the off-stage performers recolors the figures and creates a simple color scheme of complementary red-orange and green hues.

Two of the figures repeat poses of a model who appears in a unique set of three photographic negatives. Photographed between about 1895 and 1898, the original plates solarized into colors that resemble, in reverse, the oranges and greens in *Four Dancers*. Degas owned the photographic plates and may even have shot the pictures. The same model, hair piled on her head and features indistinct or hidden, posed for all three photographs, and the four dancers in the painting resemble her. The arrangement of the four dancers may also have been influenced by Eadward Muybridge's sequential photographs, particularly his 1887 book, *Animal Locomotion*. Their poses, a succession of preparatory gestures, depict a progression of intricate movements.

As Degas' eyesight worsened, the artist increasingly preferred pastels to oil paints. In *Four Dancers*, Degas used oils to imitate the color effects and matte surface of pastels.

EDGAR DEGAS
(1834–1917)

Four Dancers, c.1899

Canvas. 151.1 × 180.2 cm.
(59½ × 71 in.)

Chester Dale Collection
1963.10.122

American Painting
OF THE XVIII–EARLY XIX CENTURIES

P ortraiture formed the mainstay of subject matter in colonial and federal American art, as emigrants to the New World attempted to bring a semblance of Old World civilization to their wild or, at best, provincial surroundings. Early portraitists such as Winthrop Chandler called themselves "limners," related to the word "illuminate."

When Benjamin West arrived in Rome in 1760, he was the first American artist to study in Europe. Upon seeing the Vatican's famous classical statue, the *Apollo Belvedere*, West exclaimed, "My God! How like it is to a young Mohawk warrior!" His astute comparison between the "noble savage" and the "glory that was Greece" won hearty applause from the connoisseurs. West soon emerged as Europe's foremost history painter, dropping the allegorical trappings from classical antiquity and basing his work on historical research.

John Singleton Copley followed West's example in depicting past and present occurrences with believable accessories and settings. Gilbert Stuart, who studied with West in London, revitalized the concept of "Grand Manner" portraiture; *The Skater* is invigorated with a sense of immediacy and activity, and Stuart's portraits soon commanded higher prices than those of any painter in the capital, except for the court artists Gainsborough and Reynolds.

When the Revolutionary War ended in 1783, artists sought to create a distinctive environment for the ideals of liberty. The eighteenth century's classicizing concepts evolved imperceptibly into the nineteenth century's neoclassical style of idealized anatomy, symmetrical composition, and pure colors. The large Peale family bridges this transition toward a more scientific naturalism.

Romanticism, partly engendered by reactions to the American and French revolutions, sought to release the emotions in dynamic design, dramatic spotlighting, and virtuoso displays of palpable paint textures. Such emotional elements mark the later paintings of Benjamin West. Two of West's later pupils, Thomas Sully and John Trumbull, helped to introduce romanticism to the United States.

When the Louisiana Purchase of 1803 instantly doubled the nation's area, artists such as John James Audubon and George Catlin began to investigate the native peoples, flora, and fauna. These academically educated artists were outnumbered by unschooled artist-craftsmen, such as Edward Hicks, who painted for their own pleasure or on commission from rural patrons. After the War of 1812, landscape painting came to prominence, symbolizing America's unique natural resources and vast territory. And, with the introduction of photography to the United States in 1839, the cameraman soon usurped much of the clientele from the portrait painter.

Detail:
BENJAMIN WEST,
The Battle of La Hogue

JOHN SINGLETON COPLEY
(1738–1815)

*Epes Sargent, c.*1760

Canvas. 127.1 × 101.8 cm.
(49⅞ × 40 in.)

Gift of the Avalon Foundation
1959.4.1

John Singleton Copley, America's most important colonial painter, was born in Boston of Irish parents. In 1748 Copley's widowed mother married Peter Pelham, a painter and engraver. Copley's stepfather probably gave him some art lessons but died when Copley was only thirteen. In later years the painter claimed he was self-taught.

Copley, who was extremely observant, presumably learned about art largely by watching other English-trained painters who were working in the New World and by studying engravings imported from Europe. Much more important was his innate ability to record details objectively and to suggest character. Gilbert Stuart would later say of the uncompromising realism in Copley's *Epes Sargent,* "Prick that hand and blood will spurt forth."

About seventy years old when he posed for Copley, Sargent had dropped out of Harvard College to enter business in his native Gloucester. After the death of his first wife, this prosperous merchant and shipowner married a rich widow from Salem. Copley's portrayal shows him nonchalantly leaning on a marble pedestal as a symbol of prestige; since carved stone monuments were rather rare in the colonies, this imaginary device must be borrowed from European prints of potentates.

Such penetrating likenesses made Copley the best-paid artist in colonial America. By shipping some of his canvases to London for criticism, Copley soon became known in England.

John Beale Bordley, a close friend of Charles Willson Peale, raised the funds in 1766 to send the young artist to London, where Peale trained under Benjamin West's tutelage. In the stormy years before the American Revolution, Bordley was a Maryland planter, judge, and member of the Governor's Council. A fervent republican, he gave Peale his first major commission – for life-size, symbolic portraits that were to be exhibited in London as declarations of colonial opposition.

The portrait addresses two political issues: America's agricultural self-sufficiency, and her fair treatment. The first of these concepts is referred to in the background, which depicts Bordley's plantation on Wye Island in the Chesapeake Bay. A peach tree and a packhorse signify America's abundance, while the grazing sheep speak for freedom from imported, British woolens. The theme of tyranny dominates the foreground. Bordley, trained as a lawyer, assumes an attitude of debate, raising his hand in a gesture of argumentation. He points to a statue of British Liberty holding the scales of justice, reminding English viewers that the colonists lived under British law and, thus, were entitled to the rights it guaranteed. That Britain had violated these rights is signified by the legal document, torn and discarded at Bordley's feet. A poisonous plant at the statue's base – the native American jimson weed – warns of the deadly consequences of any attack on American civil liberties.

CHARLES
WILLSON PEALE
(1741–1827)

John Beale Bordley, 1770

Canvas. 201 × 147.6 cm.
(79⅛ × 58⅛ in.)

Gift of the Barra Foundation, Inc.
1984.2.1

JOHN SINGLETON COPLEY
(1738–1815)

The Copley Family,
1776/77

Canvas. 184.1 × 229.2 cm.
(72½ × 90¼ in.)

Andrew W. Mellon Fund
1961.7.1

In June 1774, when he was already thirty-five years old, Copley decided that he must go to Europe. Although he intended to stay abroad just long enough to acquire artistic sophistication, the American Revolution changed his plans. Studying in Rome and stopping in many continental cities, Copley arrived in London in October 1775. There he was joined by his wife, children, and father-in-law, Richard Clarke, one of the Tory merchants whose investments had been dumped overboard at the Boston Tea Party.

In 1777 at the Royal Academy, Copley exhibited *The Copley Family,* which records his delight at being reunited with his family. The artist portrayed himself turning away from a sheaf of his sketches to look at the spectator. His wife, Susanna, leans forward to hug their four-year-old son, John Junior. Mary, who was a year younger than her brother, lies on the sofa, while Betsy, aged six and the eldest of the children, stands with a serious aplomb indicative of her seniority. The baby, Susanna, tries to attract her grandfather's attention with a rattle. The background is fanciful; no carpeted room ever merged so ambiguously into a forest glen. Copley's contemporaries would have understood the idyllic landscape as a reference to the family's natural simplicity and the elaborate furnishings as an indication of their civilized propriety.

Watson and the Shark's exhibition at the Royal Academy in 1778 generated a sensation, partly because such a grisly subject was an absolute novelty. In 1749, fourteen-year-old Brook Watson had been attacked by a shark while swimming in Havana Harbor. Copley's pictorial account of the traumatic ordeal shows nine seamen rushing to help the boy, while the bloody water proves he has just lost his right foot. To lend equal believability to the setting Copley, who had never visited the Caribbean, consulted maps and prints of Cuba.

The rescuers' anxious expressions and actions reveal both concern for their thrashing companion and a growing awareness of their own peril. Time stands still as the viewer is forced to ponder Watson's fate. Miraculously, he was saved from almost certain death and went on to become a successful British merchant and politician.

Although Copley underscored the scene's tension and immediacy, the seemingly spontaneous poses actually were based on art historical precedents. The harpooner's pose, for example, recalls Raphael's altarpiece of the Archangel Michael using a spear to drive Satan out of heaven. The oil painting's enormous acclaim ensured Copley's appointment to the prestigious Royal Academy, and he earned a fortune selling engravings of its design.

JOHN SINGLETON COPLEY
(1738–1815)

Watson and the Shark,
1778

Canvas. 182.1 × 229.7 cm.
(71¾ × 90½ in.)

Ferdinand Lammot Belin Fund
1963.6.1

BENJAMIN WEST
(1738–1820)

The Battle of La Hogue,
1778

Canvas. 152.7 × 214.3 cm.
(60⅛ × 84⅜ in.)

Andrew W. Mellon Fund
1959.8.1

Seventeen years after Benjamin West settled in England, a London newspaper's review of the 1780 Royal Academy exhibition stated that *The Battle of La Hogue* "exceeds all that ever came from Mr. West's pencil." In 1692, Louis XIV of France had mounted an ill-fated attempt to return James II, a fellow Catholic, to the throne of England. In response, Britain and her Protestant allies, the Dutch, massed their fleets and engaged the enemy for five days off the northern French coast near La Hogue. Benjamin West condensed the events of the long battle into one dramatic composition that, by employing much artistic or poetic license, is largely propaganda.

Standing in a boat at the left, for instance, Vice Admiral George Rooke embodies heroic command with his upright posture and raised sword. Yet, in order to survey the maneuvers, he undoubtedly gave orders from a distance. Beached in the center distance is the French flagship, the *Royal Sun*. Actually burned and sunk a few days before this encounter, the *Royal Sun* is here deliberately refloated – only to be run against the cliffs so that West might symbolize the French defeat. This complex, multi-figured panorama is an excellent example of West's influential early style, and of the balanced designs and carefully blended brushwork of eighteenth-century neoclassicism.

Although most colonial artists traveled to find patrons, Winthrop Chandler centered his career around his native Woodstock, Connecticut. At first, he called himself a "painter," and several of his surviving works are decorative landscapes to adorn the paneling over mantelpieces. By the later 1780s, though, Winthrop Chandler referred to his profession as that of "limner," implying that he now primarily made portraits.

Captain Samuel Chandler depicts the artist's brother, a tavern keeper and a member of the Connecticut militia during the Revolutionary War. A battle between Red Coats and colonials can be seen through the open window. Wearing his captain's uniform, Samuel proudly displays a sword with silver hilt and scabbard. His military tricorn hat rests on a mahogany drop-leaf table which serves to indicate his civilian wealth.

The careful delineation of these objects gives them an importance almost equal to the forthright portrayal of the captain's stern countenance. As with many essentially self-taught artists, Winthrop Chandler compensated for his lack of expertise in anatomy and perspective by creating superbly integrated designs. The repeated ranks of horsemen in the landscape, for instance, form patterns that effectively reiterate the uniform's rows of buttons; and the rippling curves of cuffs, cravat, and tricorn hat play against the straight lines of sword, furniture legs, and window frame.

WINTHROP CHANDLER
(1747–90)

*Captain Samuel Chandler, c.*1780

Canvas. 139.4 × 121.7 cm.
(54⅞ × 47⅞ in.)

Gift of Edgar William
and Bernice Chrysler Garbisch
1964.23.1

GILBERT STUART
(1755–1828)

*The Skater (Portrait of
William Grant)*, 1782

Canvas. 245.5 × 147.6 cm.
(96⅝ × 58⅛ in.)

Andrew W. Mellon Collection
1950.18.1

In 1775, Gilbert Stuart set sail for London where Benjamin West welcomed the destitute young man into his home. *The Skater* marks the end of his five-year apprenticeship to West. Stuart's first effort at full-length portraiture, its originality brought the artist so much notice at the 1782 Royal Academy exhibition that he soon set up his own studio.

The unorthodox motif of skating – indeed, any presentation of vigorous movement at all – had absolutely no precedent in Britain's "Grand Manner" tradition of life-size society portraiture. The painter recalled that when William Grant, from Congalton near Edinburgh, arrived to have his picture painted, the Scottish sitter remarked that, "on account of the excessive coldness of the weather . . . the day was better suited for skating than sitting for one's portrait." Thus artist and sitter went off to skate on the Serpentine River in Hyde Park. When he returned to West's studio with Grant, Stuart conceived the idea of portraying his subject on ice skates in a winter landscape, with the twin towers of Westminster Abbey far in the distance.

In this innovative design, Grant glides effortlessly forward with arms crossed over his chest in typical eighteenth-century skating form. Except for his folded arms, the figure's stance derives from an ancient Roman statue, the *Apollo Belvedere*, a cast of which stood in the corner of West's studio.

JOHN TRUMBULL
(1756–1843)

Patrick Tracy, 1784/86

Canvas. 232.5 × 133.7 cm.
(91½ × 52⅝ in.)

Gift of Patrick T. Jackson
1964.15.1

Patrick Tracy demonstrates a colonial American rapidly absorbing the British "Grand Manner." The subject, a Massachusetts warehouse owner, appropriately rests his hand on an anchor and stands on a shell-strewn beach before crates and barrels. His hoary features reveal his seventy-some years, but his delicate fingers and slender calves apparently belong to a much younger man. In the colonies, John Singleton Copley had encouraged Trumbull in painting, and the face's sharp realism is an homage to Copley's American frankness. The body, however, adheres to the flattering canons for harmonized proportions that were advocated by Sir Joshua Reynolds, president of the Royal Academy.

Trumbull's account book for 1784 resolves the dilemma: "Whole length of Mr. P. Tracy (father of Nat) leaning on an anchor – head copied." Nat Tracy, the subject's son, apparently commissioned the portrait while in London on business. Since Patrick was still in America, Trumbull adapted his face from a likeness which Nat must have lent him, but did the rest in his new style.

While working on this life-size portrait, Trumbull received an unprecedented honor from Benjamin West. West, who had intended to paint a vast series of scenes illustrating the characters and events of the War of Independence, decided he was too busy and passed the idea along to his pupil. The resulting history paintings culminated in Trumbull's world-famous murals in the Capitol's Rotunda.

Charles Willson Peale was a major figure in American science and art during the revolutionary period. His faith in the educational value of art led him to establish a painting academy in Philadelphia as early as 1795. When that venture failed, Peale combined his scientific and artistic interests in a museum.

In 1788, the Lamings had asked him to do this double portrait. Peale's diary records his activity from 18 September, when he "sketched out the design" after dinner, to 5 October, when he added the final touches. Besides working on the picture, Peale studied natural history at the family's estate outside Baltimore.

Peale cleverly devised a leaning posture for the husband so that his bulk would not overshadow his petite wife. Moreover, this unusual, reclining attitude binds the couple closer together, telling of their love.

The setting, "view of part of Baltimore Town," is appropriate for a wealthy Maryland merchant. The spyglass indicates Laming's interest in shippage by sea, and the green parrot perched behind his leg may recall his birth in the West Indies. Mrs. Laming's fruit and flowers, although traditional emblems of innocence and fertility, could also refer to her own gardening. The detailed attention paid to the bird, plants, scenery, and telescope attests to Peale's encyclopedic knowledge.

CHARLES
WILLSON PEALE
(1741–1827)

*Benjamin and Eleanor
Ridgely Laming,* 1788

Canvas. 106.6 × 152.9 cm.
(42 × 60¼ in.)

Gift of Morris Schapiro
1966.10.1

BENJAMIN WEST
(1738–1820)

*The Expulsion of Adam
and Eve from Paradise,*
1791

Canvas. 186.8 × 278.1 cm.
(73⅝ × 109½ in.)

Avalon Fund and Patrons'
Permanent Fund
1989.12.1

By 1779, Benjamin West had conceived his life's "great work," intending to rebuild the Royal Chapel at Windsor Castle as a shrine to Revealed Religion. After sponsoring the elaborate scheme for two decades, George III abruptly canceled it in 1801. Though the overall project was abandoned, many individual paintings, including this nine-foot-long *Expulsion*, were completed.

The Book of Genesis does not state how the first man and woman were expelled from Eden, but artists usually portray the Archangel Michael as the agent of the Lord's wrath. The sinners wear fur robes because God clothed them in "coats of skins" so that they could stand unashamed in his presence. The serpent, now cursed among creatures, slithers away on its belly to eat dust. The sharp beam of light overhead refers to the "flaming sword" in Genesis.

West's *Expulsion* contains two motifs not found in Genesis or any traditional pictures of the theme: an eagle swoops upon a helpless bird, and a lion chases frightened horses. In general terms, such beasts of prey imply the destruction of harmony that resulted from Original Sin. Regardless of any further symbolism, West's artistic treatment foretells the new romantic style with its theatrical gestures, rich paint textures, and clashes of blinding light and shadowy darkness.

hen Stuart returned to America in 1793, the artist found himself in a homeland that was foreign to him. Politically, here was now a United States instead of thirteen separate colonies. Artistically, the fashionable style he had adopted for British and Irish sitters was highly inappropriate for Yankee merchants' forthright tastes.

Complaining about the literalness required of him in America, Stuart quipped, "In England my efforts were compared with those of Van Dyck, Titian, and other great painters – here they are compared with the works of the Almighty!" The Almighty had given Catherine Yates a bony face and an appraising character, and that is exactly what Stuart had to portray. Not wishing to waste time posing for an artist, this wife of a New York importer industriously attends to her sewing.

Yet Stuart's brilliant paint manipulation generates a verve few other artists on either side of the Atlantic could have matched. Every passage contains some technical tour de force, employing a variety of thick or thin, opaque or translucent oil paints for the fabrics, needle, thimble, wedding band, flesh, and fingernails. It is little wonder that *Mrs. Richard Yates* has become one of America's most famous paintings, both as an artistic masterpiece and as a visual symbol of the early republic's rectitude.

GILBERT STUART
(1755–1828)

Mrs. Richard Yates,
1793/94

Canvas. 77 × 63 cm.
(30¼ × 25 in.)

Andrew W. Mellon Collection
1940.1.4

GILBERT STUART
(1755–1828)

George Washington
[Vaughan portrait], 1795

Canvas. 73.5 × 60.5 cm.
(29 × 23¾ in.)

Andrew W. Mellon Collection
1942.8.27

Gilbert Stuart was exclusively a portraitist; in his five-decade career, he produced well over 1100 pictures, less than ten of which were not likenesses. Of these portraits, nearly one-tenth are images of George Washington, to whom he was introduced by their mutual friend Chief Justice John Jay. Stuart's 104 known likenesses of the first president are divided into categories named after the owners of Stuart's originals, from which he made his own replicas: the National Gallery's *George Washington [Vaughan portrait]* was purchased by Samuel Vaughan, a London merchant who was the president's close friend.

A charming conversationalist, Stuart would chat while painting, thereby entertaining his sitters to maintain the freshness of their expressions during the long hours of posing. To the serious and taciturn Washington, however, Stuart's glib wit was annoying. The artist claimed, "An apathy seemed to seize him, and a vacuity spread over his countenance, most appalling to paint." Nevertheless, this image has spontaneity because of its quick, sketchy handling. To impart the sixty-three-year-old subject's imposing physical presence, Stuart placed the head high in the design. Finally, he added the crimson glow that complements Washington's ruddy complexion and surrounds his head like a superhuman aureole.

Edward Savage's *The Washington Family* quickly became a veritable icon of our early national pride. In the winter of 1789–90, President Washington and his wife posed for Savage in New York City, then the nation's capital. Mrs. Washington's grandchildren, adopted by the Washingtons after the deaths of their parents, probably also sat for their oil portraits in New York. Savage began to incorporate the separate life studies of their faces into a group portrait engraved on a copper plate. After a stay in England, he resumed the family portrait in Philadelphia – this time, however, in large format as an oil on canvas. *The Washington Family* was exhibited in 1796.

Savage's catalogue states that Washington's uniform and the papers beneath his hand allude to his "Military Character" and "Presidentship" respectively. With a map before her, Martha Washington is "pointing with her fan to the grand avenue," now known as Pennsylvania Avenue. A servant overdressed in livery and a supposed vista down the Potomac complete the imaginary scene.

Savage's self-taught ability to distinguish between satins, gauzes, and laces is nothing short of astonishing. However, the anatomy alternates between wooden and rubbery, and the family strangely avoids eye contact. Despite Savage's lack of experience, his huge *Washington Family* remains one of the most ambitious projects ever undertaken by a federal artist.

EDWARD SAVAGE
(1761–1817)

The Washington Family,
1796

Canvas. 213.6 × 284.2 cm.
(84⅜ × 111⅞ in.)

Andrew W. Mellon Collection
1940.1.2

REMBRANDT PEALE
(1778–1860)

*Rubens Peale with a
Geranium*, 1801

Canvas. 71.8 × 61 cm.
(28¼ × 24 in.)

Patrons' Permanent Fund
1985.59.1

Charles Willson Peale christened most of his seventeen children after famous artists and scientists; however, there is little consistency between the sons' and daughters' namesakes and their adult careers. While Rembrandt Peale did become a painter and the portraitist of this work, Rubens Peale, who sat for this likeness at the age of seventeen, was a botanist.

Painted in Philadelphia, the work could be described as a double portrait because the geranium, reputed to be the first specimen of this exotic plant ever grown in the New World, is as lovingly portrayed as the painter's brother is. The Peale family often collaborated in their endeavors, and here Rembrandt commemorated his brother's horticultural triumph. Rembrandt's own skill is evident in the clearly defined pools of light on Rubens' cheeks. In a phenomenon familar to all, his glasses focus the beams passing through them, thereby forming the brighter disks of light under his eyes.

Rubens Peale with a Geranium is a supreme example of the unaffected naturalism which typified the artist's early maturity. Combining firm, clear drawing, carefully modulated color, and an intense devotion to detail, twenty-three-year-old Rembrandt Peale produced an eloquent expression of his family's philosophical orientation.

The eldest son of Charles Willson Peale, one of the most important and influential artists of the early American republic, Raphaelle Peale was not only a versatile painter, but also one with a particular speciality. As William Dunlap, the first historian of American art, wrote in 1834, he was, like his father, "a painter of portraits in oil and miniature, but excelled more in compositions of still life. He may perhaps be considered the first in point of time who adopted this branch of painting in America." That Raphaelle Peale chose still-life painting was unusual, for aestheticians such as England's Sir Joshua Reynolds ranked it far below history painting as a lowly form of artistic expression. In Peale's hands, however, still life was invested with a sense of timeless beauty and gravity that gave it meaning and weight far beyond that which accrued to the simple forms he depicted. He became one of the greatest American artists ever to work in the genre.

A Dessert is perhaps Peale's most beautifully realized expression of the possibilities of the subject of still life. The humble objects included – fruits, nuts, glassware, and a ceramic dish – are rendered with a fidelity that suggests the specific and the immediate, but the way they are arranged in a balanced and harmonious composition and the way they are strongly lit with illumination falling from the left and outlining their contours give the whole a sense of the permanence and timelessness that is truly transcendent.

RAPHAELLE PEALE
(1774–1825)

A Dessert, 1814

Wood. 34 × 48.3 cm.
(13⅜ × 19 in.)

Gift (Partial and Promised) of Jo Ann and Julian Ganz, Jr., in memory of Franklin D. Murphy
1999.44.1

223

THOMAS SULLY
(1783–1872)

Lady with a Harp: Eliza
Ridgely, 1818

Canvas. 214.5 × 142.5 cm.
(84⅜ × 56⅛ in.)

Gift of Maude Monell Vetlesen
1945.9.1

When Thomas Sully painted fifteen-year-old Eliza Ridgely in the spring of 1818, he was widely regarded as America's leading artist. Particularly noted for his graceful images of women, he was a natural choice to paint this Baltimore merchant's daughter.

In painting Eliza, Sully emphasized her privileged social status as well as her delicate, youthful charm. Her family affluence is indicated by her up-to-the-minute hair style and dress, inspired by contemporary European designs in the neo-Grecian manner. The satin of her Empire gown is carefully described through fluid brushwork and brilliant highlights. Eliza, as a young lady of cultural accomplishment, posed with her European pedal harp. She idly plucks the harp strings and gazes dreamily into space, as if musing on the lyrical chord she strikes. A fiery sunset heightens the romantic reverie.

Although she may very well have possessed luminous eyes, arched brows, and a porcelain complexion, Miss Ridgely's figure has been greatly idealized. Sully, for the sake of fashionable elegance, exaggerated her legs to half again as long as any conceivably normal proportion. Sully once wrote, "From long experience I know that resemblance in a portrait is essential; but no fault will be found with the artist, at least by the sitter, if he improve the appearance."

Abandoning his career as a barrister, George Catlin moved to Philadelphia and set up shop as a portrait painter. A visiting delegation of Indians rekindled his lifelong interest in native Americans, and shortly thereafter, he began making plans to travel west.

Inspired by the examples of Charles Willson Peale's art, work on natural history, and ethnographic museum, the explorer-artist set out with easel and paints strapped to his back on a mission to record the vanishing tribes. After exhibiting his work in several East Coast cities, Catlin set sail for Europe in 1839 with eight tons of Indian artifacts as well as his own pictures. His spirited lectures and his collections captivated audiences in London and Paris.

In 1847, King Louis Philippe commissioned him to do a series of paintings illustrating the voyages of La Salle, the seventeenth-century French explorer of the Great Lakes and Mississippi River. *La Salle's Party Feasted in the Illinois Village* re-creates an event that took place on 2 January 1680. With his firsthand experience of contemporary Indians, Catlin captured the mood of the ceremony, while his quick, feathery method of painting exquisitely conveys the effect of snow frosting the trees, tepees, and wigwams.

GEORGE CATLIN
(1796–1872)

La Salle's Party Feasted in the Illinois Village,
1847/48

Canvas. 37.8 × 56.2 cm.
(14⅞ × 22⅛ in.)

Paul Mellon Collection
1965.16.325

225

EDWARD HICKS
(1780–1849)

The Cornell Farm, 1848

Canvas. 93.3 × 124.4 cm.
(36¾ × 49 in.)

Gift of Edgar William
and Bernice Chrysler Garbisch
1964.23.4

Edward Hicks, having apprenticed to a Pennsylvania coachmaker at thirteen, became a minister in 1811. He was torn between his calling as a Quaker minister and his love of painting, worrying that his art kept him from "the Lord's work."

Hicks precisely identified this subject with a long inscription along the bottom of the canvas: "An Indian summer view of the Farm & Stock of JAMES C. CORNELL of Northampton Bucks county Pennsylvania. That took the Premium in the Agricultural society, October the 12, 1848 Painted by E. Hicks in the 69th year of his age." Though the punctuation and capitalization are inconsistent, the quality of the lettering proves that Edward Hicks was schooled in sign painting.

Having no background in academic art, Hicks employed the direct approach of a primitive or folk painter. The horizontal band of livestock across the foreground, although childlike in its simplicity, clearly presents each prize-winning animal as an individual portrait. Hicks' delight in creating ornamental pattern is evident in the arrangement of fences, while the rich red and bright white of the house and barn symmetrically flank this central landscape. Although the stark silhouettes of figures and buildings seem naive, Hicks softly blended his paints over the orchard to give the impression of space existing well beyond what the eye can see.

George Caleb Bingham was one of America's first important painters to specialize in genre paintings, which depict scenes of everyday life. His early years were spent in Missouri, and he knew at first hand the life of the frontier, especially the comings and goings of the boatmen who ferried cargo on the great rivers of the Midwest. Bingham's paintings were intended for audiences in eastern cities such as New York and Philadelphia, and the boatmen he portrayed were already by the 1850s emblematic of the rough and tumble characters who were pushing American civilization ever farther westward. They were also considered disreputable characters who were fond of drunken carousing in the towns they passed while en route downriver.

The men portrayed in Bingham's river pictures are usually young, but here we are presented with an older, scowling individual who looks out at us with undisguised ill humor. This solitary figure seems confrontational, even threatening, establishing a mood of unease that is unique in Bingham's work. Perhaps the nature of the narrative – an old man left to guard the cargo while his companions enjoy themselves in town – dictated he be depicted in this way. But Bingham, who was actively engaged in politics and who was staunchly antislavery, may have also intended the troubled visage of this boatman to be a mirror of the difficult times the nation was facing in the years leading to the Civil War.

GEORGE CALEB BINGHAM
(1811–79)

Mississippi Boatman, 1850

Canvas. 61.3 × 43.7 cm.
(24⅛ × 17³⁄₁₆ in.)

John Wilmerding Collection
2004.66.1

American Painting
OF THE XIX–EARLY XX CENTURIES

As nineteenth-century Americans sought an appropriate vehicle to express their national zeal, artists turned to images of the land. Thomas Cole, the leader of the "Hudson River School," portrayed a once-pristine environment threatened by the onslaught of civilization. Spurred on by his romantic idealism, some of Cole's followers created pastoral, idyllic views, while others took a more reportorial stance. During the 1850s, an intimate approach to landscape also evolved in New England. The twilight marine paintings of Fitz Hugh Lane are paradigms of this elegiac style, which some scholars have termed "luminism." Artists seeking nature's more awesome aspect often traveled far afield: Frederic Church journeyed from the arctic to the equator, while other peripatetic painters explored the far western United States, giving tangible expression to America's dream of Manifest Destiny.

Lighthearted genre paintings depicting everyday life also gained popularity around mid-century; however, the mood of the nation quickly darkened following the outbreak of Civil War. Eschewing such overt sentimentality, Thomas Eakins and Winslow Homer expressed a starkly realistic world view. Their mature art demonstrates an uncompromising commitment to truth.

As Americans traveled abroad in increasing numbers, a newfound cosmopolitanism emerged. Avant-garde movements such as impressionism were embraced by American painters who found the style's look, if not its underlying theory, consistent with their artistic aims. Familiarity with traditional European art also may have inspired a renewed interest in still-life painting and aristocratic portraiture at century's end; the popularity of such paeans to wealth and acquisition reflects the prevailing spirit of materialism.

At the opposite end of the social spectrum, optimistic immigrants flocked to America, only to confront the sobering reality of urban blight and poverty. Robert Henri, an influential artist and teacher, urged his followers to address these pressing issues. Their ostensibly crude subject matter offended critics, who dubbed the New York group "the Ash Can School."

Violence, anxiety, and alienation became dominant themes in the twentieth century, as artists expressed dissatisfaction with the dehumanizing aspects of modern life. Whether phrased in the representational idiom of Bellows and Hopper, or in the language of pure abstraction, these disturbing works seem a far cry from the idyllic aspirations of early nineteenth-century Americans, who – for a brief time – truly believed their country held the promise of paradise.

Detail:
JOHN SINGER SARGENT,
Repose

THOMAS COLE
(1801–48)

The Notch of the White Mountains ("Crawford Notch"), 1839

Canvas. 110.6 × 156 cm.
(40 × 61½ in.)

Andrew W. Mellon Fund
1967.8.1

Crawford Notch gained notoriety in 1826 when a catastrophic avalanche took nine lives. Nathaniel Hawthorne wrote a short story commemorating the tragedy, which may have piqued Cole's interest in the New Hampshire site. Rather than concentrating on the human drama, the artist minimized figurative elements to underscore man's insignificance and vulnerability in the face of nature's unleashed fury. Amid a seemingly idyllic autumnal setting, the barely discernible settlers, a lone rider, and the stagecoach passengers all seem oblivious to the impending cataclysm. Only the brooding storm clouds gathering at the upper left offer a portentous hint of the disaster to come.

In addition to its oblique reference to a specific historical event, *Crawford Notch* also reflects a prevailing romantic belief: that the destruction of America's virgin forests was tantamount to sacrilege. By juxtaposing gnarled trees with freshly hewn stumps, Cole vividly underscored the environmental consequences of man's conquest of the wilderness.

Cole's renowned four-part series traces the journey of an archetypal hero along the "River of Life." Confidently assuming control of his destiny and oblivious to the dangers that await him, the voyager boldly strives to reach an aerial castle, emblematic of the daydreams of "Youth" and its aspirations for glory and fame. As the traveler approaches his goal, the ever-more-turbulent stream deviates from its course and relentlessly carries him toward the next picture in the series, where nature's fury, evil demons, and self-doubt will threaten his very existence. Only prayer, Cole suggests, can save the voyager from a dark and tragic fate.

From the innocence of childhood, to the flush of youthful overconfidence, through the trials and tribulations of middle age, to the hero's triumphant salvation, *The Voyage of Life* seems intrinsically linked to the Christian doctrine of death and resurrection. Cole's intrepid voyager also may be read as a personification of America, itself at an adolescent stage of development. The artist may have been issuing a dire warning to those caught up in the feverish quest for Manifest Destiny: that unbridled westward expansion and industrialization would have tragic consequences for both man and nature.

THOMAS COLE
(1801–48)

The Voyage of Life: Youth, 1842

Canvas. 134.3 × 194.9 cm. (52⅞ × 76¾ in.)

Ailsa Mellon Bruce Fund
1971.16.2

ALBERT BIERSTADT
(1830–1902)

Lake Lucerne, 1858

Canvas. 182.9 × 304.8 cm.
(72 × 120 in.)

Gift of Richard M. Scaife and
Margaret R. Battle, in Honor of the
Fiftieth Anniversary of the National
Gallery of Art
1990.50.1

Best known for his panoramic views of the Rocky Mountains, Albert Bierstadt began his career as a painter of European landscapes. In 1856, during a period of study abroad, he spent time in Switzerland and completed the plein air sketches he would later use to compose *Lake Lucerne*, the most important painting of his early career.

In the spring of 1858 he sent the painting to New York for the annual exhibition at the National Academy of Design. The picture caused a sensation. Bierstadt was hailed as a bright new star on the American art stage and was elected an honorary member of the Academy.

Bierstadt's painting offers a sweeping view of Lake Lucerne with the village of Brunnen in the middle distance and the alpine peaks Ematten, Oberbauen, Uri-Rotstock and St. Gotthard in the distance. Though an image of mountain grandeur, *Lake Lucerne* also contains numerous pastoral vignettes – a harvest scene near the center, a religious procession at the right, and a gypsy camp at the left.

One year after completing *Lake Lucerne* Bierstadt traveled to the Rocky Mountains for the first time. During the decade that followed he produced the western landscapes that brought him his greatest success. These views of the west, so often described as distinctly American, were born of Bierstadt's experience abroad and frequently duplicate the composition of the first of his large-scale landscapes, *Lake Lucerne*.

Rather than celebrating nature in the tradition of the Hudson River School, George Inness' *Lackawanna Valley* seems to commemorate the onset of America's industrial age. While documenting the achievements of the Delaware, Lackawanna, and Western Railroad, Inness has also created a topographically convincing view of Scranton, Pennsylvania. The artist took relatively few liberties with his composition, but in compliance with the wishes of his corporate patron, he intentionally exaggerated the prominence of the railroad's yet-to-be-completed roundhouse. His inclusion of numerous tree stumps in the picture's foreground, although accurate, lends an important note of ambiguity to the work.

Whether it is read as an enthusiastic affirmation of technology or as a belated lament for a rapidly vanishing wilderness, this painting exemplifies a crucial philosophical dilemma that confronted many Americans in the 1850s; expansion inevitably necessitated the widespread destruction of unspoiled nature, itself a still-powerful symbol of the nation's greatness. Although it was initially commissioned as an homage to the machine, Inness' *Lackawanna Valley* nevertheless serves as a poignant pictorial reminder of the ephemeral nature of the American Dream.

GEORGE INNESS
(1825–94)

The Lackawanna Valley,
1855

Canvas. 86 × 127.5 cm.
(33⅞ × 50¼ in.)

Gift of Mrs. Huttleston Rogers
1945.4.1

JASPER FRANCIS CROPSEY
(1823–1900)

*Autumn – On the Hudson
River*, 1860

Canvas. 152.5 × 274.3 cm.
(60 × 108 in.)

Gift of the Avalon Foundation
1963.9.1

This monumental view of the Hudson River Valley was painted from memory in the artist's London studio. Cropsey adopted a high vantage point, looking southeast toward the distant Hudson River and the flank of Storm King Mountain. A small stream leads from the foreground, where three hunters and their dogs gaze into the sunlight. All along the meandering tributary there are signs of man's peaceful coexistence with nature: a small log cabin, grazing sheep, children playing on a bridge, and cows standing placidly in the water. Here, man neither conquers nor is subservient to nature; both coexist harmoniously. In fact, the landscape is depicted as a ready arena for further agricultural expansion. While autumnal scenes traditionally are associated with the transience of life, Cropsey's painting is more a celebration of American nationalism. As a critic wrote in 1860, the picture represents "not the solemn wasting away of the year, but its joyful crowning festival."

The painting created a sensation among many British viewers who had never seen such a colorful panorama of fall foliage. Indeed, because the autumn in Britain customarily is far less colorful than in the United States, the artist decided to display specimens of North American leaves alongside his painting to persuade skeptical visitors that his rendition was botanically accurate.

L ike his teacher, Thomas Cole, Church conveyed a sense of awe-some sublimity in his landscapes by celebrating the seemingly infinite wonders of the natural world. The artist devoted a great deal of time to scientific study, believing that a knowledge of optics, mete-orology, botany, and geology would greatly enhance his work. After reading the journalistic accounts of the German naturalist Alexander von Humboldt, Church explored wilderness regions from the arctic to the equator.

El Rio de Luz is a fanciful pastiche based on numerous sketches and notations that Church had made during an 1857 trip to South America. Despite the time-lapse of twenty years, the tightly focused realism, the overall tonal harmony and restrained colorations, and the compositional unity all lend a remarkable cohesiveness to the work. Church rendered the verdant foliage with exquisite attention to detail, and his virtuoso treatment of tropical sunlight diffused by morning mist makes the atmosphere seem tangible. Red-breasted hummingbirds, a flock of waterfowl, and a distant canoeist occupy the scene, but they do not disturb the overall mood of tranquility. Confronted with the glowing light and heavy vapors of this raw landscape, the viewer is invited to liken daybreak in the tropical rain-forest to the dawn of creation itself.

FREDERIC EDWIN
CHURCH
(1826–1900)

El Rio de Luz (*River of Light*), 1877

Canvas. 138.1 x 213.7 cm.
(54⅜ x 84⅛ in.)

Gift of the Avalon Foundation
1965.14.1

FITZ HUGH LANE
(1804–65)

*Lumber Schooners at
Evening on Penobscot Bay,*
1863

Canvas. 62.5 × 96.8 cm.
(24⅝ × 38⅛ in.)

Andrew W. Mellon Fund and Gift of
Mr. and Mrs. Francis W. Hatch, Sr.
1980.29.1

Despite its meticulous draftsmanship and precise detail, Lane's work is far more than a simple inventory of harbor activity. The diminutive figures and carefully rendered vessels remain secondary to the vast expanse of sky, where shimmering light creates a tranquil, idyllic mood. Lane's rarefied landscapes epitomize man's harmonious union with the natural world.

Some scholars have used the term "luminism" to describe the artist's subtle use of light and atmospheric effects to convey nature's intangible spirit. Ralph Waldo Emerson, the foremost exponent of American Transcendentalism, believed that poets and painters should serve as conduits through which the experience of nature might be transmitted directly to their audience. With a similarly self-effacing artistic temperament, Lane minimized his autographic presence, using translucent glazes rather than heavily impastoed surfaces to underscore the scene's pervasive stillness. His elegiac paintings differ profoundly from the more explosive exuberance expressed by Cole and Church, though he shared these artists' reverence for nature and their belief in its inherent divinity.

Worthington Whittredge was one of the most artistically exper-imental painters of America's Hudson River school. A con-temporary of other key school figures such as Jasper Francis Cropsey, Sanford Robinson Gifford, and Frederic Edwin Church, Whittredge created landscapes that were still critically and popularly admired in the 1870s and 1880s, long after the earlier style had fallen out of fash-ion. Unlike many of his fellow painters, Whittredge had firsthand knowledge of European landscape painting, and he was especially receptive to the aesthetics of French Barbizon and impressionist art. In painting this radiant and freely brushed work, the artist demon-strated his mastery of these newer styles of landscape painting and also created one of the outstanding American landscapes of the era.

By the time Whittredge painted *Second Beach*, it had long been one of the favored recreational sites of wealthy Americans who built their lavish summer homes in the town of Newport, Rhode Island. Here we see fashionably dressed figures testing the waters and enjoying the splendors of a beautiful day; in the background a horse-drawn car-riage ferries others from one end of the beach to the other. Stopped in time and fixed indelibly through the clarity of artistic vision, this scene was recorded by Whittredge with a sensibility that perfectly matched its ineffable beauty.

WORTHINGTON
WHITTREDGE
(1820–1910)

Second Beach, Newport,
c. 1878/80

Canvas. 76.8 × 127.6 cm.
(30¼ × 50¼ in.)

Paul Mellon Fund and Gift of Juliana
Terian in memory of Peter G. Terian
2004.58.1

When Whistler submitted *The White Girl* to the Paris Salon in 1863, the tradition-bound jury refused to show the work. Napoleon III invited avant-garde artists who had been denied official space to show their paintings in a "Salon des Refusés," an exhibition that triggered enormous controversy. Whistler's work met with severe public derision, but a number of artists and critics praised his entry. In the *Gazette des Beaux-Arts*, Paul Manz referred to it as a "symphony in white," noting a musical correlation to Whistler's paintings that the artist himself would address in the early 1870s, when he retitled a number of works "Nocturne," "Arrangement," "Harmony," and "Symphony."

Whistler used variations of white pigment to create interesting spatial and formal relationships. By limiting his palette, minimizing tonal contrast, and sharply skewing the perspective in a manner reminiscent of Oriental art, he flattened forms and emphasized their abstract patterns. This dramatic compositional approach reflects the influence of Japanese prints, which were becoming well-known in Paris as international trade increased.

Clearly, Whistler was far more interested in creating an abstract design than in capturing an exact likeness of the model, his mistress Joanna Heffernan. His radical espousal of a purely aesthetic orientation and the creation of "art for art's sake" became a virtual rallying cry of modernism.

JAMES MCNEILL
WHISTLER
(1834–1903)

The White Girl
(Symphony in White,
No. 1), 1862

Canvas. 214.7 × 108 cm.
(84½ × 42½ in.)

Harris Whittemore Collection
1943.6.2

MARTIN JOHNSON HEADE
(1819–1904)

*Cattleya Orchid and
Three Brazilian
Hummingbirds*, 1871

Wood. 34.8 × 45.6 cm.
(13¾ × 18 in.)

Gift of the Morris and Gwendolyn
Cafritz Foundation
1982.73.1

Heade offered viewers an intimate glimpse into the exotic recesses of nature's secret garden. Lichen covers dead branches; moss drips from trees; and, a blue-gray mist veils the distant jungle. An opulent pink orchid with light-green stems and pods dominates the left foreground. To the right, perched near a nest on a branch, are a Sappho Comet, green with a yellow throat and brilliant red tail feathers, and two green-and-pink Brazilian Amethysts.

Inspired by the writings of Charles Darwin, the artist studied these subjects in the wild during several expeditions to South America. The precisely rendered flora and fauna seem alive in their natural habitat, not mere specimens for scientific analysis. Defying strict categorization as either still life or landscape, Heade's work reflects the artist's unerring attention to detail and his delight in the infinitesimal joys of nature.

Homer developed a penchant for forceful realism early in his career. Following an apprenticeship in a Boston lithography shop, he supported himself as a freelance illustrator, creating a wide variety of popular images that subsequently were published as wood engravings in national periodicals like *Harper's Weekly*. During the early 1860s, his themes ranged from stylish seaside-resort life to the horrors of the battlefield. Following an extended trip to Europe in 1866–67, Homer adopted a warmer palette, a looser brush technique, and an interest in painting outdoor scenes that owed much to the influence of contemporary French artists such as Courbet, Manet, and Monet.

Upon his return to the United States, Homer turned his attention to lively scenes of sports and recreation, painting warm and appealing images that perfectly suited the prevalent post-war nostalgia for a simpler, more innocent America. *Breezing Up*, painted during the country's centennial year, has become one of the most well-known and beloved artistic images of life in nineteenth-century America.

WINSLOW HOMER
(1836–1910)

Breezing Up, 1876

Canvas. 61.5 × 97 cm.
(24⅛ × 38¼ in.)

Gift of the W. L. and May T. Mellon Foundation
1943.13.1

THOMAS EAKINS
(1844–1916)

Baby at Play, 1876

Canvas. 81.9 × 122.8 cm.
(32¼ × 48⅜ in.)

John Hay Whitney Collection
1982.76.5

Baby at Play is the final work in a series of intimate portraits of family and friends created by Eakins between 1870 and 1876. The painting depicts the artist's two-and-a-half-year-old niece, Ella Crowell. Dressed in an intricately embroidered white frock, her legs clad in red-and-white striped stockings, the child is soberly absorbed at play.

According to one recent interpretation, Eakins was depicting Ella's initial foray into the adult world of education and learning. Having temporarily cast aside her more infantile toys in favor of alphabet blocks – the tools of language – the child now seems ready to enter the next critical stage in her intellectual development.

The monumentality of her painted form may seem surprising considering the diminutive stature of Eakins' model. Her life-sized figure is arranged in a stable pyramidal block at the composition's center and the deft handling of light and shadow further emphasizes spatial volume. Eakins' choice of a lowered vantage point encourages the spectator to adopt a child's point of view. His penetrating psychological insight elevates this picture from a sentimental genre scene to a highly serious portrayal of an earnest, intelligent child.

William Michael Harnett was the most influential still-life painter in America in the last quarter of the nineteenth century. As the acknowledged master of *trompe l'oeil*, he was well known for his use of exquisitely rendered textures, and precise effects of light to create still lifes in which objects seemed deceptively real. *The Old Violin* was in its time perhaps his most famous work.

The Old Violin was painted shortly after Harnett's return from a six-year stay in Europe. The subject is deceptively simple; a violin, two sheets of music, a small newspaper clipping, and a blue envelope are shown against a background formed by a green wooden door. These few objects are, however, arranged with such order and balance that none could be moved without upsetting the equilibrium of the image.

The painting is a work of multi-layered meanings involving the relationships between illusion and reality, between old and new, and between the momentary and the enduring. At the heart of such meanings is the transience of time, which the artist illustrated by showing signs of wear and age throughout the painting. Even the sheets of music, one from Bellini's *La Sonnambula*, and the other the popular song "Hélas, Quelle Douleur," are concerned with temporal change. But it is the violin itself, now mute, but worn with use and still dusted with rosin, that speaks most evocatively of past pleasures.

WILLIAM MICHAEL
HARNETT
(1848–92)
The Old Violin, 1886

Canvas. 96.5 × 61 cm.
(38 × 24 in.)

Gift of Mr. and Mrs. Richard
Mellon Scaife in Honor of Paul
Mellon 1993.15.1

ALBERT PINKHAM RYDER
(1847–1917)

Siegfried and the Rhine Maidens, 1888/91

Canvas. 50.5 × 52 cm.
(19⅞ × 20½ in.)

Andrew W. Mellon Collection
1946.1.1

By his own account, Ryder was so enthralled by a five-hour performance of Wagner's *Götterdämmerung* that he rushed home and began painting this rendition of the opera's narrative, working without sleep or food for forty-eight hours. Galloping down a moonlit path, the legendary Norse hero Siegfried encounters a group of Rhine Maidens who beckon seductively from the phosphorescent river. They warn the hero that the magical ring he won by slaying a dragon was forged from stolen gold and bears a deadly curse. Siegfried defiantly proclaims he would rather die than give up his prize. By the opera's dramatic climax, the nymphs' apocalyptic prophecy is fulfilled: Siegfried is killed; overcome by grief, the heroine Brünnhilde sacrifices herself on her lover's funeral pyre, the other gods and heroes of Valhalla are consumed by the spreading conflagration, and the Ring of the Nibelung, now purified by the flames, is returned to the river from whence it came.

Wagner's orchestration engulfed listeners with an overwhelming torrent of sound, and Ryder's composition offers a visual counterpart to this rhapsodic aesthetic experience. Although Ryder's technical naiveté and his unorthodox methods have caused the surfaces of his once-luminous paintings to crack and darken over time, the expressive power and emotional intensity of his art endures.

William Merritt Chase, an influential art teacher and one of the leading exponents of American impressionism, captured the genteel, privileged life of polite society in the 1890s. *A Friendly Call*, set in Chase's elegant summer house at Shinnecock Hills, Long Island, shows two fashionably dressed women in a large, airy room decorated with prints, paintings, hanging textiles, and a large, gilt-framed mirror. The artist's wife Alice, on the right, listens attentively to her visitor, who is still wearing her hat and gloves and carrying a parasol.

Chase's rendering of light, his facile brushwork, and his choice of everyday subject matter all recall the work of the French impressionists; yet, unlike his European contemporaries, the artist carefully composed his paintings to underscore abstract elements. Simple rectangular patterns of the floor, wall, and couch are echoed in the framed pictures and wall hangings while they are contrasted to the more curvilinear figures, chair, and plump pillows. The mirror framing Mrs. Chase offers a surprising reflection of a wall behind the viewer; Chase's compositional arrangement and his use of reflected imagery suggest that he may have been paying homage to the seventeenth-century Spanish artist Velázquez, whose much-admired painting *Las Meninas* displays a similarly inventive studio interior.

WILLIAM MERRITT
CHASE
(1849–1916)

A Friendly Call, 1895

Canvas. 76.5 × 122.5 cm.
(30⅛ × 48¼ in.)

Gift of Chester Dale
1943.1.2

GEORGE BELLOWS
(1882–1925)

Both Members of This Club, 1909

Canvas. 115 × 160.5 cm.
(45¼ × 63⅛ in.)

Gift of Chester Dale
1944.13.1

*B*oth *Members of This Club* was inspired by the fights Bellows attended at Tom Sharkey's Athletic Club in New York. At the time, public boxing matches were illegal in the city. Private organizations like Sharkey's made prospective fighters temporary members of the "club" on the night of the event to circumvent the law.

In the painting one can almost sense the atmosphere of stale cigar smoke and body heat that typified these back-room bouts. At the match's frenzied climax, the victorious fighter on the right lunges forward, while the nearly vanquished boxer on the left, his face contorted with pain, weakly resists the blow and momentarily postpones his imminent defeat. Bellows' rapid, slashing brushwork, his characteristic use of dramatic lighting and lurid color, his selection of stark angles and dramatic close-ups all enhance the scene's immediacy. Members of the audience, their faces horribly disfigured by vicarious passion, display an animalistic bloodlust that reveals much about the darker aspects of human nature. The artist is suggesting that the men in the ring, teamed in their physical struggle, also must contend with the larger, perhaps even more brutal adversary of social injustice.

246

*R*ight and Left, painted a year before the artist's death, is the culminating achievement of Winslow Homer's extraordinary career. The title, provided by a viewer during the work's first public showing, refers to the act of shooting the ducks successively with separate barrels of a shotgun. Some scholars have suggested that the dull expression, the slackened feet, and the diving posture of the duck on the right indicate that it is the one which has been hit by the hunter's initial blast. Its mate is attempting to escape the second shot which has just been fired – as evidenced by the vermilion flash and billowing gray smoke barely visible at the middle left. Yet the downward posture may be an effective escape maneuver, while the arrested motion of the duck on the left might indicate that it is the one which has been hit. Homer may have conveyed an ambiguous message deliberately, in order to illustrate that crucial moment of transition between life and death.

We witness the scene from the ducks' elevated vantage point, a precarious perspective that encourages empathy with the threatened creatures. By underscoring the fleeting nature of these birds' existence, Homer reminds viewers of the fragility of their own.

WINSLOW HOMER
(1836–1910)

Right and Left, 1909

Canvas. 71.8 × 122.9 cm.
(28¼ × 48⅜ in.)

Gift of the Avalon Foundation
1951.8.1

247

JOHN SINGER SARGENT
(1856–1925)

Repose, 1911

Canvas. 63.8 × 76.2 cm.
(25⅛ × 30 in.)

Gift of Curt H. Reisinger
1948.16.1

Sargent's inordinate technical facility, coupled with his ability to portray elegant sitters in sumptuous surroundings, made him extremely popular with wealthy patrons on both sides of the Atlantic. Despite his success as one of the most sought-after portraitists of the late Victorian era, Sargent eventually became exasperated by the whims and vanities of prominent sitters. By 1909 he had abandoned conventional portraiture in order to "experiment with more imaginary fields."

The woman in *Repose* is Sargent's niece, Rose-Marie Ormond Michel. In keeping with his newfound preference for informal figure studies, Sargent did not create a traditional portrait; rather, he depicted Rose-Marie as a languid, anonymous figure absorbed in poetic reverie. The reclining woman, casually posed in an atmosphere of elegiac calm and consummate luxury, seems the epitome of nonchalance – the painting's original title. Sargent seems to have been documenting the end of an era, for the lingering aura of *fin-de-siècle* gentility and elegant indulgence conveyed in *Repose* would soon be shattered by massive political and social upheaval in the early twentieth century.

patriotic whirlwind overtook mid-town Manhattan as America entered the First World War in the spring of 1917. On Fifth Avenue, the British Union Jack, the French Tricolor, and Stars and Stripes were displayed prominently during parades honoring America's allies. The colorful pageantry inspired Childe Hassam, who dedicated this picture "to the coming together of [our] three peoples in the fight for democracy." Hassam's flag paintings were first shown as a group in New York's Durand-Ruel Gallery in November 1918, just four days after the armistice was declared. Thus, the works, originally created to herald America's entry into the war, also served to commemorate its victorious resolution.

Hassam had studied in Paris from 1886–89 and was strongly influenced by the impressionists. In many respects, *Allies Day* resembles the vibrant boulevard paintings of Monet and Pissarro. Like these contemporary French artists, Hassam selected a high vantage point overlooking a crowded urban thoroughfare to achieve an illusion of dramatic spatial recession. But, rather than using daubs of shimmering pigment to dissolve form, he applied fluid parallel paint strokes to create an architectonic patterning. Although he shared the impressionists' interest in bright colors, broken brushwork, and modern themes, Hassam's overall approach was less theoretical and his pictorial forms remained far more substantial than those of his European contemporaries.

CHILDE HASSAM
(1859–1935)

Allies Day, May 1917,
1917

Canvas. 93.5 × 77 cm.
(36¾ × 30¼ in.)

Gift of Ethelyn McKinney in memory of her brother, Glenn Ford McKinney
1943.9.1

JOHN SLOAN
(1871–1951)

*The City from Greenwich
Village*, 1922

Canvas. 66 × 85.7 cm.
(26 × 33¾ in.)

Gift of Helen Farr Sloan
1970.1.1

The City from Greenwich Village is a lyrical celebration of the vitality and excitement of life in lower Manhattan. Looking south over Sixth Avenue from the artist's Washington Place studio on a rainy winter evening, electric light merges with moonlight, casting an evocative golden glow over the city. At the far left, New York's skyscrapers seem to hover over the city like a shimmering celestial vision. Sloan's painting conveys a nostalgic, romanticized mood, one that contrasts strongly with the scenes of tenement life, teeming city streets, and desolate back alleys that he and fellow members of the "Ash Can School" had produced during the first decade of the century.

The artist's ambiguous reference to "moonshine" on the billboard in the left foreground both documents the city's commercialization and lends a poetic aura to the scene. This urban imagery may be seen as a precursor to American art of the 1960s, when Pop artists appropriated advertising motifs and Photo-realists immortalized the architectural richness of New York.

"My aim in painting," explained Edward Hopper, "has always been the most exact transcription possible of my most intimate impressions of nature." Claiming the figures in *Cape Cod Evening* were done almost entirely without models, and the dry, blowing grass could be seen from his studio window in the late summer or autumn, Hopper continued: "In the woman I attempted to get the broad, strong-jawed face and blond hair of a Finnish type of which there are many on the Cape. The man is a dark-haired Yankee. The dog is listening to something, probably a whippoorwill or some evening sound."

Despite his matter-of-fact account, Hopper also has endowed this ostensibly straightforward work with a strong, albeit ambiguous, emotional undercurrent. The sense of eerie calm is due, in part, to the serene effect of the golden twilight sun that illuminates the grass in front of the Victorian house, but fails to penetrate the dense forest beyond. The middle-aged rural couple seem to lack any emotional rapport; they project a mood of self-absorption, futility, and alienation that typifies much of Hopper's figurative work.

EDWARD HOPPER
(1882–1967)

Cape Cod Evening, 1939

Canvas. 76.8 × 102.2 cm.
(30¼ × 40¼ in.)

John Hay Whitney Collection
1982.76.6

Painting and Sculpture
OF THE XX CENTURY

Throughout the twentieth century vanguard artists have repeatedly challenged convention by exploring new avenues of expression and seeking alternative forms to embody new ideas. In the early years of the century, the so-called *fauve* artists (or "wild beasts") in France, led by Henri Matisse, experimented with vivid, highly saturated colors and bold brushwork to evoke intense emotional responses. Later, artists such as the Russian Wassily Kandinsky carried these experiments further, creating abbreviated shapes that, however abstract, were meant to stand for specific concepts or forms.

Although he intermittently painted in a realist style, Pablo Picasso, along with Georges Braque, was responsible for one of the most radical innovations of the century. In their cubist paintings these artists defied the notion that painting provided a "window" into a deep fictional space. Instead they fractured forms and space into shifting planes and reduced their palette to a few muted tones. While Picasso never favored absolute abstraction, Piet Mondrian eliminated any reference to visual reality from the rigorous compositions of straight lines and primary colors that he intended as the expression of an ideal and universal order.

Through a variety of styles and media, surrealist artists sought to exploit the internal world of imaginings and the unconscious. René Magritte, for example, employed precise illusionism to subvert our expectations about reality. Others like Joan Miró employed the technique of automatism, making doodles or random marks on paper or canvas to trigger associations in the viewer's imagination. European surrealists provided critical examples for post-war American artists such as David Smith and Jackson Pollock. In his welded metal sculpture Smith incorporated "found" objects that, as a kind of sculptural equivalent to automatism, bore an accidental resemblance to a form or an idea. Pollock recorded his ideas and gestures on the canvas in dense webs of poured paint. Like his fellow abstract expressionists Barnett Newman and Mark Rothko, Pollock believed that abstraction could achieve all the expressive potential of representational art. By the 1960s, Pop artists Andy Warhol and Roy Lichtenstein were exploring alternatives to abstract expressionism with subjects drawn from popular culture and a style informed by mass mechanical reproduction.

As the twentieth century draws to a close, contemporary artists continue to explore these themes, simultaneously assimilating and rejecting the work of their predecessors.

Detail:
JOAN MIRÓ,
The Farm

PABLO PICASSO
(Spanish, 1881–1973)

Family of Saltimbanques,
1904/05

Canvas. 212.8 × 229.6 cm.
(83¾ × 90⅜ in.)

Chester Dale Collection
1963.10.190

From late 1904 to the beginning of 1906, Picasso's work centered on a single theme: the *saltimbanque*, or itinerant circus performer. The theme of the circus and the circus performer had a long tradition in art and in literature, and had become especially prominent in French art of the late nineteenth century. A more immediate inspiration for Picasso came from performances of the Cirque Médrano, a circus that the artist attended frequently near his residence and studio in Montmartre.

Circus performers were regarded as social outsiders, poor but independent. As such, they provided a telling symbol for the alienation of avant-garde artists such as Picasso. Indeed, it has been suggested that the *Family of Saltimbanques* serves as an autobiographical statement, a covert group portrait of Picasso and his circle.

Picasso re-worked the *Family of Saltimbanques* several times, adding figures and altering the composition. The figures occupy a desolate landscape and although Picasso has knit them together in a carefully balanced composition, each figure is psychologically isolated from the others, and from the viewer. In his rose, or circus period, Picasso moved away from the extreme pathos of his earlier blue period, but in the *Family of Saltimbanques*, the masterpiece of the circus period, a mood of introspection and sad contemplation prevails.

PABLO PICASSO
(Spanish, 1881–1973)

Nude Woman, 1910

Canvas. 187.3 × 61 cm.
(73¾ × 24 in.)

Ailsa Mellon Bruce Fund
1972.46.1

In 1909, Hamilton Easter Field, a Brooklyn painter and critic, asked Picasso to create a group of eleven paintings as a decoration for his library. Picasso accepted but, although he worked on the commission intermittently over the next several years, he never completed all eleven of the panels.

Nude Woman may be the first of the paintings Picasso did produce for Field. Its narrow, vertical format, dictated by the terms of the commission, is unusual in the artist's oeuvre, but in other respects the painting is typical of Picasso's analytic cubist style. Details of the figure, a breast, the head, may be made out, but in most respects the painting appears as disembodied shards of modeled form. Those forms are delineated by sharp lines which describe roughly geometric shapes, and which in turn make for a kind of grid pattern across the surface of the canvas. The color scheme of *Nude Woman*, limited to shades of brown, gray, and black, is also typical of analytic cubism. The muted palette allowed Picasso to concentrate upon the depiction of subtly shifting, overlapping planes in shallow space.

255

HENRI MATISSE
(French, 1869–1954)

*Open Window at
Collioure*, 1905

Canvas. 55.3 × 46 cm.
(21¾ × 18⅛ in.)

Collection of Mr. and Mrs.
John Hay Whitney
1998.74.7

Asmall but explosive painting, Matisse's *Open Window at Collioure* is one of the essential works of the so-called fauve school, a group of French artists (including André Derain, Georges Braque, and Maurice de Vlaminck) active between 1904 and 1907. Their paintings are distinguished by a startling palette of saturated, unmixed colors. The name "fauvism" – which comes from the French word *fauve* or "wild beast" – was coined by Louis Vauxcelles, an art critic reviewing the landmark Salon d'Automne exhibition in 1905 at which *Open Window at Collioure* appeared in a room dedicated to the new painters.

This painting was created at a small town in the south of France to which Matisse traveled in the summer of 1905. In it lyrical beauty and seeming spontaneity of style belie conceptual complexity. Conventions of representation, for example, are subordinated by an abstract opposition of colors, such as blue-green and fuchsia, derived from the contrast of complementary hues on the color wheel. Further, each area of the view is represented with a distinctly different handling of the brush, from long blended marks to short staccato touches, creating an overall surface effect of buzzing and pulsating cross-rhythms. Finally, the composition itself is a series of frames nested within frames: the wall enframes the window; the window contains the terrace and balcony; and the balcony crops the view of sailboats on the water. The image of the open window, which Matisse introduced with this painting, would become a central motif in his oeuvre over the course of the next fifty years.

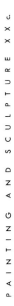

The title "Improvisations" refers to a series of works that Kandinsky painted between 1909 and 1913 which was, according to the artist, "a largely unconscious, spontaneous expression of inner character, non-material nature." Although the amorphous shapes and colorful washes of paint in *Improvisation 31 (Sea Battle)* may at first appear entirely abstract, they form a number of recognizable images the artist invented to represent his often biblical subject matter.

The central motif of *Improvisation 31 (Sea Battle)* is a pair of sailing ships locked in combat, their tall masts appearing as slender black lines. Cannons blast as the ships are tossed upon turbulent waves, and, at the upper left, a city of white towers appears on the verge of toppling. Kandinsky's subject, found in a number of the *Improvisations*, was probably inspired by the apocalyptic imagery of the Book of Revelations.

Although this work was painted on the eve of the First World War, Kandinsky denied that his paintings referred to any specific war but rather to "a terrible struggle . . . going on in the spiritual atmosphere." Kandinsky, who fervently believed that humanity stood on the brink of a new spiritual era, avowed that art could help to sever human attachment to the material world and usher in the new age.

WASSILY KANDINSKY
(Russian, 1866–1944)

*Improvisation 31
(Sea Battle)*, 1913

Canvas. 145.1 × 119.7 cm.
($55\frac{3}{8} \times 47\frac{7}{8}$ in.)

Ailsa Mellon Bruce Fund
1978.48.1

257

JOAN MIRÓ
(Spanish, 1893–1983)

The Farm, 1921/22

Canvas. 123.8 × 141.3 cm.
(49¾ × 55⅝ in.)

Gift of Mary Hemingway
1987.18.1

Miró moved from Barcelona to Paris in 1920, determined to participate in the artistic vanguard of the French capital. Nevertheless, he remained deeply attached to his native Catalonia, and returned each summer to his family's farm in the village of Montroig. In 1921, he determined to make a painting of this farm, a painting that he came to regard as one of the key works in his career.

The Farm represents a brilliant amalgamation of an intense, even primitive realism with the formal vocabulary of cubism. The painting is a compendium of separate details, each carefully observed and precisely described. This detailed realism, however, is matched by a tendency to simplify forms into abstract, geometric shapes. Moreover, space in *The Farm* is defined by a ground plane that tilts sharply upward, while individual forms are similarly tilted, so that they sit silhouetted, parallel to the picture plane.

By the mid-1920s, Miró had abandoned the realist manner of *The Farm,* and had created a surrealist style of automatism and abstraction. Elements from *The Farm* continued to appear in his work, however, and the intensity of vision found in this painting remained a standard for all of his later art.

P iet Mondrian intended his abstract or so-called "neo-plastic" paintings to express his fundamentally spiritual notion that universal harmonies preside in nature. The horizontal and vertical elements of his compositions, assiduously calibrated to produce a balanced asymmetry, represented forces of opposition that parallel the dynamic equilibrium at work in the natural world. By 1921 Mondrian had distilled his compositions into black lines that intersect at right angles, defining rectangles painted only in white or gray and the three primary colors.

In 1918 the artist turned one of these square canvases 45 degrees to rest "on point," doing so without rotating the linear elements within the composition. Approximately three years later he merged that format with the elemental color scheme of his mature works to produce this monumental painting, the earliest of the neo-plastic diamond or lozenge compositions. Repainted around 1925, when the black lines were thickened, this picture relates to several other works of the 1920s, where color is restricted to the periphery. Mondrian said the diamond compositions were about cutting, and indeed the sense of cropping here is emphatic. Forms are incomplete, sliced by the edge of the canvas, thus implying a pictorial continuum that extends beyond the physical boundary of the painting.

PIET MONDRIAN
(Dutch, 1872–1944)

Diamond Painting in Red, Yellow and Blue,
c. 1921/25

Canvas. 142.8 × 142.3 cm.
(56¼ × 56 in.)

Gift of Herbert and Nannette Rothschild
1971.51.1

259

CONSTANTIN BRANCUSI
(Romanian, 1876–1957)

Bird in Space, 1925

Marble, stone, and wood.
Height 344.6 cm. (136½ in.)

Gift of Eugene and Agnes Meyer
1967.13.3

With his many versions of *Bird in Space*, Constantin Brancusi achieved a lifelong ambition to convey through sculpture the essence of flight. Through its harmonious blend of serenity and soaring energy, this streamlined marble form seems to defy gravity.

The elegant shape of *Bird in Space* evolved gradually from Brancusi's earlier sculptures of the magical *Maiastra* or "master bird" from Romanian folklore. Brancusi filled in the area below the bird's breast, reduced the open beak to a tilted oval plane, and tapered the feet to a simple flared cone. His solution combines a dynamic compression of forms with an emphatic verticality.

Brancusi designed his own bases, viewing them not just as a means of enhancing the upward thrust of the sculpture, but as a transition between the spiritual realm of the bird and the mundane environment of the physical world. A roughly hewn, x-shaped wooden base is topped first by a cruciform-shaped stone, and then a stone cylinder.

In 1930, Georgia O'Keeffe painted a series of six canvases depicting a jack-in-the-pulpit. The series begins with the striped and hooded bloom rendered with a botanist's care, continues with successively more abstract and tightly focused depictions, and ends with the essence of the jack-in-the-pulpit, a haloed black pistil standing alone against a black, purple, and gray field.

Jack-in-the-Pulpit No. IV represents a midpoint in this process of concurrently increasing detail and abstraction. If O'Keeffe consistently found her strongest inspiration in nature, she believed that the immanence of nature could be discovered in and through the refinement of form. Thus in the jack-in-the-pulpits, abstraction becomes a metaphor of, and an equivalent for, knowledge – the closest view of the flower yields an abstract image; the most profound knowledge of the subject reveals its abstract form.

O'Keeffe bequeathed *Jack-in-the-Pulpit II–VI* to the National Gallery in 1987. Also included in that bequest were three paintings ranging in date from 1927 to 1963.

GEORGIA O'KEEFFE
(American, 1887–1986)

Jack-in-the-Pulpit No. IV, 1930

Canvas. 101.6 × 76.2 cm.
(40 × 30 in.)

Alfred Stieglitz Collection. Bequest of Georgia O'Keeffe
1987.58.3

RENÉ MAGRITTE
(Belgian, 1898–1967)

The Human Condition,
1934

Canvas. 100 × 81 cm.
(39⅜ × 31⅞ in.)

Gift of the Collectors Committee
1987.55.1

Two of Magritte's favored themes were the "window painting" and the "painting within a painting." *The Human Condition* is one of Magritte's earliest treatments of either subject, and in it he combines the two, making what may be his most subtle and profound statement of their shared meaning.

The Human Condition displays an easel placed inside a room and in front of a window. The easel holds an unframed painting of a landscape that seems in every detail contiguous with the landscape seen outside the window. At first, one automatically assumes that the painting on the easel depicts the portion of the landscape outside the window that it hides from view. After a moment's consideration, however, one realizes that this assumption is based upon a false premise: that is, that the imagery of Magritte's painting is real, while the painting on the easel is a representation of that reality. In fact, there is no difference between them. Both are part of the same painting, the same artistic fabrication. It is perhaps to this repeating cycle, in which the viewer, even against his will, sees the one as real and the other as representation, that Magritte's title makes reference.

In *One Year the Milkweed*, one of several so-called color veil paintings Gorky made in 1944, films of paint have been washed unevenly across the canvas, and evocative but indistinct forms have been brushed in. Overall green and brown hues suggest a landscape, but there are no identifiable landscape forms and no spatial recession. Instead, vertical drips and the alternation of light and deep tones create a shifting, shimmering effect across the entire picture surface.

Gorky spent most of 1944 at the country estate of his wife's parents in Hamilton, Virginia, drawing, painting, and observing the changes of the seasons. His mood in *One Year the Milkweed* is one of lyricism and ease, and the painting could be described as a kind of abstract pastoral. The loose, wash technique of *One Year the Milkweed* reflects Gorky's interest in the surrealist procedure of automatism, which exploited apparently accidental effects arrived at by painting and drawing without premeditation. In surrealist theory, those accidental effects were seen as revelatory of unconscious thought processes. The title of *One Year the Milkweed* was given to the painting by Gorky's friend, the great surrealist poet and theorist André Breton.

ARSHILE GORKY
(American, 1904–48)

One Year the Milkweed,
1944

Canvas. 94.2 × 119.3 cm.
(37 × 47 in.)

Ailsa Mellon Bruce Fund
1979.13.2

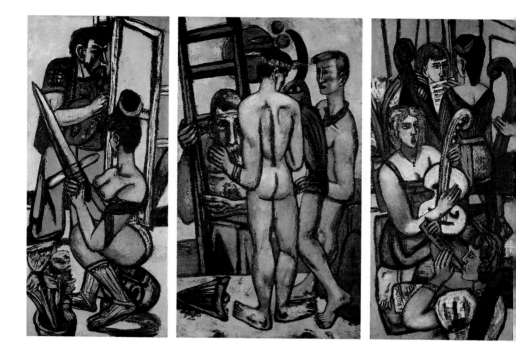

MAX BECKMANN
(German, 1884–1950)

The Argonauts, 1949/50

Canvas. Three panels,
184.1 × 85.1, 205.7 × 121.9,
185.4 × 85.1 cm. (72½ × 33½,
81 × 48, 73 × 33½ in.)

Gift of Mrs. Max Beckmann
1975.96.1 a–c

Max Beckmann planned to paint a ninth and final triptych called "The Artists," with the left panel representing painting, the right panel music, and the middle panel, with its central, garlanded figure, poetry. He was moved by a dream to rename it *The Argonauts*, after the heroes of Greek mythology who traveled with Jason in search of the Golden Fleece. Beckmann's middle panel has at its center the poet Orpheus, at his right Jason, and at his left the sea god Glaucus, who in one ancient account foretells the future to Jason and Orpheus. The woman brandishing a sword in the left panel represents Medea, and the women in the right panel serve as a chorus.

The painting's title may also allude to a group of poets and painters with whom Beckmann associated during his years in Amsterdam, 1937–47, who called themselves "the Argonauts." Indeed, multiple references to Beckmann's art and his life are evident throughout the three panels, making *The Argonauts* a complex autobiographical allegory as well as a broader allegory of the life of the artist; a saga of worldly travail and eternal reward.

ALBERTO GIACOMETTI
(Swiss, 1901–66)

The Chariot, 1950

Bronze with wood base.
164.1 × 68.6 × 67 cm.
(64⅝ × 27 × 26¾ in.)

Gift of Enid A. Haupt
1977.47.2

After 1935, when he broke with the surrealist circle of André Breton, Alberto Giacometti embarked on a thorough revision of his art, prompted by a renewed interest in the human figure. By the end of World War II, he had established the essential elements of what would remain for two decades his distinctive sculptural style. Working in plaster (which would later be cast in bronze), he modeled his sculptures roughly, leaving intact the spontaneous bumps, furrows, and gouges formed by his fingers or knife. The figures themselves became skeletal and elongated and, with their corrugated surfaces, were widely seen as expressing the ravages and atrocities of war and the fragility of human life.

According to the artist, the idea for *The Chariot* was prompted by the medicine carts that were wheeled about by nurses when he was in hospital in 1938. He also explained the sculpture in formal terms, claiming that it was also made to establish "a figure in empty space in order to see it better and to situate it at a precise distance from the floor." The isolated figure of a woman constitutes a mysterious, totemic presence, one that calls to mind ancient bronzes such as the renowned *Charioteer* of Delphi. The sculpture's monumental character was intentional, for it was originally designed as a public commemorative sculpture, one that was rejected by the city of Paris.

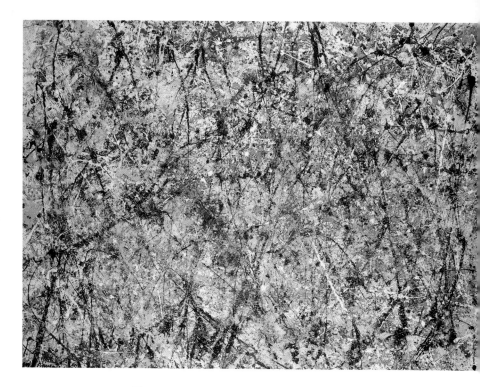

JACKSON POLLOCK
(American, 1912–56)

Number 1 (Lavender Mist), 1950

Canvas. 221 × 229.7 cm.
(87 × 118 in.)

Ailsa Mellon Bruce Fund
1976.37.1

In 1947 Jackson Pollock introduced a radically innovative method of painting in which he poured paint directly onto unprimed canvas that he tacked to the studio floor. Deploying sticks or hardened brushes, Pollock circled around the canvas, flinging, dripping, and splashing skeins of paint onto its surface, layer upon layer, until a dense web of colour was formed. Although his process, which was filmed in 1950 by the photographer Hans Namuth, was spontaneous and intuitive, Pollock exercised remarkable control over it and insisted, "there is no accident."

Number 1 (Lavender Mist), one of Pollock's most important "drip" paintings, attests to the artist's pure virtuosity of paint handling. One can trace his rhythmic movements in the long arcs, staccato dribbles, or coagulated pools of color that accrue into a rich, shimmering interlace. With only a few hues he achieved a soft tonal effect, not by the actual use of lavender but with aluminum and salmon-colored paint. The weave of long black and white strokes implies an inherent linear structure, but the "allover" composition exhibits an even density throughout, with no discernible focal points. Pollock, who spoke of being "in" his paintings, left very literal traces of his presence in the multiple handprints at the upper edges of the canvas.

The *Stations of the Cross* comprises fourteen paintings produced over the course of eight years (plus the painting *Be II*, which Newman added when the paintings were shown for the first time as a cycle at the Solomon R. Guggenheim Museum in 1966). In most of his work from this period, Newman eliminated color, creating a number of paintings in black and white – or gray, in the case of the twelfth *Station* – with large areas of exposed canvas (which the artist likened to the medium of light). The impression in the *Stations* is one of internal formal logic drawn from limited means through which the individual canvases tightly cohere as a series, although rigorous seriality – a principle of permutation that was being employed by younger artists of the minimal art generation beginning in the mid-1960s – is not Newman's concern. Indeed, the *Stations* was not originally devised as a group; only gradually did Newman decide to produce fourteen paintings of identical dimension and to name them together in allusion to the Passion of Christ. Newman's interest was less in precisely correlating his canvases to the narrative of the Passion than in making claims for the profound content in his work. Clearly, however, much like the pictorial representation of this subject in Byzantine and medieval church interiors, Newman's *Stations* was also intended to implicate the beholder in a processional experience through which formal, emotional, or allegorical impact would emerge in episodic, and perhaps cumulative, fashion over time.

BARNETT NEWMAN
(American, 1905–70)

Stations of the Cross,
1958–66

Fourteen canvases, each approx.
198.1 × 152.4 cm. (78 × 60 in.);
and *Be II*, canvas,
204.5 × 183.5 cm. (80½ × 72¼ in.)

Robert and Jane Meyerhoff
Collection
1986.65.1–15

HENRI MATISSE
(French, 1869–1954)

*Large Composition with
Masks*, 1953

Paper mounted on canvas.
353.6 × 996.4 cm.
(139¼ × 392½ in.)

Ailsa Mellon Bruce Fund
1973.17.1

During the last fifteen years of his life Matisse developed his final artistic triumph by "cutting into color." First, his studio assistants would brush opaque and semi-transparent watercolor pigments onto small sheets of white paper. The artist would then cut the sheets freehand in bold shapes that would be pinned to the white studio walls, adjusted, recut, combined and recombined with other elements. Later, the elements were glued flat to large white paper backgrounds for shipping or display.

Large Composition with Masks, the largest of Matisse's cutouts, was originally conceived as a full-scale preliminary study for a ceramic mural. It is architectural in scale, symmetrical in structure. Columns at either side enclose a composition of rosettes arranged in groups of four that form a grid pattern across the nearly thirty-three-foot expanse.

If the design of *Large Composition with Masks* is relatively static, that is compensated by a lively distribution of color. Bright, vivid tones, profiled against the white ground, are dispersed across the surface. They keep the viewer's eye moving, engaged in a composition of paradoxically ordered calm and dynamic energy.

By 1949 Mark Rothko had developed the classic compositional mode that he would explore with astonishing variety and invention over the next two decades. These large, vertical paintings, in which stacked rectangles of richly saturated color hover equivocally in space, realized the artist's long quest for the "simple expression of the complex thought." Rather than the gestural brushwork of his contemporaries, Willem de Kooning and Jackson Pollock, Rothko relied on glowing fields of thinly applied and subtly manipulated layers of color. The moods created by these chromatic relationships range from the gently atmospheric and meditative to the profoundly tragic, and were intended to provoke a transcendental experience in the sensitive viewer.

Untitled is a superb example of Rothko's mature style. Against a cool gray field, a narrow magenta rectangle floats above a larger black one. Just above and below the black run narrow bands of brilliant orange that have been loosely brushed in. Rothko is careful to leave the spatial relationships ambiguous, as planes of color seem to shift slightly in our field of vision. The careful contrasts and transitions of tone and the tension between the effects of compression and expansion contribute to our emotional response.

MARK ROTHKO
(American, 1903–70)

Untitled, 1953

Canvas. 195.1 × 172.3 cm.
(76⅞ × 67⅞ in.)

Gift of the Mark Rothko
Foundation
1986.43.135

JOSEPH CORNELL
(American, 1903–72)

Untitled (Medici Prince),
*c.*1953

Mixed media.
43 × 27 × 11.2 cm.
(17 × 10⅝ × 4⅜ in.)

Gift of the Collectors Committee
1982.54.1

The highly personalized work of Joseph Cornell consists of whimsical assemblages, usually housed in small boxes, which are enigmatic in meaning and nostalgic in inspiration. *Untitled (Medici Prince)* belongs to a group of objects called the Medici Slot Machine series, in which each work is designed around a personage from the Italian Renaissance. This box has at its center a reproduction of a sixteenth-century Italian painting of Piero de' Medici as a young boy. The artist found the reproduction in an art magazine, made a photostat print of it and arranged it in a box built from a discarded Victorian molding. He placed a sheet of blue glass with a grid pattern over the print and, at either side, stacked miniature reproductions of the prince. Other elements in the box include colored balls, French texts, and Baedeker map fragments.

Cornell took great care in composing and constructing his boxes and despite the curious amalgamation of objects, the overall effect of the box is remarkably harmonious. The mysterious grouping of disparate objects was intended to spark unexpected associations in the viewer's imagination. Although individual elements may carry specific references, Cornell was careful to keep his imagery evocative on a more general level: here a sense of distance and sadness prevails

In 1960 Andy Warhol began making the paintings of comic strips, newspaper advertisements, and mass-produced items that would quickly earn him the reputation as a leader of the new Pop movement. The straightforward depiction of these banal subjects became a hallmark of his style, one that marked a substantial departure from the heavily worked surfaces of many abstract expressionist canvases.

Early in 1962 the artist created a number of paintings that reproduce the front pages of newspapers. Lifting this ready-made imagery wholesale from its source, Warhol replicated the close-up photos and dramatic headlines of the tabloid, here announcing the birth of Princess Margaret's son. Designed for immediate accessibility and maximum dramatic impact, the tabloid format also provided the artist with a tightly organized, rectilinear structure. The reproductive nature of the subject and the generalized treatment of the imagery, rendered with a minimum of detail, belie the fact that the canvas was painted by hand.

A Boy for Meg capitalizes on a national obsession with the lives of celebrities, whether members of the royal family or popular personalities such as Frank Sinatra, and foreshadows the silkscreened depictions of celebrities that the artist would commence later the same year.

ANDY WARHOL
(American, 1928–87)

A Boy for Meg, 1962

Canvas. 182.9 × 132 cm.
(72 × 52 in.)

Gift of Mr. and Mrs. Burton Tremaine
1971.87.11

271

David Smith
(American, 1906–65)

Three Circles, 1962

Painted steel.
Circle I:
200.6 × 273.6 × 45.7 cm.
(79 × 107 × 18 in.).
Circle II:
267.9 × 281.2 × 60 cm.
(105½ × 110¾ × 23⅝ in.).
Circle III:
242.5 × 182.8 × 45.7 cm.
(95½ × 72 × 18 in.).

Ailsa Mellon Bruce Fund
1977.60.1–3

America's leading modern sculptor, David Smith belongs to the generation of abstract expressionist artists that included Jackson Pollock and Willem de Kooning. In 1934 Smith set up a studio at Terminal Iron Works, a machinist shop in Brooklyn, where he translated the industrial materials and methods of that trade into his art. Inspired by the welded sculptures of Pablo Picasso and Julio Gonzalez from the late 1920s, Smith incorporated machine parts, scrap metal and found objects into his innovative and remarkably diverse structures.

Smith only adopted the circle as a single compositional focus in the early sixties, perhaps in response to the target paintings then being created by his friend Kenneth Noland. Although these planar circles are obviously related, they are subtly differentiated in color, the size of the interior diameter, and the geometric shapes that have been welded to either side of the circle. Typically, the polychromed surfaces are sensitively treated; one can easily trace the path of the artist's brush. Smith probably intended the circles as a kind of triptych from their inception, but the definitive arrangement of the group was achieved only when he moved the circles about in the fields of his studio at Bolton Landing, eventually aligning them so that they could be viewed concentrically.

One of the key figures in the history of so-called Pop art, Roy Lichtenstein shared with his contemporary Andy Warhol a fascination for the visual languages of mass print media and consumer culture during the 1960s. Lichtenstein was especially preoccupied with cheap newspaper advertising and cartoon or comic book illustration, which he enlarged and transposed – making subtle alterations – directly into paint on canvas. At the time, the simplistic narratives and boldly graphic visual mannerisms of comics and advertising were understood to resist the powerful post-war legacy of abstract expressionist painting – the highly subjective processes and grand claims for psychic content that characterized the work of Jackson Pollock, Mark Rothko, Willem de Kooning, and other New York school artists whose achievement had recently placed American art at the center of a world stage. Substituting the banalities of resolutely flat printed commercial imagery in black, white, red, yellow, and blue for layered, complex, rarefied efforts in large-scale abstraction, Pop, by implication, also challenged the conventional hierarchies of visual "art." Irreverent in its day, *Look Mickey* is now recognized as a Pop art classic: Mickey and Donald in a ready-made figural composition extracted from a bubble-gum wrapper and transformed into the hand-painted imitation of an image that is, in its original form, mechanically reproduced. Lichtenstein, like Warhol, would continue to pursue the implications of this procedure.

ROY LICHTENSTEIN
(American, 1923–97)

Look Mickey, 1961

Canvas. 121.9 × 175.3 cm.
(48 × 69 in.)

Dorothy and Roy Lichtenstein, Gift of the Artist, in Honor of the 50th Anniversary of the National Gallery of Art
1990.41.1

273

ALEXANDER CALDER
(American, 1898–1976)

Untitled, 1976

Painted aluminum and steel.
910.3 × 2315.5 cm.
(358½ × 911½ in.)

Gift of the Collectors Committee
1976.76.1

Alexander Calder created his first motorized abstract sculptures or "mobiles" in the early 1930s. After he visited the Paris studio of Piet Mondrian, Calder painted these assemblages of wire and small spheres or disks in black and white with bright, primary colors. By developing an ingenious system of weights and counter-balances, the sculptor eventually designed his constructions so that, when suspended, they moved freely with the air currents, embodying a temporal dimension as well as the possibility of chance.

In 1972, when the East Building of the National Gallery was under construction, the artist was asked to create a large mobile that would complement the monumental atrium space of the building. Calder's giant mobile, which maintains a sense of lightness and delicacy in spite of its architectural scale, demonstrates the artist's ability to orchestrate the ever-shifting relations between forms in space. The individual elements have a source in the biomorphic shapes Calder admired in the art of Joan Miró and Jean Arp. Originally planned in steel, the sculpture was too heavy when enlarged and the artist-engineer Paul Matisse transformed the design into an aluminum construction that weighed a mere 920 pounds. The artist died one year before the sculpture was hoisted up to the space frame of the roof on 18 November 1977.

Beginning in the late 1960s, within the context of minimal and process art, Richard Serra abandoned the notion that sculpture must be either figural or abstract per se, creating work instead that offers the beholder an intense perceptual encounter with properties of weight, mass, gravity, balance, and duration. Largely produced in lead and steel – materials familiar to him from early working experience in industrial mills – Serra's work radically departs from the history of sculpture as a carved, modeled, cast, or constructed object sitting on a pedestal or base. *Five Plates, Two Poles* is one of seven "plate-and-pole" pieces that Serra created in 1970 and 1971, during a time when he began producing work on an expanded scale, including projects specifically designated for various outdoor sites. The plate-and-pole series elaborates principles first explored in Serra's early "props." *Five Plates, Two Poles* is the largest and most complex: it consists of five eight-foot square standing steel plates that are partly supported by slotted steel poles. These heavy elements rest directly on the floor and are held erect by the force and counterforce of the leaning plates (which are not welded but touch each other at various points), an essential premise of Serra's work from this period. Walking around it allows one to grasp a sequence of shifting planar and spatial relationships manifested by the configuration of the plates; the power of this encounter is heightened by scale and implied weight. *Five Plates, Two Poles* represented a breakthrough for the artist, introducing essential concerns that he would continue to pursue throughout his career.

RICHARD SERRA
(American, born 1939)

Five Plates, Two Poles,
1971

Hot-rolled steel. Overall size:
243.8 × 548.6 × 701 cm.
(96 × 216 × 276 in.)

Gift of The Morris and Gwendolyn Cafritz Foundation © 2001 Richard Serra/Artists Rights Society (ARS), New York
2001.27.1

JASPER JOHNS
(American, born 1930)

Perilous Night, 1982

Encaustic on canvas with
objects. 170.5 × 244.2 × 15.9 cm.
(67⅛ × 96⅛ × 6¼ in.)

Robert and Jane Meyerhoff
Collection,
1995.79.1

Perilous Night is composed as a diptych. The right half of the composition contains objects and images that are variously representational: three fragmented wax casts of a human arm (taken at various ages from a single person) hanging by hooks from the top of the canvas; a wooden slat – perhaps a painter's maulstick – sprung along the right-hand edge; a handkerchief copied from Picasso's images of the Weeping Woman, "attached" to the canvas by an illusionary nail; the silk-screened musical score of "Perilous Night," a song composed by John Cage; painted trompe l'oeil wood grain; an image of a "crosshatch" drawing by Johns himself painted to look like a collage element; and a traced detail from Matthias Grünewald's Isenheim altarpiece, which Johns has transformed into a dark, illegible pattern. Enlarged and rotated, the Grünewald detail also occupies the entire left side of the painting. Together these elements represent individual systems of representation coexisting in a limbo state of unresolved relationships. Indeed, *Perilous Night* possesses an iconographical complexity that was new to the artist's work at that time. One realm to which it alludes is that of the artist's studio, a setting that was often depicted in the history of Western art since the Renaissance; another is that of the New Testament (already implicated by the Grünewald image, which was lifted from the figure of a fallen Roman soldier at Christ's Resurrection), especially – given the helpless arms, wooden planks, and nails – the Crucifixion.

Fanny/Fingerpainting, a portrait of Close's mother-in-law, represents one of the largest and most masterly executions of a technique the artist developed in the mid-1980s. That technique involved the direct application of pigment to a surface with the artist's fingertips. By adjusting the amount of pigment and the pressure of his finger on the canvas, Close could achieve a wide range of tonal effects. Typically, he worked from a black and white photograph which he would divide into many smaller units by means of a grid. He then transposed the grid onto a much larger canvas and meticulously reproduced each section of it. The result is a monumental, close-up view that forces an uncomfortable intimacy upon the viewer.

Seen from a distance, the painting looks like a giant, silver-toned photograph that unrelentingly reveals every crack and crevice of the sitter's face. Closer up, the paint surface dissolves into a sea of fingerprints that have an abstract beauty, even as they metaphorically suggest the withering of the sitter's skin with age. The fingerpaintings provide a far more literal record of the artist's touch than most abstract expressionist brushwork – but are at the same time dictated by an abstract, distinctly impersonal system.

CHUCK CLOSE
(American, born 1940)

Fanny/Fingerpainting, 1985

Canvas. 259.1 × 213.4 cm. (102 × 84 in.)

Gift of Lila Acheson Wallace
1987.2.1

European Sculpture
OF THE XIV–XIX CENTURIES

Along with the splendors of its great painting collections, the National Gallery of Art boasts approximately 2100 works of Western sculpture, many of them of spectacular quality. This selection has aimed to include many of the finest examples from the period 1300–1900; it covers a wide range of materials and techniques, and gives some idea of the variety of purposes that sculpture has traditionally served.

The earliest works here – the Pisan *Annunciation* pair and the English *Saint George* – were devotional sculptures, made to stand on an altar or elsewhere in a church or chapel, to teach religious lessons, inspire faith, and invite divine favor for the donors. Another major task for sculptors throughout history was the portrait bust, especially in demand during the Renaissance when it would be set on the mantelpiece or above the door of a home to commemorate a family member. Renaissance portrait medals, of which the Gallery holds many fine examples, were made as gifts for friends or political allies, often to commemorate important events. Such medals might be worn or kept as desk or pocket objects.

From statues of mythological subjects for the palaces and gardens of the powerful, sculptors turned to the production of great civic monuments in the nineteenth century, of which Rodin's bronze *Jean d'Aire* is a small version. The most revolutionary sculpture in the present group is the last – the wax *Tub* by Degas – a highly personal and experimental study combining freely modeled naturalistic forms with geometric composition, and incorporating everyday objects.

The sculptures selected can be roughly divided between figures in the round and reliefs, though some works with very high relief – such as those of Riccio and Andrea della Robbia – have qualities of both. Color has historically played a significant part in sculpture; careful painting of hair, flesh, and clothing enhances resemblance to natural appearance on the Benedetto da Maiano *Saint John the Baptist*, for example. Different ideas about what makes a figure beautiful reflect both the artist's personality and the values of his time. Compare, for instance, the very different ideals of feminine beauty in the Mino *Virtues*, the Milanese bronze *Venus*, or the Lemoyne *Companion of Diana*. It is worth considering why, in some cases, as in Degas' *The Tub*, conventional beauty ceased to be the sculptor's chief preoccupation.

Detail:
JEAN-LOUIS LEMOYNE,
A Companion of Diana

In the dimensions given for individual works, height appears first, followed by width, and then depth.

PISAN, 14th century

The Archangel Gabriel and *The Virgin Annunciate*, c.1325/50

Wood, polychromed and gilded. 159.4 × 47.3 × 36 cm. (62¾ × 18⅝ × 14⅛ in.) and 162.3 × 53.8 × 39.9 cm. (63⅞ × 21⅛ × 15¾ in.)

Samuel H. Kress Collection 1961.9.97 and 1961.9.98

Among the National Gallery's earliest life-size sculptures (and few medieval works in wood) is this monumental pair of figures. Mary and the archangel, who brings her the miraculous tidings as described in the Gospel of Saint Luke, turn calmly toward each other, expressing their emotions by subtle movements and gestures of their hands. Their slender proportions, fine, sharply delineated facial features, sinuously waving hair, and the deep, curving folds of their costumes, are typical of the Gothic style.

These wooden figures are copied from a pair of fourteenth-century marble statues in the church of Santa Caterina in Pisa, Italy. Carbon-14 tests on samples of the wood have indicated that each piece was carved from a tree cut down at least six hundred years ago.

Such Annunciation pairs would perhaps have flanked the entrance to the high-altar area of a church or the altar itself. While they might also have been set into tabernacles, the carving completely in the round suggests a position in which viewers could move around them. Their surfaces were once completely polychromed, and traces of the colors remain – red, blue, green, and a red-and-gilt pattern on the borders of the mantles.

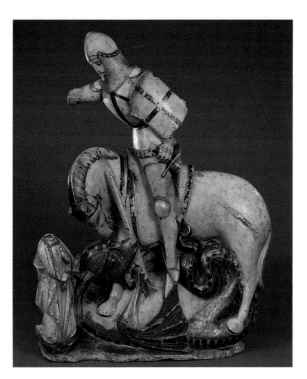

ENGLISH, late 14th to early 15th century

Saint George and the Dragon, c. 1370/1420

Painted and gilded alabaster.
81.5 × 60.5 × 20.5 cm.
(32 × 23¾ × 8⅛ in.)

Samuel H. Kress Collection
1953.2.2

English sculptors in the fourteenth and fifteenth centuries made extensive use of alabaster, a stone readily available in the British Isles, which they enlivened with polychromy. Much religious sculpture was destroyed in England and elsewhere in iconoclastic attacks that accompanied the Protestant Reformation. This statuary group, fully carved both in front and back, is therefore a great rarity. Its survival no doubt owes much to the fact that it was preserved, from an unknown early date until after 1880, at the Dominican convent of San Juan at Quejana in the province of Alava, Spain.

The sculptor has designed a saint who seems to tower over his elegantly curving horse as he plunges a lance (now mostly destroyed) into the resisting dragon. These figures are united in a wonderfully compact composition, with a graceful silhouette that survives in spite of important losses like the head of the rescued princess, who holds the dragon by a leash made from her belt. Noteworthy is the sculptor's decision to carve the figures with large, smooth surfaces, leaving the textures of chain mail, horse hair on the mane, and scales on the dragon to be applied in paint.

FLORENTINE,
early 15th century

Madonna and Child,
c.1425

Painted and gilded terra cotta.
120.8 × 47.2 × 33.5 cm.
(47½ × 18½ × 13¼ in.)

Andrew W. Mellon Collection
1937.1.112

With this terra-cotta statue, slightly under life-size, we encounter figures that demonstrate the beginnings of the Italian Renaissance admiration for the human body. Earlier statues in the collection like the Pisan *Annunciation* pair (p. 280), present the figure as a relatively simple and static form, with drapery arranged in graceful decorative patterns that tell little about the body it covers. Here, while some decorative folds remain, the clothes work more effectively to describe the form and movement of the body beneath them. Projecting folds wrap around Mary's bent right leg, and deep pockets of space penetrate the sculptural mass, articulating the figure of a young woman with the strength to move vigorously in her heavy garments and support a sturdy child. For a fifteenth-century audience the child's nudity would have represented Christ's humility in entering the world as a small, poor, and helpless human being.

The mother, whose costume details recall ancient sculpture – classical sandals, a fillet around the head, and palmette ornament on the sleeve cuffs – shares much with images conceived by the Florentine master Donatello (1385/86–1466), the greatest sculptor of the early Renaissance.

L eone Battista Alberti, among the most broadly talented men of the Renaissance, is celebrated for his treatises on painting, sculpture, and architecture. He was also accomplished in the fields of law, philosophy, mathematics, and science. Besides experimenting with painting and sculpture, he designed great churches in the north Italian cities of Rimini and Mantua, whose rulers he advised on the arts. He also served as architectural advisor to Pope Nicholas V.

This bronze is probably cast from a wax model, in a shape and design inspired by an ancient Roman carved gem. The folds around the neck suggest classical drapery. The closely cropped cap of hair can be associated both with Roman and mid-fifteenth-century styles. Its fluffy tufts recall the mane of Alberti's namesake, the lion (*leone*).

The clean, continuous lines, proudly lifted head, and distant gaze give Alberti's features a noble, idealized character. Under his chin is his personal emblem, a winged eye. Alberti wrote of the eye as the most powerful, swift, and worthy of human parts, reminding us to be ever vigilant in the pursuit of what is good. The image is also meant to represent the all-seeing eye of God.

LEONE BATTISTA ALBERTI
(Florentine, 1404–72)

*Self-Portrait, c.*1435

Bronze. 20.1 × 13.6 cm.
(7$\frac{7}{8}$ × 5$\frac{3}{8}$ in.)

Samuel H. Kress Collection
1957.14.125

283

PISANELLO
(Italian, c.1395–1455)

*Leonello d'Este 1407–50,
Marquess of Ferrara 1441*
(obverse); *A Lion Being
Taught by Cupid to Sing*
(reverse), 1444

Bronze. 10.3 cm. diam. (4 1/16 in.)

Samuel H. Kress Collection
1957.14.602a,b

Pisanello, who was a painter as well as a medalist, is generally credited with having invented the Renaissance medal form, as well as having brought it to its highest potential. He made several medals of the Marquess of Ferrara, this one being for the occasion of Leonello's marriage to Maria of Aragon in 1444. The composition of the reverse side alludes to their marriage, with Leonello (in the guise of a lion; his name means "little lion") being taught to sing by Cupid, who here represents matrimonial love. The artist has dated this reverse composition (MCCCCXLIIII, or 1444) on the pillar in the background, and has signed it OPVS PISANI PICTORIS ("the work of Pisano the Painter").

The inscription across the field and around the bottom of the obverse, LEONELLVS MARCHIO ESTENSIS D(ominus) FERRARIE REGII ET MUTINE, identifies Leonello as Marquess of Este and Lord of Ferrara, Reggio, and Modena. The truncated inscription around the top, GE R AR, is an abbreviation of GENER REGIS ARAGONUM, identifying him (through his marriage) as the son-in-law of King Alfonso V of Aragon, ruler of Naples; Leonello's marriage to Maria brought him a bride who increased his prestige by associating him with the powerful Neapolitan court.

This work reflects the relief style of the great Florentine sculptor Donatello, whose approach to statuary is glimpsed in the terra-cotta *Madonna and Child* of *c.*1425 (p. 282). In both marble and bronze, Donatello had devised ways of using very low, flat relief to suggest figures in a deep space. The able and intelligent follower of Donatello who produced this small image has suggested an architectural setting receding into space behind the Madonna and Child.

The figures appear in a close-up view on a balcony or parapet. The Child stands on the ledge in a lively pose that combines a forward shift of his weight with a twist backward to cling to his mother. With delicate modulations of his wax model, the sculptor varied the textures of crumpled cloth, fine fringe, and feathery hair, set against powerful architecture. The gestures of the Madonna's and Child's hands, paralleling each other with choreographic grace, recall those of Donatello's statues at the Basilica of Saint Anthony in Padua. Here the figures seem to reach out in greeting toward acclaiming worshippers. One scholar has named the composition "The Madonna of Welcome."

Follower of DONATELLO, mid-15th century

Madonna and Child within an Arch, mid-15th century

Gilded bronze.
20.3 × 15.2 cm. (8 × 6 in.)

Samuel H. Kress Collection
1957.14.131

*Saint Jerome in the
Desert, c.*1461

Marble. 42.7 × 54.8 cm.
(16¾ × 21½ in.)

Widener Collection
1942.9.113

Desiderio da Settignano, born in a small village in the hills above Florence, numbers among the most brilliant marble sculptors of the Renaissance. His mastery of relief sculpture is apparent in this pictorially rich image, with its complicated space in which figures move in different planes, all suggested by the subtlest manipulations of the marble surface.

Clearly Desiderio had learned much from the low-relief technique of Donatello. The sculptor invented a rocky, wilderness landscape with a cloud-streaked sky and tall, pointed cypress trees receding into the distance among the cliffs. In the foreground, Saint Jerome kneels in penitential prayer before a crucifix. He wears only a few crumpled wisps of drapery, and his gaunt face tells of fervent, ascetic devotion. On the right, in particularly fine low relief, suggesting he is some distance in the background, a terrified boy flees from the lions that emerge from the rocks on the left behind the cross.

According to legend, Jerome tamed a lion by removing a thorn from its paw, and the lion therefore often appears as his attribute in art. The lions here, clearly no threat to the saint, suggest his harmonious relationship with nature, achieved through solitary meditation, prayer, and penance.

Like Desiderio, Antonio Rossellino probably came from Settignano. He was the most accomplished sculptor among five brothers, all trained in the important workshop led by the eldest brother Bernardo. Widespread admiration for Antonio's skill may explain why his nickname *Rossellino*, "little redhead," came to be attached to all his brothers, replacing the family name Gambarelli.

John the Baptist, portrayed by Antonio in this graceful bust, was a patron saint of the city of Florence and a favorite figure in Florentine painting and sculpture. The Florentine theologian, Cardinal Giovanni Dominici, recommended around 1410 that parents display images of the Christ Child and the young John together in their homes, as religious and moral examples for their children. When it was first made, this bust may have served just such a purpose in a Florentine home. But for at least the 180 years before 1940, it was in a Florentine religious building, the oratory of San Francesco of the Vanchettoni, together with Desiderio da Settignano's bust of the Christ Child, now exhibited in the same gallery. The Desiderio boy is considerably younger, with plump cheeks and silky hair; Rossellino's John is close to adolescence. His richly waving curls and the fine curving lines of his lips suggest the beauty of a young classical god.

Antonio Rossellino
(Florentine, c.1427–79)

*The Young Saint John the Baptist, c.*1470

Marble. 34.7 × 29.8 × 16.1 cm.
(13⅝ × 11¾ × 6¼ in.)

Samuel H. Kress Collection
1943.4.79

MINO DA FIESOLE
(Florentine, 1429–84)

Charity and *Faith*,
c.1475/80

Marble.
Each 126 × 43 cm.
(49¾ × 17 in.)

Andrew W. Mellon Collection
1937.1.118 and 1937.1.117

In the art of the Middle Ages and Renaissance, the Virtues were often personified by human figures carrying identifying attributes. Charity typically holds one or more children, while Faith in this case had a chalice and a cross, now broken. As represented by Mino da Fiesole, a contemporary of Desiderio da Settignano and Antonio Rossellino, these Virtues appear as slender young girls in clinging, layered gowns with fine pleats. Their heavy mantles are carved in distinctive, angular folds. Typical of Mino's style is the fine, precise, sharp-edged treatment of textile folds and locks of hair, giving these features an ornamental quality different from the softer approach of Desiderio and Antonio Rossellino.

Set in arched niches, the figures must have been intended as part of a monument combining architecture and sculpture, probably a wall tomb inside a church. The Virtues would represent reasons for the deceased person's good memory on earth and hopes for Paradise.

Faith and *Charity* stand on bases treated as little banks of clouds, as if they were already in heaven themselves. Hope, the third theological Virtue mentioned in Saint Paul's first letter to the Corinthians, might have completed such a group.

A ndrea della Robbia carried on the popular and lucrative production of terra-cotta sculpture covered with enamel glaze, a technique developed in the 1430s and 1440s by his uncle Luca. The glazed coating gave the colors of della Robbia's works a degree of durability impossible for sculpture that was simply painted. Their white-glazed figures, set off against deep blue grounds and sometimes surrounded by multicolored garlands of fruit or flowers (as in Andrea's *Adoration of the Child* in the same gallery), were in demand as devotional images for churches, homes, and outdoor shrines.

The half-length treatment of the Virgin brings us close to the figures, whose attitudes combine tenderness and solemnity. The Virgin holds the Child gently, her forehead grazing his hair. The child rests his left arm against her chest and clutches her left hand, as he clings to a corner of her veil. Yet for all their physical closeness, they do not look at each other, and their expressions are grave. The Virgin's downcast gaze suggests meditation on the child's fate. The child turns his face toward the world, but his eyes, with pupils drifting upward, also suggest contemplation. Their thoughts seem to converge on the same sorrowful theme: the coming Passion and death of Christ.

ANDREA DELLA ROBBIA
(Florentine, 1435–1525)

*Madonna and Child with Cherubim, c.*1485

Glazed terra-cotta. Diameter 54.7 cm. (21½ in.)

Andrew W. Mellon Collection 1937.1.122

BENEDETTO DA MAIANO
(Florentine, 1442–97)

Saint John the Baptist,
*c.*1480

Painted terra cotta.
48.9 × 52 × 26 cm.
(19¼ × 20½ × 10¼ in.)

Andrew W. Mellon Collection
1937.1.130

The popular Florentine subject of the young John the Baptist is here presented in a different conception from that of Antonio Rossellino's delicately beautiful marble bust (p. 287). The difference is not only in the medium, painted terra cotta, which has retained much original coloring that contributes to an immediate naturalism. The sculptor of this bust also has given it a particular psychological intensity. The face is thinner; the features relatively individualized, and the gaze distant in a way that from some angles suggests inward concentration on his message, from others suggests focus on some far-away listener. The long, richly modeled and differentiated hair is at once elegant in its swirling waves and unruly in its loose wisps, suggesting passionate energy that is reiterated by the cloak sweeping across the chest to twist into a knot at one side. The open mouth implies the saint is already preaching.

Benedetto da Maiano was primarily a sculptor in marble, but a number of his terra-cotta productions survive, both sketch models and independent works. An almost life-size, marble statue of the young Saint John the Baptist by Benedetto, datable *c.*1480/81, is part of a marble doorway in the Sala dei Gigli in the Palazzo della Signoria, Florence's town hall.

At High Mass in Florence Cathedral on 26 April 1478, henchmen of the Pazzi family drew their daggers to assassinate the heads of the family that dominated Florence, Lorenzo de' Medici and his younger brother Giuliano. Giuliano, aged only twenty-five, fell victim to the attack. Lorenzo, although wounded, escaped to suppress the conspiracy and consolidate his power. To commemorate these events and offer public thanksgiving for his salvation, life-size wax images of Lorenzo were placed in several churches. Andrea del Verrocchio, a favorite sculptor of the Medici, supervised the production of these images. The terra-cotta bust on the right may perpetuate one of them in more permanent material.

Whatever the occasion for its production, this portrait is as much about power as about an individual personality. Over life-size, solid and compact, the bust is composed of massive, simple forms. The plain costume of a Florentine citizen and the bluntly cropped hair contribute to this simplicity. Lorenzo's overhanging brows, projecting chin, and grimly set mouth convey force and determination. His brooding look suggests one who has survived the worst attack his enemies could mount and warns them not to try again. Lorenzo makes a striking contrast with Verrocchio's terra-cotta bust of Giuliano de' Medici. Wearing richly ornamented armor, Giuliano embodies a buoyant, supercilious charm unclouded by threats.

ANDREA DEL
VERROCCHIO
(Florentine, 1435–88)

Giuliano de' Medici,
*c.*1475/78

Terra cotta. 61 × 66 × 28.3 cm.
(24 × 26 × 11⅛ in.)

Andrew W. Mellon Collection
1937.1.127

FLORENTINE,
15th or 16th century,
probably after a model
by Andrea del Verrocchio
and Orsino Benintendi

Lorenzo de' Medici

Painted terra cotta.
65.8 × 59.1 × 32.7 cm.
(25⅞ × 23¼ × 12⅞ in.)

Samuel H. Kress Collection
1943.4.92

291

TILMAN
RIEMENSCHNEIDER
(German, c.1460–1531)

*Saint Burchard of
Würzburg*, c.1510/23

Painted linden wood.
82.3 × 47.2 × 30.2 cm.
(32¾ × 18½ × 11⅞ in.)

Samuel H. Kress Collection
1961.1.1

Burchard, the English-born first bishop of Würzburg, Germany, died in 754. In this imaginary portrait, he raises his right hand in blessing. His left hand once held a curving crozier. The figure's facial type occurs repeatedly in the wood and stone sculptures of this famous German master: prominent nose and cheekbones, strong chin, long, sunken cheeks, and finely outlined, downturned mouth and eyes, suggesting a mood of slightly sorrowful contemplation. In this careworn, sensitive face, Riemenschneider explored the psychology of a man on whom spiritual authority seems to weigh heavily.

Hollowed out to make it light, the bust may once have been carried in religious processions. It has experienced some alterations since it was carved; the square, diamond-shaped cut on the chest was certainly made well after the sculpture was finished, possibly in order to fill the recess with relics.

Tiny traces of original coloring, removed long ago, may be noticed, for instance on the cope (mantle), where bits of blue and yellow remain. Although this particular bust was polychromed, Riemenschneider was a pioneer in the use of bare, unpainted wood for the sculpture on his major altarpieces. The black rings around the pupils, however, so important to the dreamy expression of the eyes, are typical of Riemenschneider's figures.

In the north Italian city of Padua, a major center of Renaissance bronze production, Riccio stood out as the most brilliant master. The Entombment of Christ is a recurring subject in his reliefs. This is his largest single relief and his masterpiece on the theme.

Riccio modeled his crowd of mourners in such high relief that many emerge almost as separate statuettes. To an astonishing degree, space penetrates the crowd and the landscape, flowing behind the freestanding trees. People of all ages join in the funeral procession, their faces and costumes rendered with strength and precision. Their expressions range from stoic sorrow to wild outbursts, with streaming hair, gesticulating arms, and mouths open in howls. These frantic attitudes had precedents in the art of antiquity and in the works of Donatello and his pupil Bellano that Riccio could see in Padua. The scene also recalls the funeral of the mythological hero Meleager, depicted on many Roman sarcophagi and recommended to artists by the theorist Alberti as a convincing portrayal of a dead man weighing down his bearers.

The man just in front of Christ's feet carries an urn inscribed AERDNA, "Andrea" spelled backwards. The presence of this barely disguised signature has led to speculation that the artist intended this relief to mark his own tomb.

ANDREA BRIOSCO,
called RICCIO
(Paduan, c.1470–1532)

The Entombment,
c.1500/30

Bronze. 50.4 × 75.5 cm.
(19⅞ × 29¾ in.)

Samuel H. Kress Collection
1957.14.11

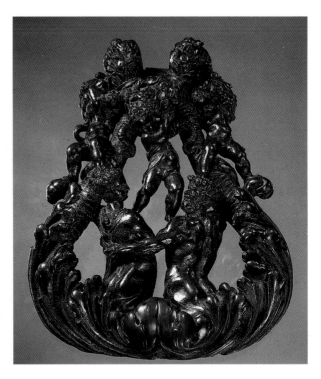

JACOPO SANSOVINO
(Florentine/Venetian,
1486–1570)

*Doorknocker with Nereid,
Triton and Putti, c.*1550

Bronze. 35.6 × 28.8 × 8.5 cm.
(14 × 11⅜ × 3⅜ in.)

Pepita Milmore Memorial Fund
1979.10.1

Renaissance bronze sculpture often served practical functions. This doorknocker is one of the finest examples of a specialty of the city of Venice, where Jacopo Sansovino dominated sculptural and architectural projects for some forty years. Gifted, prolific, and well-connected, Sansovino introduced the dynamic and heroically proportioned human types of central Italian High Renaissance art to Venetian sculpture.

Typical of its kind, this doorknocker has a broad base of lush acanthus leaves, from which horns curve upward and converge toward the top in a form suggesting a lyre. A nereid and triton, half-human sea creatures whose lower bodies are understood to disappear into fish-tails hidden in the foliage, gaze delightedly at each other. The male's outstretched left arm unites them, and each figure's outer arm winds up under and around the horns that rise out of the leaves. Above them, robust little putti twist about beneath their burden of dense fruit garlands, splaying their legs and planting their feet impudently on the adults' heads and chests. The whole, brilliantly interwoven antiquarian invention alludes in a direct and playful way to love and fertility, appropriate to the door of a home. The smooth, worn lower leaves indicate that the knocker received many years of use.

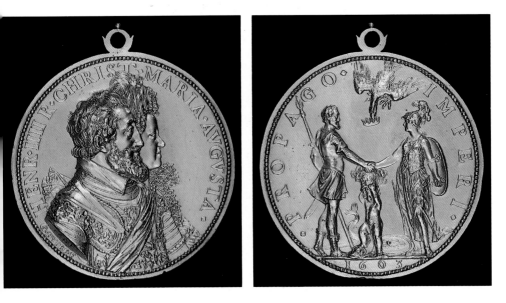

In contrast to the more personal significance of Pisanello's *Leonello d'Este* (p.284), this medal is a political commentary on the union of King Henri IV of France and his wife Marie, and their resulting offspring, the future King Louis XIII. Henri and Marie are shown in a double portrait on the obverse, he in a superb armorial breastplate, she in a court dress with an extensive lace collar. The inscriptions around the top, HENR(icus) IIII R(ex) CHRIST(ianissimus), and MARIA AVGVSTA, identify the two as "Henri the fourth, most Christian King," and "Empress Marie." The maker, Guillaume Dupré, was the most brilliant practitioner of the medallic arts in France during this period and a great favorite of the ruling monarchs.

On the reverse, the distinctive profiles of the two rulers are recognizable in the two standing figures holding hands. These represent Henri as Mars, the god of war, and Marie as Pallas, the goddess of wisdom and the arts. Beneath their clasped hands stands the young child, their son Louis. The inscription around the top, PROPAGO IMPERI, "the offspring of the empire," reflects the dynastic aspirations of Henri and Marie, based on their hopes for young Louis' future.

GUILLAUME DUPRÉ
(French, *c.*1576–1643)

Henri IV and Marie de Médicis (obverse);
Louis XIII as Dauphin between Henri IV as Mars and Marie as Pallas (reverse), 1603

Gilded bronze. 6.8 cm. diam.
without suspension
loop (2¾ in.)

Samuel H. Kress Collection
1957.14.1151

MILANESE, cast from a
model attributed to
FRANCESCO BRAMBILLA
(1530–99)

Venus, c.1580/90

Bronze. 166 × 44 × 33.7 cm.
(65½ × 17¼ × 13¼ in.)
Andrew W. Mellon Collection
1937.1.132

This *Venus* is among the few life-size Renaissance bronze statues in the United States and, certainly, one of the best. Her proportions recall classical ideals of feminine beauty, but are a little fuller, more rounded and compact. Standing with the weight on her left leg, she twists in a subtle spiral. Her right hand offers a conch shell, an ancient female symbol. The luxuriant tresses of her hair, bound in knots and chased with fine lines, wind as if full of energy. The voluptuous contours and warm gaze make this statue a persuasive conception of the ancient Greco-Roman goddess of love, beauty, and procreation.

The *Venus* was once thought to be a work of Jacopo Sansovino (p. 294), probably because she is paired with a statue of *Bacchus and a Faun* that resembles Sansovino's *Bacchus* of 1511–12 in Florence. Recent research has dated the Washington *Venus* and *Bacchus* closer to 1600 and traced their ownership back as far as 1656, when they stood in the garden of a villa at Lainate, near Milan. The sculptural decoration for this garden in the late 1580s was supervised by Francesco Brambilla, chief of sculpture for Milan Cathedral. Other works produced from his designs suggest that he may have made the wax or clay model that was cast into the *Venus*.

ADRIAEN DE VRIES
(Dutch/Florentine,
c.1545–1626)

*Empire Triumphant over
Avarice*, 1610

Bronze. 77.3 × 34.8 × 31.8 cm.
(30¾ × 13⅝ × 12½ in.)
Widener Collection
1942.9.148

Adriaen de Vries was one of the leading late Renaissance masters of northern Europe. His heroic figures – female as well as male – reflect study of the antique and of Michelangelo's sculpture, with an emphasis on self-consciously complicated, twisting poses.

Adriaen devised this bronze allegory for the Holy Roman Emperor Rudolf II, who had appointed him court sculptor at Prague in 1601. Once thought simply to represent "Virtue Overcoming Vice," the bronze has recently been interpreted as a specific theme close to the Emperor's heart. The dominant female figure, crowned with laurel, symbolizes Empire. The second laurel wreath she holds high proclaims her victory over a figure with ass's ears and a bag of gold coins that identify her as Avarice (the ears and the gold come from the ancient myth of King Midas, known for his greed and bad judgment). Rudolf was fighting, none too successfully, in wars against the Turks, and also struggling with the lands he ruled that were reluctant to grant the funds he needed to continue. The bronze gives form to his wish for triumph over both adversaries. The sculptor gave psychological force to this symbolic program in the rippling tension of the torsos and in the gaze that passes between the coolly imperious victor and the distraught vanquished.

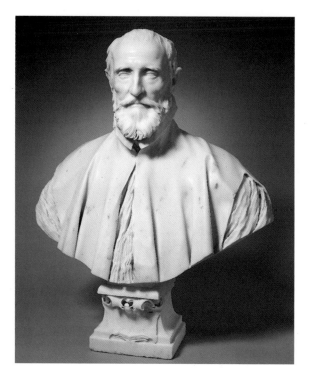

GIAN LORENZO BERNINI
(Roman, 1598–1680)

Monsignor Francesco Barberini, c.1623

Marble. 61 × 65.9 × 25.7 cm.
(31½ × 25¼ × 10⅛ in.)

Samuel H. Kress Collection
1961.9.102

The sternly reserved expression of this portrait bust may come as a surprise in a work of the great baroque sculptor and architect Bernini. The restrained treatment must owe something to the fact that the sculptor was working not from a living subject but from the painted portrait of a man who had died in 1600, when Bernini was two years old. Around 1623 Bernini's good friend Maffeo Barberini, the newly elected Pope Urban VIII, commissioned busts of his family, including this beloved uncle.

With the needs of his patron in mind, Bernini created a noble and dignified paternal presence in the ancient Roman tradition of ancestral portraiture. He chose a bust form that includes most of the chest, and curved the truncation to echo the arch of the spreading shoulders, producing an effect both of harmony and imposing physical bulk. Shadows play over Francesco's aged face, especially in the sunken temples, and beneath the bushy eyebrows. The sagging flesh of the cheeks appears soft and pliant. The sculptor's drill has pierced dark wells between the tufts of the silky beard. The mantle falls in broad folds that contrast with the crinkly pleats of the surplice below. These varied forms and textures show how successfully Bernini strove to compensate for marble's lack of color.

Algardi, Bernini's greatest rival for leadership in sculpture in seventeenth-century Rome, came to the Eternal City from Bologna, capital of the province of Emilia. His Bolognese origin is significant not only because he shared it with the Carracci family, leaders in the reform of painting in Emilia and Rome beginning around 1600, but also because Emilia is a province where sculptural stone is scarce. While Algardi nevertheless became a skilled marble carver, the modeler's technique of his earliest training, with clay and stucco, always came more naturally to him. This bust exemplifies his fluid command of modeling.

The bust may have originated as one of several studies of saintly types to be used as models for sculpture when the occasion arose. Algardi gave his bearded saint a youthful face, with harmonious, classically proportioned features. Classical too are the calm expression, the blank pupils, the drapery, and the clearly rounded head bound by a fillet. Algardi's love for gently flowing curves shows in the undulating locks of hair that seem to echo the curving outlines of the saint's wide eyes.

ALESSANDRO ALGARDI
(Bolognese/Roman,
1598–1654)

*Saint Matthew, c.*1640

Terra cotta.
38 × 32.4 × 19.8 cm.
(15 × 12¾ × 7¾ in.)

Ailsa Mellon Bruce Fund
1970.7.1

Attributed to FRANCISCO
ANTONIO GIJÓN
(Spanish, 1653–*c.* 1721)

*Saint John of the Cross
(San Juan de la Cruz),*
c. 1675

Polychromed and gilded wood
with sgraffito decoration
(*estofado*). Height: 168 cm.
(66⅛ in.)

Patrons' Permanent Fund
2003.124.1

Spanish baroque sculpture has entered the National Gallery o
Art at a high level with this statue. Saint John of the Cros
(1542–91) was a friar of the Discalced Carmelite order and a frien
of Saint Teresa of Avila, the nun portrayed in mystical ecstasy by
Bernini in a famous marble work in Rome. In his own ecstasy, Sain
John stands with arms spread, eyes wide, and mouth half-open, gaz
ing toward the sky. His attitude suggests the love of God and of spir
itual teaching that moved him to write not only theology, but poem
counted among the greatest in the Spanish language. His right han
once held a quill pen, and a dove of the Holy Spirit hovered near hi
right ear. The book in his left hand supports a small image of Moun
Carmel, originally topped with a cross.

Gijón's statue was commissioned in 1675 for the church o
Nuestra Señora de los Remedios in Seville to celebrate John's beati-
fication, a step toward the canonization that occurred in 1726. The
sculptor carved him with an empathy evident in the tensed hand
and the brows drawn together. Naturalistic flesh painting, extending
to a light beard, is set against a brown and white Carmelite habit rendered in *estofado*, a technique that called for surfaces to be gilded and
painted over in colors through which an artist scratched ornamenta
patterns that emerged in gold.

JEAN-LOUIS LEMOYNE
(French, 1666–1755)

A Companion of Diana,
1724

Marble. 182.5 × 76.5 × 57.8 cm.
(71¾ × 30⅛ × 22¾ in.)

Widener Collection
1942.9.133

A few of the National Gallery's sculptures were conceived for display outdoors; one of the finest such works is this *Companion of Diana.* Louis XIV commissioned at least ten sculptured *Companions of Diana* for the grounds of his beloved Château de Marly, between Paris and Versailles. After his death in 1715, his successor Louis XV installed some of the completed statues in the forests of La Muette, another hunting retreat.

In classical mythology Diana was goddess of the moon and of the hunt. Her woodland companions were nymphs like this one, appropriate denizens for a royal hunting preserve. Lemoyne's *Companion,* supple and long-limbed, moving with effortless grace and joy, epitomizes the rococo ideal of beauty.

With a dancing step, the girl seems barely to touch the ground as she lifts the leash to signal the beginning of the chase. In amusement and affection she smiles down at her hound and, incidentally at the viewer, who would have seen her on a high pedestal.

CLODION (Claude Michel)
(French, 1738–1814)

Model for *Poetry and Music*, 1774

Terra cotta.
27 × 23.3 × 15.6 cm.
(10⅝ × 9¼ × 6⅛ in.)

Loula D. Lasker Fund
1976.10.1

Clodion specialized in small-scale terra-cotta figure groups, ofte with playfully erotic subjects loosely based on ancient myth concerning the wine god Bacchus and his devotees. Intended fo enjoyment at close range in elegant domestic settings, these inventior were the fruits of years of study in Italy. Although signed and clearl meant to be preserved, this example was sculpted as a model for a large scale work in marble. The National Gallery also owns the finishe marble (on view in the East Sculpture Hall), one of the few suc commissions to Clodion that have survived. This rare pairing of terra-cotta model and a finished marble in one collection permits fascinating insight into the design's development.

The marble *Poetry and Music* was one of four groups symbolizing th arts and sciences, ordered by the Abbé Joseph-Marie Terray t decorate the dining room of his Parisian mansion, celebrating h appointment as Director of the Royal Buildings in 1774. In realizin these plump little figures, Clodion made knowing use of terra cotta effectiveness for representing flesh, with soft, pliant forms and even pinkish color. Particularly engaging is the children's absorbe concentration. Poetry, with head on hand, devours a book, whil Music strums his stringed instrument and sings with head thrown back

Pietro Magni's *Reading Girl* is a study in female absorption like Canova's penitent Magdalen of the end of the eighteenth century and Bartolini's kneeling girl at prayer of the 1830s; but unlike these earlier highly popular works, the subject is not religious. As we approach the girl, it quickly dawns on us that she is a "daughter of the people," for the tiles are rough, the chair rustic, and the ornament around her neck a medallion of Garibaldi, the great Italian patriot and general, suspended from a thong rather than a chain. She is absorbed, from every point of view, with an exquisite inclination of the head, slightly parted lips, her shift slipped from one shoulder, the finger of her left hand a little raised, as she reads, or rather rereads, a poem on the defeat of the Austrian Empire by a united Lombardy (a printed text was originally stuck to the book). The sculpture caused a sensation when first exhibited in Milan in 1856 and this version (the second in marble) was much acclaimed in London in 1862. It appealed because of its combination of political and domestic sentiment, but also because of its realism in the depiction of textures and its virtuosity in the carving of the marble, seen not only in the undercutting of locks of hair but in the fact that the whole figure seems unsupported from below.

PIETRO MAGNI
(Italian, 1817–77)

*The Reading Girl
(La Leggitrice)*, model
1856, carved 1861

Marble. 122 cm. (48$\frac{1}{16}$ in.)

Patrons' Permanent Fund
2003.84.1

AUGUSTE RODIN
(French, 1840–1917)

A Burgher of Calais (Jean d'Aire), designed 1884/6, reduction cast *c.*1895

Bronze. 47 × 16 × 14 cm.
(18½ × 6¼ × 5½ in.)

Gift of Mrs. John W. Simpson
1942.5.13

Rodin designed this figure as one of six colossal statues forming a monument to a group of fourteenth-century citizens of the northern French town of Calais. The six men had offered themselves as hostages to induce the English to lift a siege and spare their starving city. When modern Calais, about to tear down its medieval walls, decided to erect a monument reaffirming its ancient identity, Rodin pursued the commission eagerly and won it in 1884.

Rodin's burghers, following the conqueror's orders, are stripped down to their shirts, with halters around their necks and the keys to the city in their hands as a sign of submission. The sculptor portrayed the men as they were leaving their town for the English camp, where they expected execution. Rodin conceived the burghers less as ideally noble heroes than as ordinary men, ragged and emaciated after the ordeal of the siege, each experiencing a personal confrontation with death.

Jean d'Aire, his gaunt body visible through the sides of his shirt, stands upright as a pillar, with squared shoulders, massive clenched hands, and a stoically set jaw. In his bony face and sunken eyes one can read what his sacrifice is costing.

Degas exhibited only one sculpture during his lifetime, the wax *Little Dancer Fourteen Years Old (Dressed Ballet Dancer)*, at the Sixth Impressionist exhibition in 1881. (A plaster cast from this wax is on view at the National Gallery of Art.) Many critics reacted with shock to its subject, which they found harshly realistic and even ugly, and to its unconventional incorporation of actual, rather than sculpturally imitated, fabric and hair.

In his other sculptures, not meant for exhibition, Degas worked less in pursuit of perfect forms than in restless exploration of movement and composition. Using soft, pliable materials, he built up his figures on makeshift armatures reinforced with brush handles, matches, or whatever else was at hand. The waxes, whose lumpish surfaces leave his labor visible, have a translucent character that conveys an astonishing sense of life.

Like the *Little Dancer*, *The Tub* employs actual as well as represented materials. The figure may be wax, the water plaster, but they occupy a real lead basin resting on a wooden base covered with plaster-soaked rags. In a bird's-eye view, the circular tub and square base create a foil for the convoluted twists of the figure. The result is an intriguing interplay of two-dimensional geometric shapes and three-dimensional natural forms.

EDGAR DEGAS
(French, 1834–1917)

The Tub, 1889

Brownish red wax, lead, plaster of Paris, cloth. 24 × 47 × 42 cm. (9½ × 18½ × 16½ in.)

Collection of Mr. and Mrs. Paul Mellon
1985.64.48

Decorative Arts

As objects for daily use, decorative arts allow a close insight into cultures of the past. Among its holdings, the National Gallery has an extensive collection of European furniture, tapestries, and ceramics from the fifteenth and sixteenth centuries as well as medieval church vessels. In addition, the museum possesses a fine selection of eighteenth-century French furniture and a large group of Chinese porcelains, primarily from the Qing Dynasty of the seventeenth to nineteenth centuries. Most of these objects were gifts of the Widener family of Philadelphia.

The medieval examples are primarily ecclesiastical objects, their beauty intended to lend honor and solemnity to religious rituals. A Limoges reliquary chasse, richly enameled in blues and greens, originally held the relics of a holy site or saint. The masterpiece of the Gallery's collection of medieval art is an ancient sardonyx chalice for which the twelfth-century Abbot Suger of Saint Denis provided a jeweled silver-gilt setting.

The tapestry hall is dominated by a large fifteenth-century stone fireplace and includes furniture intended for wealthy homes in France and Italy. Tapestry weaving was held in high esteem in the late Middle Ages and Renaissance. By the fifteenth century the leading tapestry production center in Europe was Brussels, where most of the Gallery's pieces were woven. Major court painters supplied cartoons, or full-scale designs, to the weavers' workshops, where several craftsmen collaborated on most productions, ranging from the skilled masters who wove the faces through specialists in architecture, foliage or border patterns.

Detail:
Chalice of the Abbot
Suger

The production of tin-glazed earthenware, known as maiolica, constituted a lively industry in Renaissance Italy. Retaining the full freshness of their original colors, maiolica plates and bowls show the remarkable talents of the artists who painted them. Often they also record how paintings and prints by famous masters influenced the decorative arts.

A fine collection of eighteenth-century French furniture is installed in a suite of rooms adorned with carved oak wall paneling, its curving forms and foliate patterns reflecting the taste of Louis XV's Paris. Much of the furniture, whether of rococo or neoclassic style, is signed by court cabinetmakers. From the reign of Louis XVI, a lady's delicate writing table by Jean-Henri Riesener is listed in the 1784 royal inventories of the Tuileries Palace, in the queen's apartment where Marie Antoinette was imprisoned after the French Revolution.

French (12th century)

Chalice of the Abbot
Suger of Saint-Denis,
1137–40

Sardonyx cup with gilded
silver mounting,
18.4 cm. (7¼ in.)

Widener Collection
1942.9.277

This chalice, a vessel to hold wine for Mass, is one of the most splendid treasures from the Middle Ages. Acquired by Abbot Suger for the French royal abbey of Saint-Denis, near Paris, the stone cup was set in gold and probably used in the consecration ceremony for the new altar chapels of the church on 11 June 1144.

Suger, abbot of Saint-Denis from 1122 to 1151, was not only a Benedictine monk but also a brilliant administrator who served as regent of France during the Second Crusade. With objects such as this chalice and the abbey's new Gothic architecture, he aimed to create a vision of paradise on earth that would awe beholders. In his writings, Suger equated Divine Light with the real light shimmering through stained glass and glistening from gems.

The cup incorporated in Abbot Suger's chalice was carved from sardonyx, probably in Alexandria, Egypt during the second to first centuries B.C. Suger's goldsmiths mounted the cup in a gold and silver setting with delicate gold-wire filigree and adorned it with gems. On the foot, a medallion depicts the haloed Christ, flanked by the Greek letters signifying: "I am the Alpha and Omega, the Beginning and the End."

Tapestries were not only items of decoration; their ownership signified power and wealth. Whether commissioned for religious or secular patrons they were hung to adorn interiors as well as kept as treasures in vaulted storage. The themes chosen often had personal importance as well as political and diplomatic significance.

The Triumph of Christ, generally acknowledged as one of the finest surviving tapestries of its time, represents the storied interpretation of the last book of the New Testament, the Revelation of Saint John the Divine. This book expounds the idea that Christ will rule in eternal majesty as the ultimate judge of mankind. Based on the book's apocalyptic imagery, this tapestry presents its own drama of triumphant Christianity. In the tapestry's center panel Christ presides over the religious and secular world personified by representatives of church and state below him. Two flanking panels, like wings of a painted triptych, symbolize Christ's triumph over the worlds of the Old Testament and the pagans.

Although little is known about the history of this magnificent piece prior to its listing in the inventory of Cardinal Mazarin (1653), The Triumph of Christ is believed to be the product of Flemish artisans working in Brussels between 1495 and 1500.

Flemish

The Triumph of Christ ("The Mazarin Tapestry"), woven in Brussels, c.1500

Wool and silk, gold and silver.
340 × 401 cm. (134 × 158 in.)

Widener Collection
1942.9.446

Chinese, Qing Dynasty
(1644–1912)

Peach-bloom Semi-
globular Water Pot,
dated in the reign of
Emperor Kangxi,
1662/1722

Porcelain. 8.3 × 12.7 cm.
(3¼ × 5 in.)

Widener Collection
1942.9.514

The Chinese had developed by the seventh century AD a true porcelain – a ceramic which is pure white, lustrously translucent, and so dense that it rings when struck. The sheer technical excellence of this medium culminated in the eighteenth century under the Manchus, the conquering Manchurian emperors of the Qing Dynasty.

Peach-bloom ware, made exclusively for the imperial court, constitutes one of the rarest types of Qing monochromes. Invented in the early 1700s, peach-bloom glazing was primarily confined to two decades during the reign of the Emperor Kangxi, a contemporary of France's Louis XIV. Peach blooms were admired for their distinctive green mottling, reminiscent of a fruit just approaching the moment of pink ripeness. Virtually all known examples are furnishings for scholars' desks, where they would have accompanied the finest calligraphy and painting.

Among the best of the Gallery's twenty-five peach blooms is a reservoir for clean water. After being thrown on a potter's wheel and allowed to dry, the clay was incised with three medallions of dragons. Kiln-firing, fourteen times hotter than the boiling point of water, converted the vessel into white porcelain. Glazes, essentially powdered glass tinted with metallic oxides, were then applied and fired.

A mong the variety of styles favored in eighteenth-century France was the taste for things Oriental, or *chinoiserie,* as exemplified in the black and gold Japanese lacquer applied to this commode. As was usual in the production of eighteenth-century French furniture, many artisans were crucial in the fabrication of the commode. In fact the role of each artisan – whether the *ébéniste* who designed the veneer, the *fondeur* who created the gilt-bronze mounts or the *marbrier* who shaped the marble top – was strictly governed by guild regulations.

Always wider than their height, commodes occupied well-defined positions in French interiors. They usually stood between two windows or opposite a fireplace. They most often were topped with marble that matched the chimneypiece, so that they harmonized with the decoration of a room. Frequently a vertical mirror hung above the commode so that the ensemble emphasized the height of the ceiling.

Characteristic of much of eighteenth-century art are the swelling, curving lines of the piece. The gilded-bronze mounts which swirl across the front of the commode accent the gentle swell of the chest's silhouette. Even the marble top gracefully repeats the rhythm. Such a preference for curves is a hallmark of the rococo style which reached a zenith during the reign of Louis XV.

Attributed to Joseph Baumhauer
(French, active 1745–72)

Chest of Drawers (commode), 1745/49

Wood, lacquer, marble, and gilded bronze.
86.8 × 153.8 × 66 cm.
(34 × 60⅝ x 26 in.)

Prints, Drawings, and Illustrated Books

The National Gallery's collection of prints, drawings, and illustrated books consists of more than 90,000 Western European and American works on paper and vellum dating from the eleventh century to the present day. It began with just 400 prints donated in 1941 by five collectors, W.G. Russell Allen, Paul Sachs, Philip Hofer, Ellen Bullard, and Lessing J. Rosenwald. Their gifts of important works by Mantegna, Schongauer, Dürer, Canaletto, Blake, and a variety of other fine printmakers were intended to lay a strong foundation for a national collection that would enhance and complement the collections of painting and sculpture installed in the public galleries. The first sizeable gift of graphics, nearly 2,000 works, came the very next year with the donation of the entire collection of Joseph E. Widener, including an extraordinary array of French eighteenth-century prints, illustrated books, and related drawings.

Lessing Rosenwald ensured the future of the Gallery's graphics collection in 1943 by giving the museum his collection of some 8,000 old master and modern prints and drawings. In the ensuing thirty-six years he gave almost 14,000 more, supplemented by such fascinating technical materials as carved woodblocks and engraved copper plates. His collection brought to the Gallery the finest gathering in America of rare German woodcuts and engravings from the fifteenth century; comprehensive surveys of the prints and some select drawings by Dürer, Rembrandt, Nanteuil, Daumier, Whistler, and Cassatt; important watercolors, drawings, prints, and engraved copper plates by William Blake; and a sizeable collection of prints by early twentieth-century printmakers.

Through the generosity of literally hundreds of other benefactors great and small, the Gallery's collection of graphic art has grown steadily and impressively over the years. The collection of old master and modern prints benefited from major gifts by R. Horace Gallatin, Addie Burr Clark, Rudolph Baumfeld, C.V.S. Roosevelt, and Mrs. Robert A. Hauslohner. The donation of the Samuel H. Kress Collection and the bequest of the Chester Dale Collection, both in 1963, added excellent French and Italian drawings and prints of the eighteenth and nineteenth centuries. More recently, a series of important donations from Mr. and Mrs. Paul Mellon has further strengthened the nineteenth- and twentieth-century holdings. At the same time, the gift and bequest of Armand Hammer's drawing collection, several superb gifts from Robert and Clarice Smith, and important gifts and promised gifts from the Woodner Family Collection have added dramatic peaks and important strengths to the collection of European old master drawings. The twentieth-century

Page from GIORGIO VASARI's *Libro de' Disegni*, with drawings by FILIPPINO LIPPI (1457–1504) and SANDRO BOTTICELLI (1445–1510)

Pen and brown ink, brown and gray wash, metalpoint, gouache, and white heightening. 56.7 × 45.7cm. (22⅜ × 18in.)

Woodner Family Collection, Patrons' Permanent Fund, 1991.190.1

collection, too, has shown spectacular growth with the help of gifts from Jacob and Ruth Cole Kainen, Mr. and Mrs. Stanley Woodward, Mrs. Max Beckmann, Norma B. Marin and John Marin, Jr., Dorothy and Herbert Vogel, and the Mark Rothko Foundation. Through the founding of the Gemini G.E.L. Archive at the National Gallery in 1981, the Graphicstudio U.S.F. Archive in 1986, and the Crown Point Press Archive in 1997, the Gallery has also become a leading repository of contemporary prints.

Since 1966, the Gallery has maintained an active presence in the prints and drawings market, using a variety of purchase funds to acquire important individual works for the collection. Among the most significant purchases made to date are rare prints by Mantegna, Callot, Piranesi, and Munch, and exceptional drawings by Dürer, Carpaccio, Bruegel, Goltzius, Rubens, Castiglione, Watteau, Fragonard, and Picabia. Purchase funds have also enabled the Gallery to acquire whole collections through combination gift/purchase arrangements, including the American drawings collection of John Davis Hatch, the old master and modern drawings collection of Dr. Julius S. Held, and the library of rare books and architectural prints formed by Mark J. Millard. The most spectacular purchase of all, made in 1991, was the acquisition of two of the greatest old master drawings in America, a page from Giorgio Vasari's *Libro de' Disegni* containing drawings by Botticelli and Filippino Lippi, and Benvenuto Cellini's *Satyr*, both from the Woodner Family Collection.

Since works on paper are highly susceptible to damage by overexposure to light, they can only be exhibited for short periods. For that reason, the Gallery maintains a schedule of changing exhibitions drawn from its own collection or borrowed from other institutions and private collections. Works of graphic art that are not on display are divided between two public study rooms and storage facilities, with European art in the East Building and American art in the West Building. Both study rooms are open to individuals as well as to classes and special groups by appointment.

ALBRECHT DÜRER
(German, 1471–1528)

*An Oriental Ruler Seated
on his Throne, c.*1495

Pen and black ink.
30.6 × 19.7cm. (12 × 7¾in.)

Ailsa Mellon Bruce Fund,
1972.22.1

ALBRECHT DÜRER
(German, 1471–1528)

Melencolia I, 1514

Engraving. 24.0 × 18.7cm.
(9$\frac{7}{16}$ × 7¾in.)

Gift of R. Horace Gallatin,
1949.1.17

RAPHAEL SANZIO
(Italian, 1483–1520)

*The Prophets Hosea and
Jonah, c.*1520

Pen and brown wash,
heightened with white, over
black chalk and stylus, squared
with red chalk and stylus.
26.2 × 20cm. (10$\frac{5}{16}$ × 7⅞in.)

The Armand Hammer Collection,
1991.217.4

317

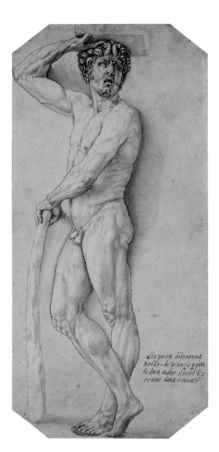

BENVENUTO CELLINI
(Italian, 1500–71)

Satyr, c.1542

Pen and brown ink, with light
brown and golden-brown
wash, over black chalk.
41.4 × 20.2cm. (16¼ × 7¹⁵⁄₁₆in.)

Woodner Family Collection,
Patrons' Permanent Fund,
1991.190.2

CLAUDE LORRAIN
(French, 1600–82)

Landscape with a Bridge,
1630/35

Pen and brown ink with
brown wash over graphite.
21.5 × 26.9cm. (8⁷⁄₁₆ × 10⁵⁄₈in.)

Gift of Mr. and Mrs. Ronald S.
Lauder, 1981.68.1

**GIOVANNI BENEDETTO
CASTIGLIONE**
(Italian, in or before
1609–64)

*Alexander at the Tomb of
Cyrus*, c.1650

Oil heightened with white.
58 × 42.9cm. (22⅞ × 16⅞in.)

Pepita Milmore Memorial Fund and
Edward E. MacCrone Fund,
1981.10.1

REMBRANDT VAN RIJN
(Dutch, 1606–69)

*Self-Portrait, c.*1637

Red chalk. 12.9 × 11.9cm.
($5\frac{1}{8}$ × $4\frac{3}{4}$in.)

Rosenwald Collection,
1943.3.7048

REMBRANDT VAN RIJN
(Dutch, 1606–69)

*Christ Crucified between
the Two Thieves (The
Three Crosses),* 1653

Drypoint and burin.
38.5 × 45cm. ($15\frac{1}{8}$ × $17\frac{1}{4}$in.)

Gift of R. Horace Gallatin,
1949.1.50

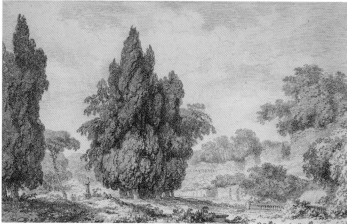

GIOVANNI BATTISTA PIRANESI
(Italian, 1720–78)

The Pier with a Lamp,
1749/50

Etching, engraving, sulphur tint or open bite, burnishing.
41.5 × 55.8cm. (16⅜ × 22in.)

W.G. Russell Allen, Ailsa Mellon Bruce, Lessing J. Rosenwald, and Pepita Milmore Funds, 1976.35.13

JEAN-HONORÉ FRAGONARD
(French, 1732–1806)

A Stand of Cypresses in an Italian Park, c.1760

Red chalk. 23.5 × 37.7cm. (9¼ × 14⅞in.)

Patrons' Permanent Fund, 1991.4.1

WILLIAM BLAKE
(British, 1757–1827)

*The Great Red Dragon
and the Woman Clothed
with the Sun, c.1805*

Pen and ink with watercolor
over graphite. 40.8 × 33.7cm.
(16$\frac{1}{16}$ × 13$\frac{1}{4}$in.)

Rosenwald Collection,
1943.3.8999

EDGAR DEGAS
(French, 1834–1917)
and VICOMTE LUDOVIC
NAPOLÉON LEPIC
(French, 1839–89)

*The Ballet Master (Le
Maître de ballet)*, *c.*1874

Monotype (black ink) touched
with white.
56.5 × 70cm. (22¼ × 27½in.)

Rosenwald Collection,
1964.8.1782

WINSLOW HOMER
(American, 1836–1910)

*Incoming Tide, Scarboro,
Maine,* 1883

Watercolor. 38.1 × 54.8cm.
(15 × 21½in.)

Gift of Ruth K. Henschel in memory
of her husband, Charles R. Henschel,
1975.92.8

EDVARD MUNCH
(Norwegian, 1863–1944)

*Two Women on the
Shore (Frauen am
Meeresufer)*, 1898

Woodcut in blue, green, black,
and ocher with crayon,
45.4 × 51.1cm. (17⅞ × 20⅛in.)

Gift of the Sarah G. Epstein and
Lionel C. Epstein Family Collection,
in honor of the Fiftieth Anniversary
of the National Gallery of Art,
1991.31.1

ERNST LUDWIG
KIRCHNER
(German, 1880–1938)

*Five Tarts (Fünf
Kokotten)*, 1914

Woodcut on blotting paper,
48.5 × 37cm. (19 × 14½in.)

Ruth and Jacob Kainen Collection,
1985.46.1

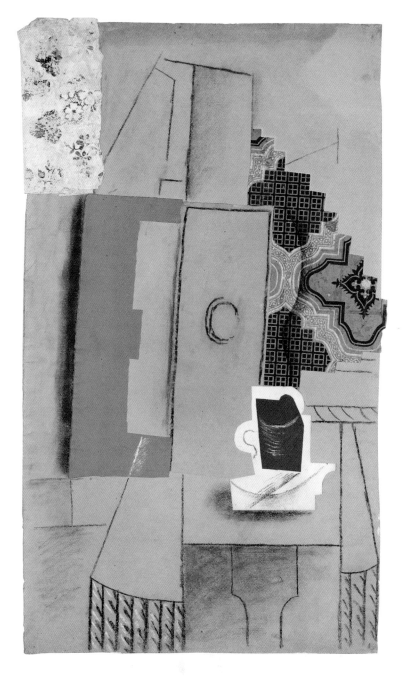

PABLO PICASSO
(Spanish, 1881–1973)

The Cup of Coffee, 1913

Collage with charcoal and
white chalk. 60.5 x 35 cm.
(23¾ x 13¾ in.)

Collection of Mr. and Mrs. Paul Mellon,
1985.64.105

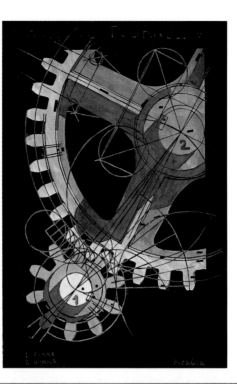

FRANCIS PICABIA
(French, 1879–1953)

*Machine tournez vite
(Machine Turn Quickly),*
1916/1918

Brush and ink with watercolor
and shell gold. 49.6 x 32.7 cm.
($19\frac{1}{2}$ x $12\frac{7}{8}$ in.)

Patrons' Permanent Fund,
1989.10.1

JASPER JOHNS
(American, born 1930)

*Untitled (from Untitled
1972),* 1975/76

Pastel and graphite on gray
paper. 38.5 × 95.9cm.
($15\frac{3}{16}$ × $37\frac{3}{4}$in.)

Gift of Jasper Johns, in honor of the
Fiftieth Anniversary of the National
Gallery of Art, 1990.107.1

RICHARD DIEBENKORN
(American, 1922–93)

Untitled (related to Club/
Spade Group '81–82),
1982

Gouache, pastel, crayon, and
graphite. 96.5 x 63.5 cm.
(38 x 25 in.)

Gift of Mr. and Mrs. Richard
Diebenkorn,
1992.90.1

Photographs

In 1948, when Georgia O'Keeffe was deciding where to place the largest and most significant collection of photographs by her late husband, the seminal American photographer Alfred Stieglitz, she visited the National Gallery of Art. Noting that "Stieglitz worked for the recognition of photography as a fine art – the National Gallery means something in relation to that," O'Keeffe and the Alfred Stieglitz Estate, one year later, donated more than 1,600 works by Stieglitz.

Since 1990, when the Gallery began to collect photographs, its holdings have grown to nearly 9,000 works that span the range of photographic history, from the medium's beginning in 1839 through the present. Among the earliest works is a choice group by an inventor of the medium, William Henry Fox Talbot. Other nineteenth-century photographers represented include Julia Margaret Cameron, David Octavius Hill and Robert Adamson, Roger Fenton, Francis Frith, Peter Henry Emerson, Gustave Le Gray, Charles Nègre, Henri Le Secq, Édouard-Denis Baldus, and Charles Marville.

Among the collection's greatest strengths are groups of photographs by several major twentieth-century American practitioners: Paul Strand, Ansel Adams, Walker Evans, André Kertész, Frederick Sommer, Robert Frank, Harry Callahan, Irving Penn, and Lee Friedlander. Modeled after the Stieglitz collection, each of these holdings includes works from throughout the photographer's career. For example, the Strand collection ranges from the 1910s through the 1970s, while the core of the Adams collection is the "Museum Set," seventy-five photographs representing Adams' finest landscape views of the American West. The Walker Evans holdings range from his earliest New York cityscapes, made in the late 1920s, to Polaroids from the end of his life five decades later. The Robert Frank collection is especially impressive, reaching from Frank's early career in photojournalism to his highly personal compositions of the 1990s.

The Gallery has further expanded its early twentieth-century American and European holdings with works by photographers such as Eugène Atget, Aleksandr Rodchenko, and Charles Sheeler as well as built a significant collection of work by women photographers, including Berenice Abbott, Ilse Bing, Lotte Jacobi, and Alma Lavenson. Finally, contemporary photographers, such as James Casebere and Richard Misrach, have also been added to the collection.

With the opening of galleries for the permanent display of photographs in the West Building, works from the photography collection will be on view in temporary exhibitions.

Detail:
GUSTAVE LE GRAY, *Beech Tree, Forest of Fontainebleau*

Gustave Le Gray
(French, 1820–82)

*Beech Tree, Forest of
Fontainebleau, c. 1856*

Albumen print from collodion
negative. 31.8 × 41.4 cm.
(12¾ × 16¼ in.)

Patrons' Permanent Fund
1995.36.93

Charles Sheeler
(American, 1883–1965)

*Doylestown House –
The Stove, 1917*

Gelatin silver print.
23.7 × 17 cm. (9$\frac{5}{16}$ × 6$\frac{11}{16}$ in.)

Pepita Milmore Memorial Fund
1998.19.3

ALFRED STIEGLITZ
(American, 1864–1946)

Georgia O'Keeffe, 1918

Platinum print.
24.2 × 19.2 cm. (9½ × 7 9/16 in.)

Alfred Stieglitz Collection
1980.70.12

ROBERT FRANK
(American, born
Switzerland, 1924)

London, 1952–53

Gelatin silver print.
27.3 × 39.9 cm. (10¾ × 15 11/16 in.)

Robert Frank Collection, Gift of
Robert Frank 1990.28.4
© Robert Frank
Courtesy Pace/MacGill Gallery,
New York

Index of Artists